HESPERIA: SUPPLEMENT XXIII

HELLENISTIC RELIEF MOLDS
FROM THE ATHENIAN AGORA

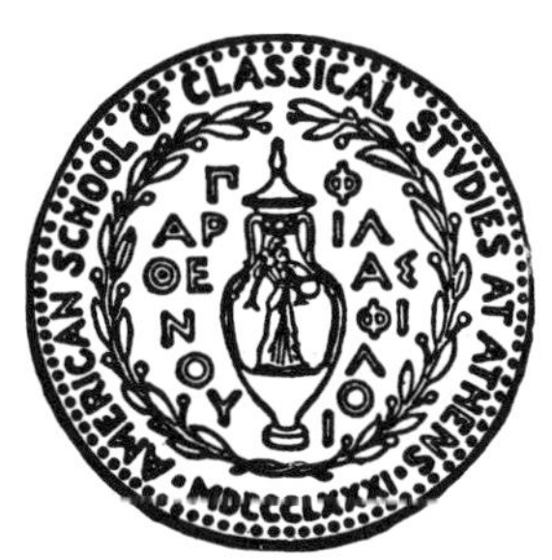

BY
CLAIRÈVE GRANDJOUAN

COMPLETED BY
EILEEN MARKSON AND SUSAN I. ROTROFF

AMERICAN SCHOOL OF CLASSICAL STUDIES AT ATHENS
PRINCETON, NEW JERSEY
1989

Library of Congress Cataloging-in-Publication Data

Grandjouan, Clairève.
    Hellenistic relief molds from the Athenian Agora / by Clairève Grandjouan ;
completed by Eileen Markson and Susan I. Rotroff.
      p.   cm. — (Hesperia. Supplement ; 23)
    Includes bibliographical references.
    ISBN 0-87661-523-X : $25.00
    1. Agora (Athens, Greece)—Antiquities—Catalogs. 2. Athens (Greece)—
Antiquities—Catalogs. 3. Modeling—Catalogs. 4. Art, Hellenistic—Greece—
Athens—Catalogs. I. Markson, Eileen. II. Rotroff, Susan I., 1947– . III. Title.
IV. Series: Hesperia (Princeton, N.J.). Supplement ; 23.
DF287.A23G73   1989
733′.3′09385–dc20

                                    89-17655
                                        CIP

TYPOGRAPHY BY THE AMERICAN SCHOOL OF CLASSICAL STUDIES PUBLICATIONS OFFICE
C/O INSTITUTE FOR ADVANCED STUDY, PRINCETON, NEW JERSEY
PLATES BY THE MERIDEN-STINEHOUR PRESS, MERIDEN, CONNECTICUT
PRINTED IN THE UNITED STATES OF AMERICA
BY THE JOHN D. LUCAS PRINTING CO., BALTIMORE, MARYLAND

FOREWORD

This corpus of terracotta molds for the making of small rectangular plaques found an ideal interpreter in the late Clairève Grandjouan. Born in Paris, Professor Grandjouan was taught by her mother, among the wartime vicissitudes of life in the French Caribbean, up to the level of admission to Bryn Mawr College. After taking her degree of A.B. from Bryn Mawr in 1950 she proceeded as a student to the American School of Classical Studies at Athens. From 1953 to 1957 she was closely associated with the Agora Excavations. After two seasons of field work she concentrated on the study of terracotta figurines and plastic lamps of the Roman period. The results of this research were incorporated in a Ph.D. dissertation presented to Bryn Mawr (1955) and subsequently published in a somewhat abbreviated form as Volume VI in the *Athenian Agora* series (1961). The book drew scholarly attention to Athenian products of the 3rd and 4th centuries: "debased" but often strikingly vivid and evocative of much contemporary production in western Europe.

While at the Agora Clairève became intrigued by the terracotta molds that are the theme of the present publication. Although a few comparable pieces had turned up elsewhere in the Greek world, the Agora collection was much the largest assemblage known. Little had been written on the subject, and questions abounded. This situation appealed to the love of exploration and imaginative enquiry that marked all Clairève's scholarship. Having accepted an invitation to prepare a comprehensive study of the genre, she worked on it for the rest of her life in the slender interstices left free in the busy career of teaching and administration that followed on her return to the U.S.A.

The fact that not one example of the Agora molds had survived intact served only as a challenge to Clairève's artistic sensitivity in recovering the designs. Nor was she dismayed by her failure to find a single cast that might have been made from one of these molds. Her reaction is represented by an illuminating discussion of the various possible materials and uses of the plaques. Dating was difficult, for few of the pieces had been found in significant chronological contexts, but the assiduous study of comparanda in other media such as metalwork and mosaics enabled her to propose for the genre a floruit in the late 4th and early 3rd centuries B.C. This dating, incidentally, validates the molds as evidence for the much discussed question of Athenian contacts in this period with South Italy and South Russia.

Recognizing that the products of the molds must in many cases have fallen short of the technical perfection that we have come to expect of Athenian work of the Classical period, our author reminds us that we are fortunate to have here an instructive sample of Athenian household art of the early Hellenistic age.

The actual body of material representing the terracotta molds is not large and would be insufficient for a separate volume in the *Athenian Agora* series, but it is too distinct and too important to attach to some larger corpus as an appendix. Presented with the alternative of publication as a long article in *Hesperia*, the Committee on Publications suggested that the comparanda in other minor arts and their implications for cultural history be studied in greater detail and appropriately illustrated; the expanded work would then be of a length suitable for a *Hesperia* Supplement. Clairève welcomed the proposal eagerly, and the manuscript was accepted provisionally for publication in that format. Although she was unable to complete the augmented study as planned, the Committee wished to honor the agreement to give the corpus independent publication.

At the time of her death in 1982 Clairève had completed a draft of her text which was left in the hands of her friend, Miss Eileen Markson. The text is indeed complete and in a style redolent of her own characteristic flavor. Some of the footnotes, however, required completion, as did also a list of acknowledgments. These needs have been taken care of by Miss Markson of the Bryn Mawr College Library with the assistance of other friends of the late author, as explained below in her preface.

In view of the lapse of time between the author's death in 1982 and the date when publication became possible (1989) it seemed well to take account of progress that had occurred in the relevant scholarship in that interval. This has been done by Professor Susan Rotroff, Clairève's academic successor at Hunter College, in addition to some work on the author's footnotes as described in the note below (p. xvii). Professor Rotroff, a recognized authority on Athens of the Hellenistic period, is also a fellow contributor with Clairève to the *Athenian Agora* series, being the author of Volume XXII, *Hellenistic Pottery: Athenian and Imported Moldmade Bowls* (1982).

The readiness, indeed the eagerness of these and many other fellow scholars to assist in preparing Clairève's manuscript for publication speaks eloquently of the admiration and affection that she had inspired within the profession.

Quite extraordinary devotion to Clairève is attested also by the speedy response to an appeal for financial assistance toward the cost of publishing this Supplement. The appeal was organized by members of the faculty of Hunter College: Professor Tamara M. Green, a colleague over many years, and Professor Susan Rotroff. Contributions were received from colleagues, former students, friends, and admirers, all of whose lives had been brightened by contact with this glowing personality.

Homer A. Thompson
Field Director Emeritus,
Agora Excavations

Publication of this Supplement has been aided by contributions from:

A. Edward Alexander
Ronnie Ancona
Yoël L. Arbeitman
Shirley I. Aronoff
Beryl Barr-Sharrar
Anna S. Benjamin
Jean Bram
Blanche R. Brown
Jeanny Vorys Canby
Virginia Marshall Carson
John E. Coleman
Ellen N. Davis
G. Roger Edwards
Angela Fortuna
Alison Frantz
Gerald Freund
Geraldine C. Gesell
Catherine E. Gorlin
Tamara M. and Martin Green
Anni Gutmann
Adele J. Haft-Zinovich
Ruth Hardinger
Evelyn B. Harrison
Suzanne Heim
Filia Holtzman
Richard Hubbard Howland
Judith B. Huertas
Spyros E. Iakovidis
Martha C. Joukowsky
Guenter Kopcke
Elizabeth Marshall Kraft
    and Rebecca F. Marshall
Anna Marguerite McCann
Mabel Lang
Lynn R. Lidonnici
Mary Aiken Littauer
The Kenneth J. Maas Fund
Dana S. Matera

William J. Mayer
Mr. and Mrs. James R. McCredie
Machteld J. Mellink
Joan R. Mertens
Mary B. Moore
David Moyer
The Barbara and Eric Pleskow Fund
Jerome J. Pollitt
Robert L. Pounder
The Luther I. Replogle Foundation
Brunilde S. Ridgway
Fay E. Robison
Linda Jones Roccos
Susan I. Rotroff
Julia and Nino Russo
Phyllis Saretta
James N. Settle
Theresa Shirer
Morton Smith
Evelyn Lord Smithson
Patricia Sonkin
Doreen C. Spitzer
Jacob and Susan Stern
Michele Stetz
Homer A. Thompson
    and Dorothy Burr Thompson
Margaret Thompson
Marie M. Tolstoy
Elizabeth L. Tourtellot
Marjorie Venit
Emily Townsend Vermeule
Livingston V. and Harriet B. Watrous
Jane G. White
Robert J. White
Matthew I. and Martha H. Wiencke
Malcolm Wiener
Jordan Zinovich

TABLE OF CONTENTS

LIST OF ILLUSTRATIONS

FIGURES IN TEXT

PLATES

PLAN

BIBLIOGRAPHY AND ABBREVIATIONS

Andronikos, M., «Βεργίνα. Οἱ βασιλικοὶ τάφοι τῆς Μεγάλης Τούμβας», *AAA* 10, 1977, pp. 1–72

Andronikos, *Vergina* = M. Andronikos, *Vergina: The Royal Tombs*, Athens 1984

Artamanov, *Treasures* = M. I. Artamanov, *Treasures from Scythian Tombs in the Hermitage Museum, Leningrad*, London 1969 [1966]

BerlWinckProg = *Winckelmannsprogramm der Archäologischen Gesellschaft zu Berlin Archäologischen Gesellschaft zu Berlin*

Besques, *Louvre* III = S. Besques, *Musée national du Louvre. Catalogue raisonné des figurines et reliefs en terre cuite grecs, étrusques et romains*, III, *Époques hellénistique et romaine. Grèce et Asie Mineure*, Paris 1971–1972

Besques, *Louvre* IV = S. Besques, *Musée national du Louvre. Catalogue raisonné des figurines et reliefs en terre cuite grecs, étrusques et romains*, IV, i, *Époques hellénistique et romaine. Italie méridionale—Sicile—Sardaigne*, Paris 1986

Boardman, "Votive Plaques" = J. Boardman, "Painted Votive Plaques and an Early Inscription from Aegina," *BSA* 49, 1954, pp. 183–201

Bonghi Jovino, M., "Una tabella capuana con ratto di Ganimede ed i suoi rapporti con l'arte tarantina," in *Collection Latomus*, CIII, *Hommages à Marcel Renard* III, Brussels 1969, pp. 66–78

Borbein, *Campanareliefs* = A. H. Borbein, *Campanareliefs: typologische und stilkritische Untersuchungen*, *RömMitt-EH* XIV, Heidelberg 1968

Corinth XII = G. R. Davidson, *Corinth*, XII, *The Minor Objects*, Princeton 1952

Daszcwski, W., *Corpus of Mosaics from Egypt*, I, *Hellenistic and Early Roman Period*, Mainz 1985

Delplace, C., "A propos de nouvelles appliqués en terre cuite dorée représentant des griffons trouvées à Tarente," *BInstHistBelgRom* 39, 1968, pp. 31–46

Dentzer, *Banquet* = J. M. Dentzer, *Le motif du banquet couché dans le Proche-Orient et le monde grec du VIIe au IVe siècle avant J.-C.*, Rome 1982

Dentzer, J. M., "Un nouveau relief du Pirée et le type du banquet attique au Ve siècle av. J.-C.," *BCH* 94, 1970, pp. 67–90

―――――, "Reliefs au 'Banquet' dans l'Asie Mineure du Ve siècle av. J.-C.," *RA* 1969, pp. 195–224

Ducrey, P., "La maison aux mosaïques à Érétrie," *AK* 22, 1979, pp. 3–13

―――――, "La maison aux mosaïques," *UniLausanne* 22, April 1978, pp. 23–31

EAA = *Enciclopedia dell'arte antica, classica e orientale*

Einzelaufnahmen = P. Arndt *et al.*, *Photographische Einzelaufnahmen antiker Skulpturen*, Munich 1893–1940

Flagge, I., *Untersuchungen zur Bedeutung des Greifen*, Sankt Augustin 1975

Floren, J., *Orbis antiquus*, 29, *Studien zur Typologie des Gorgoneion*, Münster 1977

Forster, "Plaques" = E. S. Forster, "Terracotta Plaques from Praesos," *BSA* 11, 1904–1905, pp. 243–257

Fuchs, *Vorbilder* = W. Fuchs, *Die Vorbilder der neuattischen Reliefs*, *JdI-EH* XX, Berlin 1959

Gioure, E., Ὁ κρατήρας τοῦ Δερβενιοῦ, Athens 1978

Herbig = R. Herbig, *Die jüngeretruskischen Steinsarcophage*, Berlin 1952

H. Herdejürgen, *Die tarentinischen Terrakotten des 6. bis 4. Jahrhunderts v. Chr. im Antikenmuseum Basel*, Basel 1971

Higgins, R. A., *Catalogue of the Terracottas in the Department of Greek and Roman Antiquities, British Museum*, London 1954

Kahil, L., "Moule en terre cuite figurant une danseuse au calathiskos," Δελτ 20, 1965, Β' (1967), pp. 283–284

Kontoleon, N. M., «Ἀρχαϊκὴ ζωφόρος ἐκ Πάρου», in Χαριστήριον εἰς Ἀναστάσιον Κ. Ὀρλάνδον I, Athens 1965, pp. 348–418

A. Laumonier, *Exploration archéologique de Délos*, XXIII, *Les figurines de terre cuite*, Paris 1956

C. Letta, *Piccola coroplastica metapontina*, Naples 1971

LSJ[9] = H. G. Liddell, R. Scott, and H. S. Jones, *A Greek–English Lexicon*, 9th ed., Oxford 1940, with Supplement, 1968

Lullies, "Addenda" = R. Lullies, "Addenda zu 'Vergoldete Terrakotta-Appliken aus Tarent', RM. 7. Ergänzungsheft 1962," *RömMitt* 84, 1977, pp. 235–260

————, *Tarent* = R. Lullies, *Vergoldete Terrakotta-Appliken aus Tarent, RömMitt-EH* VII, Heidelberg 1962

————, "Vergoldete Terrakotta-Appliken aus Tarent," *AA* 1958 [*JdI* 78], pp. 143–155

MAAR = *Memoirs of the American Academy in Rome*

Makaronas, Ch., «Τάφοι παρὰ τὸ Δερβένι Θεσσαλονίκης», Δελτ 18, Β' 2, 1963 (1965), pp. 193–196

Neumann, G., "Ein frühhellenistisches Golddiadem aus Kreta," *AthMitt* 80, 1965, pp. 143–151

Pinelli, P. and A. Wasowicz, *Musée du Louvre. Catalogue des bois et stucs grecs et romains provenant de Kertch*, Paris 1986

Pnyx I = G. R. Davidson and D. B. Thompson, *Hesperia*, Suppl. VII, *Small Objects from the Pnyx I*, Princeton 1943

RE = A. F. von Pauly, rev. G. Wissowa, *Real-Encyclopädie der klassischen Altertumswissenschaft*

Richter, "Phiale" = G. M. A. Richter, "A Greek Silver Phiale in the Metropolitan Museum," *AJA* 45, 1941, pp. 363–389

Robinson, *Olynthus* V = D. M. Robinson, *Olynthus, V, Mosaics, Vases, and Lamps of Olynthus*, Baltimore and London 1933

Rönne-Linders, T., "A Hellenistic Tombstone in the Ashmolean," *OpusAth* 10, 1971, pp. 85–90

Salzmann, D., *Untersuchungen zu den antiken Kieselmosaiken*, Berlin 1982

Schefold, *Untersuchungen* = K. Schefold, *Untersuchungen zu den kertscher Vasen*, Berlin and Leipzig 1934

Schmidt, E. E., "Convivium Coniugale," in *Mansel'e Armagan: Mélanges Mansel*, Ankara 1974, pp. 589–605

G. Schneider-Herrmann, "Zur Grypomachie auf apulischen Vasenbildern," *BABesch* 50, 1975, pp. 271–272

"Scythians" = "From the Lands of the Scythians," *BMMA* 32(5), special issue, 1973–1974

M. C. Sturgeon, "A Hellenistic Lion-Bull Group in Oberlin," *Allen Memorial Art Museum Bulletin* 33, 1975–1976, pp. 28–43

Thönges-Stringaris, "Totenmahl" = R. Thönges-Stringaris, "Das griechische Totenmahl," *AthMitt* 80, 1965, pp. 1–99

Vaulina and Wasowicz, *Bois* = M. Vaulina and A. Wasowicz, *Bois grecs et romains de l'Ermitage*, Wroclaw 1974

Vermeule, C., "Greek Funerary Animals, 450–300 B.C.," *AJA* 76, 1972, pp. 49–59

Von Rhoden-Winnefeld = H. Von Rhoden and H. Winnefeld, *Architektonische römische Tonreliefs der Kaiserzeit*, Berlin and Stuttgart 1911

Waywell, G. B., "A Four-Horse Chariot Relief of the Fifth Century B.C.," *BSA* 62, 1967, pp. 19–26

Zervoudaki, "Reliefkeramik" = E. A. Zervoudaki, "Attische polychrome Reliefkeramik des späten 5. und des 4. Jahrhunderts v. Chr.," *AthMitt* 83, 1968, pp. 1–88

Züchner, *Klappspiegel* = W. Züchner, *Griechische Klappspiegel, JdI-EH* XIV, Berlin 1942

ABBREVIATIONS OF PERIODICALS

AA	= *Archäologischer Anzeiger*
AAA	= *Athens Annals of Archaeology*
Acme	= *Acme. Annali della Facoltà di Filosofia e Lettere dell'Università statale di Milano*
AJA	= *American Journal of Archaeology*
AK	= *Antike Kunst*
ArchCl	= *Archeologia Classica*
'Αρχ'Εφ	= *'Αρχαιολογικὴ 'Εφημερίς*
ASAtene	= *Annuario della R. Scuola Archeologica di Atene*
AthMitt	= *Mitteilungen des deutschen archäologischen Instituts, Athenische Abteilung*
AW	= *Antike Welt*
BABesch	= *Bulletin van de Vereeniging tot Bevordering der Kennis van de antieke Beschaving*
BCH	= *Bulletin de correspondance hellénique*
BdA	= *Bollettino d'Arte*
BInstHistBelgRom	= *Bulletin de l'Institut historique belge de Rome*
BMMA	= *Bulletin of the Metropolitan Museum of Art*
BSA	= *Annual of the British School at Athens*
BSR	= *Papers of the British School at Rome*
CRAI	= *Comptes rendus de l'Académie des inscriptions et belles lettres*
Δελτ	= *'Αρχαιολογικὸν Δελτίον*
"Εργον	= *Τὸ ἔργον τῆς 'Αρχαιολογικῆς 'Εταιρείας*
IJNA	= *International Journal of Nautical Archaeology and Underwater Exploration*
JdI	= *Jahrbuch des deutschen archäologischen Instituts*
JdI-EH	= *Jahrbuch des deutschen archäologischen Instituts, Ergänzungsheft*
JHS	= *Journal of Hellenic Studies*
JHS-AR	= *Journal of Hellenic Studies,*
MarbWinckProg	= *Marburger Winckelmann-Programm Archaeological Reports*
MdI	= *Mitteilungen des deutschen archäologischen Instituts*
MonPiot	= *Monuments et mémoires publiés par l'Académie des inscriptions et belles lettres, Fondation Piot*
NSc	= *Notizie degli scavi di antichità*
ÖJh	= *Jahreshefte des österreichischen archäologischen Institutes in Wien*
OpusArch	= *Opuscula Archaeologica*
OpusAth	= *Opuscula Atheniensia*
OpusRom	= *Opuscula Romana*
QAL	= *Quaderni di archeologia della Libia*
RA	= *Revue archéologique*
RivIstArch	= *Rivista dell'Istituto Nazionale d'Archeologia e Storia dell'Arte*
RomaMedioRep	= *Roma medio repubblicana, Aspetti culturali di Roma e del Lazio nei sècoli IV e III a.C.*, Rome 1973
RömMitt	= *Mitteilungen des deutschen archäologischen Instituts, Römische Abteilung*
RömMitt-EH	= *Mitteilungen des deutschen archäologischen Instituts, Römische Abteilung, Ergänzungsheft*
StEtr	= *Studi Etruschi*
UniLausanne	= *Études de lettres. Bulletin de la Faculté des Lettres de l'Université de Lausanne et de la Société des Études de Lettres*

PREFACE

When Clairève Grandjouan died during Memorial Day Weekend, 1982, she had completed the text of this study on Hellenistic terracotta relief molds from the Athenian Agora. The footnotes, however, were still in rough draft form. In the year before her death, I had begun working with her on completing them. I did not know at the time that I would not have Clairève's clear and ready explanations to guide me as I helped her with the book. Since 1982 I have continued to work on the footnotes, filling in information as it came to light and as I found it in library resources at hand. Without the help of colleagues and friends, I could not have finished the work. I would like here to acknowledge the assistance I have received.

My Bryn Mawr College colleagues have been of the utmost help, giving generously of their knowledge and time. Machteld Mellink and Gloria Ferrari have clarified site names and led me to information which Clairève had not left either in the rough draft of her footnotes or in her working notebook. Brunilde S. Ridgway clarified references for me and was even kind enough to check several items for me at the American School of Classical Studies library during a visit to Athens. A. A. Donohue read the final version of the footnotes and made valuable editorial suggestions.

Homer and Dorothy Thompson have been of enormous moral and intellectual support in this work. Susan Rotroff tracked down several obscure footnote sources, checked the catalogue against the original fragments in Athens, and contributed to the editing and proofreading. Wendy Barnett Thomas took the time to go in person to the Athens National Museum to trace a reference which was vague in Clairève's rough draft. All these people have warmly and willingly helped to see Clairève's work through to completion.

Finally, a word of caution. Several footnote references were impossible to reconstruct exactly as Clairève might have intended them. The reader will understand that if these sources are not so specific as they might be, this is not due to Clairève's lack of concern for accuracy. It is simply that time was not permitted to Clairève to bring her own work to its best conclusion.

Clairève Grandjouan was also unable to complete the acknowledgments section of her book. Through my work on the footnotes, however, I have thought it possible to discern whom she would have thanked for help in her research and writing. In daring to do this for Clairève, I want to make it clear that failure to include any person or institution helpful to Clairève is entirely due to ignorance on my part, not to lack of gratitude on Clairève's.

First, I think Clairève would have thanked Dorothy Burr Thompson, under whose guidance she worked first as a graduate student and later as a mature scholar. During all the years I knew Clairève, she often mentioned that Dorothy Thompson was constantly urging her to "get on" with the publication of the terracotta molds from the Agora. There is no question of the major role played by Dorothy in Clairève's professional life. Homer Thompson was influential as well over the course of many years. He read the terracotta molds manuscript and made suggestions for its improvement.

Judith P. Binder, an old friend of Clairève's, is mentioned in the manuscript as having helped Clairève in discussions of her material and in specific references. Katerina Rhomiopoulou gave Clairève access to the collections of the museum in Thessaloniki during her writing of the book and discussed the material with her. John McK. Camp II showed her his then work-in-progress on the water supply of ancient Athens. Susan Rotroff shared illustrations from her then forthcoming volume on the Hellenistic pottery of the Agora (*The Athenian Agora* XXII). Ursula Knigge was likewise helpful. I am sure Clairève would have thanked the staff of the library of the American School of Classical Studies, where much of the research for this book was done.

Clairève would have also acknowledged the help of her mother, Renée Nora Grandjouan, whose literary and artistic talents were so generously shared with her daughter. Last, but certainly not least, Clairève would have warmly acknowledged the help of her father, Jacques-Olivier Grandjouan, whose wide-ranging scholarly interests and artistic talents were entirely at her disposal. He read her manuscript, gave her suggestions, discussed the linguistic implications of some of her text, and contributed to the illustrations.

Clairève Grandjouan was supported by a grant from the John S. Guggenheim Foundation during the year in which she wrote this book. I know she would have thanked the Foundation for its generous help.

Eileen Markson

Bryn Mawr College

NOTE

A manuscript, like a broth, runs the risk of ruin when too many people try to lend a helping hand. But since Clairève Grandjouan simply did not have sufficient time to complete the footnotes of her study herself, a number of additional cooks have become involved. Eileen Markson transformed her notes into scholarly footnotes, but there were gaps: fragmentary citations that only the author could have interpreted, or lacunae only she could have filled. I undertook to try to fill those gaps, to follow up her slight clues, or to guess at what she might have wanted to include. I also reviewed more recent archaeological literature and added references to scholarship up to 1987. But it has seemed important, while augmenting the scholarly apparatus, to leave the manuscript as much as possible unchanged. Therefore the text, with its descriptions, argumentation, and conclusions, was handed to the editor in the typescript produced by the author herself; the phraseology of the notes is also, in most cases, hers. I have felt that it was my role not to argue with or attempt to improve upon what she has written but rather to try to do what she would have done herself, if only she had had the time.

This has been a very moving experience. I succeeded Professor Grandjouan as the archaeologist in the Classics Department at Hunter College and, although I met her only once, I have grown to know her through the vivid reminiscences of colleagues and students. That process of acquaintance has continued as I have worked on this manuscript and have tried to follow her hints and divine her thoughts. It is a great privilege to have been able to help bring this project to completion.

My part of this work was completed at the Archäologisches Institut of the Universität Tübingen (where I was delighted to find the snake-footed lady on the stuccoed ceiling of the University Library) and at the American School of Classical Studies at Athens. I am grateful to those institutions for the wonderful facilities they provide and to the Alexander von Humboldt Foundation for generous financial support. Special thanks are due Nancy Winter and Wendy Thomas for advice on the bibliography of architectural terracottas and votive plaques, respectively, and to Homer and Dorothy Thompson for entrusting this work to me.

Susan I. Rotroff

Tübingen 1987

HELLENISTIC RELIEF MOLDS
FROM THE ATHENIAN AGORA

I. INTRODUCTION

During the American excavations in the Athenian Agora, 1931–1977, more than one hundred fragments of large clay molds for relief plaques were found, chiefly in the fills within the foundations of the three great Hellenistic stoas (the Middle Stoa, the Stoa of Attalos, and South Stoa II) that formalized space in the ancient civic center during the course of the 2nd century B.C. None of these fragments has been found in a meaningful context, that is, directly associated with a workshop where it had been made or used.

Another large group, comprising some thirty-five fragments, has been found in the excavations of the Athenian Kerameikos. One mold was found on the Pnyx. Outside Athens, only a few molds have been recovered in Greece: in Spata, Laurion, Corinth, Eretria, Chalkis, Halieis, and Delos.[1]

Since these fragmentary molds represent industrial debris, not possessions to be dedicated or kept for themselves, they have naturally not been found in those places that usually provide us with information on objects made of clay, that is, tombs or sanctuaries. On the other hand, since they are exceptionally sturdily made, it is curious that they should not appear more often on sites in the Greek world with carefully excavated Hellenistic levels.

[1] *Kerameikos:* Some thirty-five fragments of large coarse-clay molds for reliefs, entirely similar to Agora ones but preserving a few different types, have been found at various times in the excavations of the Kerameikos area. Dr. Ursula Knigge, Director of the Kerameikos excavations, very kindly allowed me to inspect these molds in the Kerameikos storage rooms and to mention them in the present study. They have not as yet been published, except for one in A. Brückner, *Der Friedhof am Eridanos*, Berlin 1909, p. 119, fig. 76: sow. The following types are represented: *Molds:* Dancing Maenad, Satyr and Maenad, Chariot Group, Rider(?), Banquet, Abduction, Scene with shield(?), Indeterminate scene, with humans, Flying figure, Griffin, Lion, Predator and Prey, Gorgoneion, Bull being led to sacrifice(?), and Sow; *Roman*(?): Two Nikai and Thymiaterion; *Positives:* Pegasos (miniature).

Pnyx: Pnyx I, p. 155, no. 105, and fig. 68, fragmentary mold: horses' heads, bridled, perhaps for a chariot group.

Spata: R. A. Higgins, *Catalogue of the Terracottas in the Department of Greek and Roman Antiquities, British Museum*, London 1954, no. 708, pp. 187–188, pl. 92: gorgoneion.

Laurion (Pl. 26:a): J. E. Jones, "Laurion: Agrileza, 1977–83: Excavations at a Silver-Mine Site," *JHS-AR* 1984–1985 (pp. 106–123), p. 119, fig. 29, complete mold, lions killing cow, H. 24–24.8 cm., W. 47.3–48 cm., T. 3.5 cm. Found at bottom of cistern shaft in "Room E" in northern range of *ergasterion* of Washery C.

Corinth: Corinth XII, no. 470, p. 62, pl. 44: fragmentary mold, griffin attacking deer, H. 16.8 cm.

Eretria (Pl. 26:b): L. Kahil, "Moule en terre cuite figurant une danseuse au calathiscos," Δελτ 20, 1965, Β′ (1967), pp. 283–284, pl. 335:a, b: kalathiskos dancer, H. 31.8, W. 16.0, T. 1.2–1.5 cm.

Chalkis (Pl. 25): A. Sampson, «Τὸ κοροπλαστικὸ ἐργαστήριο τῆς Χαλκίδας», Ἀρχ Ἐφ 1980 (1982; pp. 136–166), no. 46, pp. 147–148, 160, pl. 54, virtually complete mold for a maenad, very similar to Agora examples, H. 30.0, W. 22.0 cm. Found in the debris of a workshop dating to the very late Hellenistic and early Roman periods.

Halieis: M. H. Jameson, "Excavations at Porto Cheli and Vicinity, Preliminary Report, I: Halieis, 1962–1968," *Hesperia* 38, 1969 (pp. 311–342), p. 330, pl. 82: abduction, H. 25.3, W. 21.3, T. 5.5 cm.

Delos: A. Laumonier, *Exploration archéologique de Délos*, XXIII, *Les figurines de terre cuite*, Paris 1956, no. 1364, pp. 282–283, pl. 101: kalathiskos dancer, size inside border *ca.* 21.8 × 42.8 cm., perhaps as late as end of 2nd century B.C.: no. 1373, p. 284, pl. 103, approximate dimensions, W. 28.5, H. 15.5, T. 5.0 cm.: lion.

Greece (exact provenience unknown): A. Furtwängler, *Die Sammlung Sabouroff*, Berlin 1883–1887, III, vignette illustrating text for pl. 30 (unpaged): banquet.

More curious is the virtual absence of objects *made from these molds* in excavations in Athens or indeed elsewhere in Greece (see pp. 15–16 below).[2] This runs counter to all ceramic rules of thumb: objects made from molds should be more numerous than the molds from which they were made, and if we assume an absolute minimum of some 120 molds in Hellenistic Athens, it would be logical to expect to find there many hundreds of plaques and fragments of plaques as well.

II. SHAPE AND FABRIC

Agora relief molds, and those of the same type found elsewhere as far as I could ascertain, are made of Attic clay. The fabric is quite different from that used for figurine molds (particularly fine-textured clay baked harder and grayer than for figurines): clay for relief molds was mixed deliberately coarse, with crushed-tile grog and stony grit as well as occasional sand or straw temper. Two layers make up the thickness: an inner layer of finer clay follows the model's contours, an outer layer of coarser clay builds up the mold itself with its characteristic straight rim, for a typical breakfast-tray shape (Pl. 1). A fine clay slip inside and on the rim, and a slip—or more often a wipe with a wet cloth to produce a self-slip—on the outside, finish the molds which bake to a light, clear, Attic clay color, occasionally redder or grayer at the core.

Most molds are rectangular, except those for gorgoneia, which are round, and one or two of special shape. The representation may follow the vertical axis (single dancing figure) or the horizontal one (two predators attacking prey). Sizes, as estimated since we have only a single complete example, range from miniature (15.5 × 8.5 cm.) to large (30 × 60 or 40 × 70 cm.). The same subject may appear in various sizes; compare **2** and **6** below (Pl. 1). In other words, postcard to poster with many intermediate book or notebook sizes; these homely comparisons help us visualize the molds and their possible uses. The molds are 3–5 cm. thick, with a rim usually an additional 2 cm. high and 1–2 cm. wide, carefully smoothed. The back, always quite flat, may show traces of resting on a mat or a gritty surface and may bear a swirl of shallow finger grooves, perhaps some simple identification.

Agora relief molds stand out easily from collections of clay objects, either in a museum or on the plates of a publication: coarser, larger, and flatter than other molds, shallow and regular, with strong backs and thick rims, they resemble few of the usual figurine, plaque, or architectural molds, and neither do they look like the workshop molds of Olympia.[3]

---

[2] *Abdera:* D. Lazarides, Πήλινα εἰδώλια Ἀβδήρων, Athens 1960, no. B128, p. 70, pl. 29: lion (plaque), W. 13.0, H. 7.8, T. 3.0 cm., dated to second half of 2nd century B.C.; small, but allowing for shrinkage, could have come from a mold close to the Agora "miniatures".

Samos: R. Tölle-Kastenbein, *Samos,* XIV, *Das Kastro Tigani,* Bonn 1974, pp. 170–173, figs. 311–315, fragments of four reliefs of Nike driving a chariot, W. 47.9, H. 24.9 cm., second half of 4th century.

Praisos: Forster, "Plaques," p. 255, no. 31, fig. 17, kalathiskos dancer, H. *ca.* 23.0 cm.

[3] E. Kunze, "Olympia," in *Neue deutsche Ausgrabungen im Mittelmeergebiet und im Vorderen Orient,* Berlin 1959 (pp. 263–310), pp. 281–288, figs. 15–27.

The Athenian molds would produce cast plaques about 2 cm. thick with representations in relief neatly fitting within the rectangle and designed for it, each relief a separate, self-contained design, often going to the very edge of the plaque. Mold makers avoided the genre or romantic repertory of Hellenistic figurines and reached instead for a more timeless and statelier Greek one: Animal Combat, Dionysiac or Sea Thiasos, Banqueting Hero, and Chariot Group.

The grandeur of the repertory contrasts with the often careless execution of the molds themselves. Designs are sometimes blurred, there may be an imperfectly corrected crack or fold in the clay used to make the mold, the occasional squashed nose or lost detail has not been restored by hand before baking. If the body of material gives one, overall impression, it is that of being thoroughly competent and businesslike. Nothing of the hesitations or brilliant jabs found in hand-modeled terracottas, or of the elegance and careful finish of contemporary figurines: usually much less, simply a standard version of an ancient motif unimaginatively set in a rectangle, and occasionally more, a glimpse of the superb original of that motif.

Again, there is nothing tentative or pioneering about the Agora molds: they look as if they were made in large numbers according to well-known formulae (several examples of the same type), intended for well-understood purposes (sturdy and uniform construction), and often used (in two cases molds were mended with lead rivets: **42, 56**). This makes the absence of positives, or plaques, even more intriguing.

III. DATES

Both context and style help date the Agora molds. Style and repertory place the motifs used in most molds solidly in the second half of the 4th century B.C.; in art-historical terms the date that recurs most often for the closest parallels is *ca.* 330. This may be earlier than the molds themselves, both because studies in the 1970's have tended to lower dates for Attic material in the second half of the 4th century[4] and because the repertory of the Agora molds, since it belongs to the grand manner, must have needed some little time to move from major to minor arts. Style and repertory are discussed further, in the larger context of the early Hellenistic world, in Section V.

[4] Of particular importance for revisions in 4th-century and Hellenistic chronology are E. Vanderpool, J. R. McCredie, and A. Steinberg, "Koroni: A Ptolemaic Camp on the East Coast of Attica," *Hesperia* 31, 1962, pp. 26–61; *eidem*, "Koroni: The Date of the Camp and the Pottery," *Hesperia* 33, 1964, pp. 69–75; V. R. Grace, "Revisions in Early Hellenistic Chronology," and J. H. Kroll, "Numismatic Appendix," *AthMitt* 89, 1974, pp. 193–203; Stella G. Miller, "Menon's Cistern," *Hesperia* 43, 1974, pp. 194–245; F. S. Kleiner, "The Earliest Athenian New Style Bronze Coins: Some Evidence from the Athenian Agora," *Hesperia* 44, 1975, pp. 302–330 (with analysis of stoa fills); *idem*, "The Agora Excavations and Athenian Bronze Coinage 200–86 B.C.," *Hesperia* 45, 1976, pp. 1–41; J. H. Kroll, "An Archive of the Athenian Cavalry," *Hesperia* 46, 1977, pp. 83–140 (with discussion of contemporary Agora and Kerameikos deposits); S. I. Rotroff, *The Athenian Agora*, XXII, *Hellenistic Pottery: Athenian and Imported Moldmade Bowls*, Princeton 1982; *eadem*, prefaces (pp. 1–8 and 183–194) to H. A. Thompson, D. B. Thompson, and S. I. Rotroff, *Hellenistic Pottery and Terracottas*, Princeton 1987.

The evidence provided by Agora dated deposits[5] remains relatively ambiguous (see Appendix 2). This is perhaps to be expected when one deals with a hundred objects scattered throughout a large excavation rather than with a whole class of objects numbering into the thousands, such as pottery, lamps, or coins. Nevertheless, the beginning of the molds can be securely set in the second half of the 4th century, and possibly in its last quarter. There are no closed deposits with molds of typical shape and fabric all of whose objects can be definitely dated earlier than *ca.* 320 B.C. A well, U 13:1, dating from *ca.* 380 and preserving debris from a coroplast's workshop, is of particular interest in connection with the beginning of the molds: it contains an early gorgoneion circular mold of hard but fine fabric (T 4098) and a large, flattish mold for a dancing draped figure, of ill-baked figurine-mold fabric, both ancestral to the later relief molds.[6]

It is more difficult to establish the molds' end. There appears very little after the middle of the 2nd century B.C. and within that century very little that is not from a mixed deposit, that is, one containing material of the 4th to 2nd centuries; the stoa building fills that provide much of the total number of molds include a large proportion of objects belonging to the second half of the 4th century. With the evidence at hand, late 4th to mid-2nd century seems the only prudent stretch to assign to Agora molds, but the time may in fact be much shorter, with a vigorous start during the second half of the 4th century and a floruit perhaps in the 3rd.

IV. SUBJECTS

For a discussion of the repertory, see below (pp. 16–32); meantime, we shall briefly consider each identifiable subject in turn. It should be noted that the fragmentary state of many of the molds makes a positive identification difficult, but question marks indicate this doubt both below and in the catalogue.

Dancing Maenad: **1–8**; **9–14**? (see Pl. 27)

Maenads have an important place in the repertory, but the Agora favorite is a particularly ecstatic dancer,[7] seen in a bold twisted pose, partly profile and partly back view,

---

[5] With fewer than fifty fragmentary pieces coming from dated deposits, it is clear that I could make no original contribution to the dating of Agora deposits but benefited instead from both the published work of Agora colleagues, in particular B. Sparkes and L. Talcott, whose *The Athenian Agora*, XII, *Black and Plain Pottery of the 6th, 5th, and 4th Centuries B.C.*, Princeton 1970 (deposit lists on pp. 383–399) provides a fine research framework, and also from the researches of J. McK. Camp II, G. R. Edwards, V. R. Grace, F. S. Kleiner, J. H. Kroll, Stella G. Miller, S. I. Rotroff, and H. A. and D. B. Thompson. This study owes much to the generosity with which these and other colleagues, notably J. Binder, shared their findings and ideas with me. The dates used in this study and noted in Appendix 2 are generally conservative consensus dates as of the summer of 1978. [For the convenience of the reader, substantial revisions subsequent to 1978 have been noted in brackets in Appendix 2; these do not affect the author's conclusions, and the study remains based on the dates known to her in 1978. S. I. R.]

[6] The well U 13:1 is discussed briefly in T. L. Shear, Jr., "The Athenian Agora: Excavations of 1973–1974," *Hesperia* 44, 1975 (pp. 331–374), pp. 355–361. The coroplast's workshop material has been studied and will be published by R. Nicholls.

[7] The depiction closest to the Agora Maenad may be on a bronze mirror-cover relief of the second half of the 4th century, Züchner, *Klappspiegel*, no. KS 55, p. 43, fig. 16.

the young body framed in heavy swirls of drapery that have moved open in the dance and are held only by the shoulder pins. The head is tossed far back, the left hand flung up towards it, while the right holds a thyrsos whose straight line emphasizes the suppleness of the dancing figure. In mood and in the rich drapery, the Agora Maenad fits in well with the "Kallimachos" maenads known from Neo-Attic monuments and thought to derive from Classical originals.[8] The round face and the thick wavy hair gathered at the nape to spray out again are characteristic, as are the great ribbed shells of drapery along the sides, the heart-shaped, bubbling pleat-ends around the ankles, and the jetting out of drapery curves in front of the breast. It is clear that if Fuchs's Type 28 maenad[9] were to untie her belt and drop her half-fawn, something like the Agora Maenad would result. It is curious not to find the Agora Maenad, so well liked locally (at least ten molds in several sizes, counting those in the Kerameikos), in more use elsewhere; one might note a similarly denuded maenad, but turning towards the spectator and moving right instead of moving away left, on a small ivory plaque in a mid-3rd-century tomb in Palestrina.[10] The Agora Maenad is so far alone in representing the Dionysiac Thiasos, but some fragments of bodies in motion may have been satyrs, and pieces from the Kerameikos preserve a maenad and satyr dancing. The possible dancing Kourete (**18**) may also belong to the Thiasos in its Orphic interpretation.[11]

Nike: **15**?

A pair of feet moving right may seem insufficient evidence on which to build a Nike, but feet and ankles recall those of Nikai alighting, bringing a crown or trophy, such as we see in the 4th century.[12]

Kalathiskos Dancer: **16**?, **17**?

Short-skirted dancing figures among Agora molds might belong to kouretes, or kala-thiskos dancers (the young girls who dance crowned with flaring basketwork headdresses), or even, if the pose is interpreted differently, to Amazons in swift motion. Here, the absence of greaves and the delicately crinkled drapery moving as if from a pirouette suggest a kala-thiskos dancer, perhaps close to those on the Akanthos Column in Delphi, now usually recognized to date in the third quarter of the 4th century.[13] Kalathiskos Dancer molds are among the few to have been found outside Athens, once in a definite votive context.[14] Although the dance is perceived as a religious one, perhaps particularly dedicated to Apollo

[8] Fuchs, *Vorbilder*, pp. 73–90.

[9] *Ibid.*, pp. 80–81, pl. 16:b, c.

[10] Illustrated in *RomaMedioRep*, no. 421, pp. 276–277, pl. 89; also similar to the Agora Maenad is Zer-voudaki, "Reliefkeramik," p. 12, no. 2, pl. 29, a relief lekythos in Gnathia ware.

[11] See E. Simon, "Zagreus: Über orphische Motive in Campanareliefs," *Hommages à Albert Grenier (Collection Latomus* LVIII), Brussels 1962, pp. 1418–1427.

[12] Cf. a relief on a bronze mirror, Züchner, *Klappspiegel*, no. KS 65, p. 49, fig. 56; for a later version, see the stucco relief from the Casa Farnesina, E. L. Wadsworth, "Stucco Reliefs of the First and Second Centuries Still Extant in Rome," *MAAR* 4, 1924, pl. IV, fig. 1.

[13] This is the date proposed by J. Pouilloux and G. Roux in *Énigmes à Delphes*, Paris 1963, pp. 123–145, and accepted, e.g., by A. H. Borbein in "Die griechische Statue des 4. Jahrhunderts v. Chr.," *JdI* 88, 1973, pp. 93–212.

[14] See footnote 1 above under Eretria and Delos; note also a positive from Praisos (footnote 2 above); for a bibliography of such representations and the possible meanings of the dance, see Laumonier (footnote 1 above), p. 282.

and Artemis, its full significance and occasion remain obscure. Kalathiskos dancers are found in votive (the plaques above and the Akanthos Column itself), secular (mirrors, see p. 20 below), and funerary contexts.[15]

Kourete: **18**?

Kouretes, supernatural young warriors who protected the infant Zeus in Crete by dancing a war dance around him and clashing their weapons to cover his cries, were a favorite subject in 1st-century Campana plaques (see footnote 11 above), but are seldom found represented in Greek art before the late Hellenistic period. Pausanias saw them "below the images" of the divinities sculptured by Damophon in the 2nd century B.C. in the sanctuary of Despoina at Lykosoura (VIII.37.6), and the inventory, dated to the second quarter of the 2nd century, of statuary in an Athenian gymnasium mentions them.[16] A kourete is at least a possible explanation for the Agora mold fragment preserving two greaved legs in what appears to be violent dancing motion.

Amazon: **19**

Among the many two-person groups from scenes of combat between Amazons and Greeks, one in particular stands out, beginning in the late 5th but especially during the 4th century: a Greek has seized an Amazon by the hair; each combatant pulls back, the Amazon to try to escape, the Greek to force her to easy striking distance. The bodies strain away from each other, heads turned towards one another with the intense involvement of conflict. The Agora fragment preserves, despite a carelessly made mold, a strong reflection of a remarkable group, breathing drama but with enough nobility to prevent it from becoming merely pathetic.[17]

[15] For funerary use of kalathiskos dancers see, e.g., N. M. Contoleon, "Monuments à décoration gravée du musée de Chios," *BCH* 71–72, 1947–1948, pp. 273–301. For the motif on jewelry see Artamanov, *Treasures*, pl. 275 (ring, South Russia); H. Hoffmann and P. F. Davidson, *Greek Gold*, Mainz 1965, nos. 16, 17, pp. 91–93 (earrings, late 4th and 3rd centuries, the latter from South Russia), and no. 106, pp. 248–249 (ring, 4th to 3rd century, perhaps Tarantine).

[16] D. Clay, "A Gymnasium Inventory from the Athenian Agora," *Hesperia* 46, 1977, pp. 259–267, face a, line 4.

[17] The closest parallel may be on a 4th-century cheekpiece from Palestrina, well illustrated with a very similar example from Siris in South Italy in P. Wuilleumier, *Le trésor de Tarente*, Paris 1930, pl. XV and published with good bibliography in E. La Rocca, "Due paragnatidi di bronzo di Palestrina," *RomaMedioRep*, no. 426 a, pp. 286–288, pl. 91; see pp. 20–21 below. For references and a brief discussion of the type in 5th-century sculpture see M. C. Sturgeon, *Corinth*, IX, ii, *Sculpture, The Reliefs from the Theater*, Princeton 1977, p. 66. The type is also treated briefly in C. Le Roy, "Réchauds déliens," *BCH* 85, 1961 (pp. 474–500), pp. 482–484, with good illustrations (figs. 11, 13). P. Bernard and J. Marcadé ("Sur une métope de la tholos de Marmaria à Delphes," *BCH* 85, 1961, pp. 447–473) publish a metope with a related but opposite representation, the Amazon winning. D. von Bothmer (*Amazons in Greek Art*, Oxford 1957) deals largely with material too early for the Agora molds, although he includes the Bassai temple frieze with three groups of Amazon and Greek ancestral to the Agora one (pl. 88, slabs 1, 4, and 5). Also related are the metopes from the Argive Heraion (C. Waldstein *et al.*, *The Argive Heraeum*, Boston 1902, pls. 30, 32:3, 34) and the pedimental sculpture of the temple of Asklepios at Epidauros (J. F. Crome, *Die Skulpturen des Asklepiostempels von Epidauros*, Berlin 1951, pls. 1, 34, 39). H. Walter ("Zu den attischen Amazonenbildern des vierten Jahrhunderts v. Chr.," *JdI* 73, 1958, pp. 36–47, esp. p. 45, fig. 8) adds a number of 4th-century

Nereid: **20**?

Nereid, Triton, and Seamonster (*ketos*) make up part of the repertory of richly decorative and evocative scenes particularly favored in the 4th century. The artists delight in Beauty-and-the-Beast contrast: Nereid and *ketos*, Andromeda and *ketos*, Amazon and griffin, Ganymede and eagle. The Sea Thiasos recurs in mosaic, metal, carved wood, and on vases. The Agora mold that might belong to a Nereid shows part of a woman whose drapery slips off her shoulder, usually the sign of a Nereid, although it might also fit an Aphrodite.[18]

Triton and Ship: **21–25** (see Pl. 28)

Agora molds record an unusual representation: several fragments appear to depict a trireme (or, more properly, a *trieres*) with two banks of oars manned (perhaps to make the small-scale representation more intelligible), being rowed among Tritons, or perhaps a whole Sea Thiasos. Careful detailing on the mold—the carved moldings on two wales, the great eye inset in the prow, the start of the outrigger for the top bank of oars, the *thranitai* themselves rowing, and the finely cambered stanchions supporting the deck—give us rare evidence of a contemporary ship, related both to the Lenormant relief and to the coins of Demetrios Poliorketes showing a ship's prow.[19] The Ship with Tritons, never a common representation, is perhaps seen more often in Roman art.[20]

---

types, but it is clear that the inspiration for the Athenian mold is a major art group of the late 5th or early 4th century, readapted for the molds' curious intermediary role between major and minor arts.

[18] Some studies on the Sea Thiasos: S. Karouzou, «Ἡ μικρὰ ζωφόρος τῶν Θερμοπυλῶν καὶ ἡ ἔννοια τοῦ θαλασσίου θιάσου», Ἀρχ Ἐφ 1974, pp. 26–44, with bibliography; also S. Lattimore, *The Marine Thiasos in Greek Sculpture*, Los Angeles 1976 (*Monumenta Archaeologica* 3 of the Institute of Archaeology, UCLA, and concurrently *Monograph* 9, Archaeological Institute of America), which explores the theme and particularly its 4th-century development in connection with Skopas; previous studies by H. Sichtermann, "Deutung und Interpretation der Meerwesensarkophage," *JdI* 85, 1970, pp. 224–238, and K. Schefold, "Zur Basis der Domitius Ahenobarbus," in *Marsyas*, Suppl. I, *Essays in Memory of Karl Lehmann*, Locust Valley 1964, pp. 279–287. See also footnote 56 below.

[19] For the Lenormant relief, M. F. Brouskari, *The Acropolis Museum, A Descriptive Catalogue*, Athens 1974, p. 176, fig. 379; also L. Beschi, "Rilievi votivi attici ricomposti," *ASAtene* 47–48, n.s. 31–32, 1969–1970, section C, "Il rilievo della trireme Paralos," pp. 117–132. Among handbooks on Greek ships, J. S. Morrison and R. T. Williams, *Greek Oared Ships*, Cambridge 1968 is perhaps most thorough and best at making available information accessible; L. Casson, *Ships and Seamanship in the Ancient World*, Princeton 1971 has the best reproduction of the Demetrios Poliorketes coin, fig. 107; K. DeVries and M. L. Katsev, "Greek, Etruscan and Phoenician Ships and Shipping," in *A History of Seafaring Based on Underwater Archaeology*, G. Bass, ed., London 1972 has large, clear illustrations, including one of the actual marble ship eyes such as are preserved in the Piraeus Museum and depicted on the Agora mold (p. 45, fig. 11). Further details elucidating the shape of the prow can be found in L. Basch, "Another Punic Wreck in Sicily: Its Ram: 1. A Typological Sketch," *IJNA* 4, 1975, pp. 201–219; *idem*, "Trières grecques, phéniciennes et égyptiennes," *JHS* 97, 1977, pp. 1–10. A. Göttlicher (*Materialien für ein Corpus der Schiffsmodelle im Altertum*, Mainz 1978) gathers a good number of related ships although he includes only models and not pictures of ships.

[20] There is a ship sailing among the Sea Thiasos on a Hellenistic moldmade relief bowl of *ca.* 225–175: Rotroff, *Agora* XXII (footnote 4 above), no. 190, p. 67, pls. 35 and 80. In Roman art, the type is used, e.g., to show the Tiber welcoming Asklepios to Rome on a medallion of Antoninus Pius: R. Bianchi Bandinelli, *Rome, the Center of Power*, London 1970, p. 20, fig. 21; the type is also found on a mosaic of the late 2nd or early 3rd century after Christ: R. Thouvenot, "La mosaïque du 'navigium Veneris' à Volubilis (Maroc)," *RA* 1977, pp. 37–52.

Nike driving Chariot: **26, 27?, 28?** (see Pl. 33)

A great mainstay of Greek numismatic and funerary art, especially in Sicily and Magna Graecia,[21] the Nike driving a chariot, with its auspicious and comforting symbolism, also seems to have taken its place among Agora molds. The design beautifully fitted a rectangle and is particularly decorative with the wide spread of wings over the busy pattern of flying hooves. Agora examples appear strong and lively compared with stylized painted contemporaries in Italy such as those from the Paestan necropolis or the Canosa hypogaeum.[22]

Chariot Group: **29–35, 36–39?** (see Pl. 33)

Mold fragments showing horses moving as a team or a chariot wheel and horses' hooves should represent some of the chariot scenes in contemporary art: Abductions, Nikai as above, Apobates as below, and perhaps just racing chariots.

Apobates Group: **40**

The *apobates* race, already a popular Athenian subject in the 5th century, is used again

---

[21] G. B. Waywell ("A Four-Horse Chariot Relief of the Fifth Century B.C.," *BSA* 62, 1967, pp. 19–26) explores the kinds and purposes of Greek chariot reliefs, finding that they fall into three main kinds (Abduction, Apobates, and Single Charioteer who may often be a Nike), and that all three are especially used as votives. We might perhaps add Apotheosis, or the driving of divinities by supernatural charioteers. In the 4th century, Nikai in chariots are favorite representations in many media, often with the sort of funerary echo still present in American spirituals. For example:

Mirrors: Züchner, *Klappspiegel*, KS 66, p. 49, pl. 18.

Metalware: Richter, "Phiale"; H. Hoffmann, "Schildfragmente von Dodona," in *Festschrift E. von Mercklin*, Waldsassen, Bayern 1964, pp. 53–55, pls. 29–30; Andronikos, *Vergina*, p. 176, fig. 141, gold furniture appliqué.

Vases: Schefold, *Untersuchungen*, no. 228, p. 26, pl. 21:1; Robinson, *Olynthus* V, nos. 112, 114, pp. 96–100, pls. 68–70, 72:1; M. Borda, *Ceramiche Apule*, Bergamo 1966, pl. XVII; M. Jatta, "Tombe canosine del Museo Provinciale di Bari," *RömMitt* 29, 1914 (pp. 90–126), pl. VIII.

Tomb and Wall Painting: G. Konstantinopoulos, "New Finds from Rhodes and Astypalaia," *AAA* 6, 1973 (pp. 114–124), pp. 121–124, figs. 11, 12, a frieze painted on stucco with a chariot race that includes a Nike (Rhodes); A. Trendall, "Archaeology in S. Italy and Sicily 1969–70," *JHS-AR* 1969–70, p. 37, fig. 8 (Paestum).

Coins: A Catalogue of the Greek Coins in the British Museum: Sicily, R. S. Poole, ed., Bologna 1963 (reprint), nos. 55–58, pp. 10–11 (Agrigento); no. 44, p. 142 (Selinus); and later nos. 430–435, pp. 200–201, no. 491, p. 206, nos. 524–533, pp. 209–211 (Syracuse).

Gems: e.g., Agora T 1035, from a Late Hellenistic context, a small clay mold made from a gem impression of a Nike and quadriga.

Jewelry: a splendid earring in the Museum of Fine Arts, Boston, well illustrated in Hoffmann and Davidson (footnote 15 above), no. 12, pp. 76–82, figs. 12:a–d.

Tomb Relief: F. Studniczka, "Aus Chios," *AthMitt* 13, 1888 (pp. 160–201), fig. on p. 200 and pl. IV.

For further discussion of Nikai as charioteers see G. Siebert, *Recherches sur les ateliers de bols à reliefs du Péloponnèse à l'époque hellénistique*, Paris 1978, pp. 260–262; T. Hölscher, *Victoria Romana*, Mainz 1967, pp. 71–74.

[22] For the Paestan necropolis, see Trendall (footnote 21 above). [For the Canosa hypogaeum, see M. De Juliis, "Il Museo archeologico di Bari," in *Archeologia in Puglia*, M. De Juliis, ed., n.p., n.d., p. 59, a reference to painted plaster decoration from the hypogaeum of St. Aloia which includes figures, dated to the 3rd century B.C.; it may be this material on exhibit in Bari that the author had in mind in referring to the Canosan hypogaeum. S. I. R.]

for some of the Agora molds, where ambition in subject matter contrasts once more with sketchiness of execution.[23]

Banquet: **41–44** (see Pls. 29, 31, and 32)

Banquet (*Totenmahl*) reliefs in stone are well known and well studied,[24] from their oriental origins and island wanderings to fine 5th- and especially 4th-century Attic examples, in turn spreading to all parts of the Greek world and continuing late into Roman times; but clay banquet reliefs are rare.[25] In stone, details vary from relief to relief, but there are some canonical recurrences: one or more banqueters, male, usually shown reclining, with bare torso and drapery from the hips down, correct symposium attire. He or they hold rhyton or phiale and may gesture in welcome or benediction. One or more women sit on the foot of the couch or on a separate chair and usually hold perfume or incense. One or more boys serve wine. A table in front of the couch holds the dessert course.[26] A dog, quail, cock, or other animal may also appear as a pet. Worshipers, often making hailing gestures, may approach the main scene, usually from the left. A snake may coil about table or couch, and the head of one or more horses may appear through a window in the wall that serves as background.

The sadly fragmentary Agora representatives of the theme show a spacious, balanced composition with diners reclining on couches, ladies seated on formal chairs with footstool, and the appropriate dessert courses in progress: fruit and cakes on the tables, and wine being brought from kraters and poured by alert servers. These scenes are meant of course for idealized family dinners: the ladies are muffled up with extreme propriety.[27] It is unfortunate that the Agora fragments so far recovered should not include either horses or snakes,

[23] The apobates race is well discussed in Waywell (footnote 21 above) and in C. Vermeule, "Chariot Groups in Fifth Century Greek Sculpture," *JHS* 75, 1955, pp. 104–113.

[24] See Thönges-Stringaris, "Totenmahl"; Dentzer, *Banquet*; see also footnote 29 below.

[25] They occur chiefly among Tarantine terracottas. See for example H. Herdejürgen, *Die tarentinischen Terrakotten des 6. bis 4. Jahrhunderts v. Chr. im Antikenmuseum Basel*, Basel 1971, which discusses at length (pp. 26–33) the possible interpretations of reclining banqueters in Tarantine terracottas, with a lucid summary of previous controversies and their bibliography; Herdejürgen concludes that, on the whole, the figurines and reliefs are likely to represent heroes. A similar discussion with some other viewpoints and a good bibliography appears in C. Letta, *Piccola coroplastica metapontina*, Naples 1971, pp. 61–73. For a survey of banqueting figurines in terracotta see Dentzer, *Banquet*, pp. 163–216. For a rare painted clay plaque (Attic red figure) with what is apparently a Banqueting Hero scene with worshipers, see R. Herbig, "Giebel, Stallfenster und Himmelsbogen," *RömMitt* 42, 1927 (pp. 117–128), p. 124, pl. 14.

[26] The stylized dessert course set out on the table usually includes fruit, often pomegranate, fig, and apple, sometimes eggs, almost invariably two kinds of cakes: tall and narrow pyramid cakes and large, round, baggy cakes with a central knob called *omphalota popana* by Thönges-Stringaris ("Totenmahl"), but in which I believe we should recognize the *plakous*, an elaborately layered cheesecake. See Appendix 1.

[27] What may be a professional entertainer, a flute player, appears on the Sabouroff collection piece which may preserve more of the scene than the Agora mold. See Furtwängler (footnote 1 above). Though common in red-figure symposium scenes, musicians are apparently absent in Greek reliefs of the *Totenmahl* type; they do appear, however, in the related banqueting scene in the Tomb of the Diver at Paestum (M. Napoli, *La Tomba del Tuffatore*, Bari 1970, fig. 3) and banqueting scenes of Roman date (E. E. Schmidt, "Convivium Coniugale," in *Mansel'e Armagan: Mélanges Mansel*, Ankara 1974, pp. 589–605, pls. 183–193).

two familiar adjuncts of heroes, nor indeed the worshipers so common on stone reliefs; it may be due to the luck of recovery, or it may mean that the clay reliefs are already meant for the ordinary dead.

Athenian relief molds with banquets, some seven different fragments if we count the one from the Kerameikos and the one from the Sabouroff collections,[28] represent a sizable component of the repertory, and very much a local one. Their products would join some thirty-five fragments of small marble votive reliefs also representing the Banquet and found in the course of the Agora excavations: together they make up a large body of material for this theme. The motif of the Banquet (more properly the Banqueting Hero, not to confuse it with a Dionysiac celebration, a specific mythological banquet, or the symposium of ordinary humans) has been the subject of a good deal of study, particularly since 1965.[29] Perhaps the most basic of these studies remains that of Thönges-Stringaris,[30] who firmly established that the Banquet is not celebrated by living humans for the dead, but that it is a picture of happy eternity: the banqueter may be a god, more often a hero, and as in the course of the 4th century hero status becomes increasingly accessible, the Banquet can be used for grave reliefs. It is indeed as tombstones of the Hellenistic and Roman periods that most of the banquet reliefs are known, but we should not lose sight of their heroic connotations.[31]

These reliefs, so much part of the later Hellenistic and Roman funerary repertory, are not, in contrast, part of the interrelated repertory of 4th-century motifs briefly analyzed in Section V. Although *Totenmahl* reliefs, mostly as votives, appear sporadically elsewhere in the 4th century, almost all are derivative from Athenian models.[32] During the late 5th and

[28] See footnote 1 above.

[29] In rough chronological order: N. Firatli, *Les stèles funéraires de Byzance gréco-romaine*, Paris 1964; N. M. Kontoleon, «Ἀρχαϊκὴ ζωφόρος ἐκ Πάρου», in Χαριστήριον εἰς Ἀναστάσιον Κ. Ὀρλάνδον I, Athens 1965, pp. 348–418, a discussion of two reliefs, one with a banqueting hero, the other with an animal combat, both perhaps from a heroön; J. M. Dentzer, "Reliefs au 'Banquet' dans l'Asie Mineure du Ve siècle av. J.-C.," *RA* 1969, pp. 195–224; *idem*, "Un nouveau relief du Pirée et le type du banquet attique au Ve siècle av. J.-C.," *BCH* 94, 1970, pp. 67–90, where I believe Dentzer misinterprets the banqueter's gesture (he is not holding a crown, as in late Hellenistic reliefs, but playing *kottabos*, an interpretation more consistent both with the position of palm and fingers and with 5th-century iconography); *idem*, "Aux origines de l'iconographie du banquet couché," *RA* 1971, pp. 215–258; Napoli (footnote 27 above), with a discussion of both banquet and *kottabos*; B. Fehr, *Orientalische und griechische Gelage*, Bonn 1971; R. Horn, *Samos*, XII, *Hellenistische Bildwerke auf Samos*, Bonn 1972, which publishes the rich collection of Samian funerary reliefs; R. C. S. Felsch, "Ein hellenistisches Totenmahlrelief aus Mytilini," *AA* (*JdI* 88) 1973, pp. 89–94; Schmidt (footnote 27 above), almost exclusively concerned with the Roman iconography of the type; M. T. Couilloud, *Exploration archéologique de Délos*, XXX, *Les monuments funéraires de Rhénée*, Paris 1974, pp. 299–304, where the iconography of the Banqueting Hero, including bare torso, phiale or rhyton, snake, presence of worshipers, is refined; M. Alexandrescu-Vianu, "Le banquet funéraire sur les stèles de la Mésie Inférieure; schémas et modèles," *Dacia* 21, 1977, pp. 139–166; E. Mitropoulou, *Corpus*, I, *Attic Votive Reliefs of the 6th and 5th Centuries B.C.*, Athens 1977, pp. 117–120; *eadem*, *Three Unusual Banquet Reliefs*, Athens 1974, and *Horses' Heads and Snake in Banquet Reliefs and their Meaning*, Athens 1976; Dentzer, *Banquet*, pp. 301–363; for the related Lakonian Hero Reliefs, see, e.g., G. Steinhauer, *Museum of Sparta*, Athens, no date but bibliography to 1972 (p. 13), and previous bibliography (p. 110).

[30] Thönges-Stringaris, "Totenmahl"; bibliography prior to 1962 is summarized in M. Guarducci, "Bryaktes: un contributo allo studio dei banchetti eroici," *AJA* 66, 1962, pp. 273–280.

[31] Dentzer (*Banquet*, pp. 362–363, 453–557, 565–566) discusses this twofold use of the banquet motif in detail.

[32] *Ibid.*, pp. 365, 390–391.

the 4th century this is very much a local, Athenian representation, with the molds using types found from the middle of the 4th century onwards in stone.[33] This unfortunately leaves the molds still ambiguous, since this is the time when Banquets can be used as both votive and funerary reliefs, and the Banquet motif cannot therefore be used to place Agora molds in one or the other category.

Assembly of Gods: **45**?

It may be rash to speak of an assembly when referring to two figures, but the two on the Agora mold have the self-conscious, posed look of divinities grouped together on votive reliefs of the late 5th and 4th centuries: gracious and relaxed, but a little formal and a little bored. This is one of the molds that could have been used for votive plaques.[34]

Abduction: **46**

There is such a wide range of choices in Attica for participants in a mythological abduction (Echeloös and Basile or Iasile; Boreas and Oreithyia; Peleus and Thetis; the Leukippidai; Theseus and the young Helen, etc.) that we can only note the occurrence of the genre, not its particular attribution in this case.[35]

Scene with Shield: **47**

Rock, drapery, and shield: a scene with a warrior or with Athena; there are possible parallels in the Warrior and Girl plaque from Medma in South Italy or the later Athena Watching Odysseus Build a Boat illustrated in Campana plaques.[36]

Indistinct, with Humans: **48–51**

In this catchall category perhaps the most interesting piece is **51**, which may preserve part of a mold in the miniature range with what does seem to be a fallen Arimasp; if so, it would be the only representative so far in Agora molds of a motif among those most used in the interrelated 4th-century repertory discussed in Section V, the Arimasp and Griffin group (pp. 21, 27, 30, 31).

Two Griffins Attack Deer: **52–55**; **56**? (see Pl. 30)

The liveliest and most richly decorative of the Agora mold designs is intricately composed after what must have been a very fine model in sculpture or in metalwork. Two lithe and ferocious griffins spring upon a deer, a complicated pattern being woven at the center of

---

[33] E.g., close parallels in stone, Thönges-Stringaris, "Totenmahl," no. 82, pl. 15:2 from Athens and now in Copenhagen, dated *ca.* 350, and no. 138, pl. 16:1 from the Roman Agora in Athens, dated *ca.* 380. But none of the stone reliefs is exactly like one of the clay ones, another indication of the popularity of the theme.

[34] For examples of 5th- and 4th-century votive reliefs with groups of divinities, see U. Hausmann, *Griechische Weihreliefs*, Berlin 1960; F. T. Van Straten, "Did the Greeks Kneel before Their Gods?" *BABesch* 49, 1974, pp. 159–189; R. A. Stucky, *Tribune d'Echmoun. Ein griechischer Reliefzyklus des 4. Jahrhunderts v. Chr. in Sidon*, *AK* Beiheft XIII, Basel 1984, pp. 12–22; for 6th- and 5th-century Attic reliefs, Mitropoulou, *Corpus* I (footnote 29 above).

[35] For a scene relatively close in pose, a Tarantine soft-limestone funerary group, see J. C. Carter, *The Sculpture of Taras* (*Transactions of the American Philosophical Society* LXV), Philadelphia 1975, no. 255, p. 79, pl. 45:d, dated probably last quarter of the 4th or first quarter of the 3rd century.

[36] Medma: S. Settis, "Bellerophon in Medma," *AA* (*JdI* 92) 1977 (pp. 183–194), p. 193, fig. 12. Campana reliefs: Von Rhoden-Winnefeld, pp. 12–14, 255, pl. XXXII.

the piece by the antlers of the deer and the spiny-crested necks of the attacking beasts, the design subsiding away into the graceful tail curves and wing plumes of the two griffins.

Agora-mold griffins show some well-defined features borrowed from three animal realms: *reptilian:* lizardlike, spiny, erectile crest, neck plates like those on the underside of most snakes; *avian* (aquiline): flat-topped head with deep-set eyes, fold between brow and beak, large hooked beak with nostrils indicated, occasional raised border to beak, large wings with long, strong primaries; *mammalian* (feline): pantherlike body with a long neck, short ruff below jaw, pointed movable ears, strong-muscled paws with retractile claws, long tufted tail.

Types of griffin representations in Greece can best be shown for the mid-6th to mid-4th centuries through the coins of Abdera:[37] almost the entire combination of Agora-mold griffin features can be found on Abderan coins starting with May's Period VII, group 120, dated *ca.* 375, except for the length of wing that later coins hint at but that we find especially in the second half of the 4th century in other media.

It is only for a short period that griffins turn pantherish, with yet something reptilian about the erectile crest and broad, interlocking neck plates, and with a great shadowing of wings above them, such wings as were not seen in Greece since the magnificent griffins of Mycenaean days. Before this short period, griffins can be angry and decorative; after it, they first turn elegant and attenuated, then settle in Roman times into something like airborne St. Bernards. But during a brief moment in the 4th century griffins are believable and dangerous, as on the great gold collar from Tolstaya Mogila, or the Boston Etruscan sarcophagus.[38] And fragmentary as the Agora molds are, it is clear that they take their inspiration from just that moment.

During the second half of the 4th century griffins were a favorite representation in the Greek repertory, appearing especially in metalwork and mosaic, but also in stone, wood, and clay relief and in wall, wood, and vase painting. The meaning of griffins and animal combats involving them has been often explored, notably by Flagge,[39] who attributed different roles to griffins at various times and in various contexts. Two of her main interpretations, that of apotropaic guardianship and that of "combative principle", might be gathered under the idea of the griffin as embodying supernatural power, which can be used in funerary art both to guard the tomb and to evoke the unanswerable and unpredictable force of fate. That this force was understood to be a liberating one by Mithraic initiates of Roman times seems clear from the silver sifter found in London and the Piazza Armerina mosaic,[40] both of which set griffins to break open cages in which men are imprisoned, but

[37] J. M. F. May, *The Coinage of Abdera*, London 1966, pls. XXI–XXIII.

[38] Tolstaya Mogila: "Scythians," no. 171, p. 126, pls. 31, 32. Boston sarcophagus: Herbig, no. 6, pp. 14–15, pls. 37, 38.

[39] I. Flagge, *Untersuchungen zur Bedeutung des Greifen*, Sankt Augustin 1975, with good illustrations and a full bibliography which will not be repeated here. The bibliography is brought up to 1977 by Lullies in "Addenda."

[40] Flagge (*op. cit.*), figs. 58–62; G. Mangarano, "Aspetti pagani dei mosaici di Piazza Armerina," *ArchCl* 11, 1959, pp. 241–250; J. M. C. Toynbee, *A Silver Casket and Strainer from the Walbrook Mithraeum in the*

how far back that sophisticated idea goes is not certain. Still, Hoffman[41] already gives an eschatological meaning to griffins (death as the way to immortality) for 4th-century representations; Karouzou[42] also considers griffins as intimating immortality. The significance of a large and varied group of animal combats with griffins among Agora molds is briefly discussed in Section V.

Griffins: **57–59**

Fragments of griffins may belong to animal combats, but single griffins are also seen in contemporary art, especially in funerary contexts.[43]

Two Lions Attack Horse: **60**

Lions attacking horses are often found in gilt clay Tarantine sarcophagus ornaments[44] but do not have so rich an ancestry in Greek art as lion-and-bull groups. It may be the tastes of Black Sea customers that encouraged the choice of animal combats with wild horses as a common prey for both lions and griffins.

Two Lions, or Lion and Griffin, Attack Bull: **61** (see Pl. 34)

Like griffins attacking deer, lions attacking bulls have a long and splendid history in Greece, dating back at least to Mycenaean times, and illustrated in Attica by pedimental and other sculpture. The groups on Agora molds are close to examples between the 5th and 3rd centuries like the metalwork group from Vouni on Cyprus[45] and the stone group now in the Allen Memorial Museum in Oberlin, Ohio.[46]

Animal Combats, Animals: **62–78**

Lions and griffins attack horses, deer, bulls, or indeterminate prey. Single lions or griffins are also shown simply walking or crouching to spring, perhaps also occasionally seated. In every case, they are fine ferocious beasts, looking alert and determined, tail lashing hind legs or waving springily behind them. Single animals, including griffins, sculptured in the round, in relief or painted, and alone or in a confrontation frieze, were among

---

City of London, Leiden 1963; see also L. Foucher, "A propos d'un griffon," in *Hommages à Marcel Renard* III (*Collection Latomus* CIII), Brussels 1969, pp. 233–238.

[41] H. Hoffmann, *Tarantine Rhyta*, Mainz 1966, p. 118.

[42] S. Karouzou, ««Ἥρωες Ἀγνοὶ» σ'ἔναν ἀττικὸ κρατῆρα», Δελτ 19, Α', 1964 (1965; pp. 1–16), pp. 12–15.

[43] E.g., Lullies, *Tarent*, pls. 5, 7, 13–16, 19, 21, 25–27; Andronikos, *Vergina*, p. 89, fig. 48; Artamanov, *Treasures*, p. 73, fig. 139; see also footnote 47 below.

[44] Lullies, *Tarent*, pls. 1:2, 3:2, 5:3.

[45] V. Karageorghis, *Cyprus*, London 1969, pl. 140, from Vouni, perhaps 5th century, bronze.

[46] Lion-and-bull groups, their ancestry, possible significance, and iconographical development to the time of the Agora molds have been reviewed in a brief but important article with good bibliography to 1975 by M. C. Sturgeon, "A Hellenistic Lion-Bull Group in Oberlin," *Allen Memorial Art Museum Bulletin* 33, 1975–1976, pp. 28–43; bibliography that appears in Sturgeon's article will not be repeated here, except to mention F. Hölscher, *Die Bedeutung archaischer Tierkampfbilder*, Würzburg 1972. For further lion-and-bull groups in Athens, see also I. Beyer, "Die Datierung des grossen Reliefgiebel des alten Athenatempels der Akropolis," *AA* (*JdI* 92) 1977, pp. 44–74, with an analysis of the motif. For an early 5th-century group found in the Agora: E. B. Harrison, *The Athenian Agora*, XI, *Archaic and Archaistic Sculpture*, Princeton 1965, no. 95, pp. 33–36, pls. 15, 16.

the favorite representations for tombs in the 5th and 4th centuries.[47] The emphasis on predators, and the position of the animal over the tomb or at the door, stress the apotropaic and guardian aspect of the motif.[48]

Bull and Person: **79**

Awkwardly broken fragments of a mold in unusual fabric, closer to figurine molds, preserve in one part a bull's head the horn of which is grasped by a human hand. The actual representation proves hard to identify, although there are a number of canonical scenes involving cattle and humans: the one most used in the 4th-century repertory is the Nike Sacrificing a Bull, but Nikai never take the bull by the horns but rather lift up the beast's muzzle to expose the throat. Bulls led to sacrifice are likewise not held by the horns but driven along or held by ropes going through the muzzle. Occasions when bulls are seized by the horns are those of combat, Herakles or Theseus with some variety of Minoan bull, but the Agora fragment seems too staid for such a scene and so remains enigmatic.

Bull: **80**

An unusual curved mold for a bull, apparently just standing, perhaps a decorative element on either side of a tile or pipe.

Boar or Sow: **81, 82**

The recovery of a mold in the Kerameikos representing a sow[49] leaves in doubt the sex of the pig from the Agora represented in head fragments. Pigs and representations of them make proper offerings, of course, to Eleusinian divinities.

Fish: **83**

A mold outside the run of Agora relief molds, but not part of the repertory of figurine molds either, possibly a food mold, oval in shape, representing a fish.

---

[47] See for example C. Vermeule, "Greek Funerary Animals, 450–300 B.C.," *AJA* 76, 1972, pp. 49–59, and, for a sample of tombs with painted or relief animals: A. S. Arvanitopoulos, Στῆλαι Δημητριάδος-Παγασῶν, Athens 1928, stele with painted griffins, p. 179, fig. 201; P. M. Fraser and T. Rönne, *Boeotian and West Greek Tombstones*, Lund 1957, the tombstones from Apollonia Illyriae on pls. 31 and 32 with animal combats; Δελτ 27, 1972, Β΄ 2 (1977), p. 321, pl. 276:*a*, tombstone with two griffins and deer, from Boiotia; Δελτ 27, 1972, Β΄ 1 (1976), p. 156, pl. 106:*β*, tombstone with two griffins above helmet, probably Attic; T. Rönne-Linders, "A Hellenistic Tombstone in the Ashmolean," *OpusAth* 10, 1971, pp. 85–90, tombstone with two lions and a review of the motif of lions on Greek tombs, with good bibliography; H. K. Tsirivakos, «Εἰδήσεις ἐκ Καλλιθέας», *AAA* 1, 1968, pp. 35–36 and pp. 108–109; *idem,* "Kallithea: Ergebnisse der Ausgrabung," *AAA* 4, 1971, pp. 108–110 (both articles by Tsirivakos discuss a remarkable built tomb of the early Hellenistic period with a sculptured frieze of animals, the "playful" type, where animals crouch, or raise a paw, like kittens playing, also favored in metal and mosaic); for the painted frieze of lion-griffins in Vergina, Andronikos, *Vergina*, pp. 87–89, figs. 46, 48. In Italy, apart from the Etruscan sarcophagus noted above (footnote 38), see F. Coarelli *et al.*, "La necropoli mediorepubblicana di Palestrina," in *RomaMedioRep* (pp. 258–304), no. 414, pp. 266–268, pl. LXXVII, sarcophagus dated to the first half of the 4th century, with gorgoneion akroteria, two griffins on pediments, and a frieze of animal pairs of "playful" type on the long sides.

[48] E.g., in addition to works cited in the preceding footnote, L. Bacchielli, "Le pitture della 'Tomba dell'Altalena' di Cirene nel Museo del Louvre," *QAL* 8, 1976 (pp. 355–383), pl. I:1, 3rd or 2nd century.

[49] See Brückner (footnote 1 above).

Gorgoneion: **84–89, 90–93**?

The most uniformly apotropaic of decorations, gorgoneia are rarely absent from any body of material made by Greek artists. The Agora Gorgoneia, remarkable for their large size, otherwise follow well-known types, especially that of the round-faced gorgoneion with short hair streaming to the sides or upwards, elaborated in Athens at the end of the 5th century.[50] Another related type, but with slightly wavier hair and more snakes, resembles a 4th-century version found, for example, on gold plaques from the Black Sea.[51] The most significant parallel may be the clay gorgoneion from the House of the Mosaics at Eretria,[52] since it hints at secular and private use for at least part of the product of molds like those recovered from the Agora.

Boukranion: **94**

A single fragment, apparently the horn for a boukranion, represents this most liturgical of ornaments, usually shown hung between garlands to indicate any kind of sacred building or structure, from temple and altar to heroön and tomb. Gilt clay boukrania are also sometimes found as sarcophagus ornaments.[53]

Uncertain: **95–105**

The reason for publishing pieces with no recognizable representation is a double one: first, readers may discover what escaped a first scrutiny, and second, additional molds may be found of which these stray pieces will be seen to make the necessary complement. Some representations, like **97**, tantalizingly crisp and elaborate, refuse to be placed in a known category; others are simply too fragmentary for reconstruction.

Positives: **106–110**

It is not entirely true to say that there are no reliefs extant susceptible of having been made from Agora molds.[54] At the Athenian Agora at least five fragments of positives, of one

---

[50] E.g., J. Floren, *Studien zur Typologie des Gorgoneion* (*Orbis antiquus* 29), Münster 1977, pp. 168–171, pl. 15:1, 2. For a good collection of examples of this type see E. Buschor, *Medusa Rondanini*, Stuttgart 1958, especially pl. 46:2, clay mold from Spata, and pl. 50:1–3, krater handles illustrating variants of the 4th-century type. For a reflection in mosaic see P. Ducrey, "La maison aux mosaïques à Érétrie," *AK* 22, 1979, pp. 3–13, pls. 1:2 and 2:4. The type appears again on clay disks used as grave jewelry: see N. C. Kotzias, «Ὁ παρὰ τὸ ἀεροδρόμιον τῆς Θεσσαλονίκης (Σέδες) Γ.' τάφος», Ἀρχ Ἐφ 1937, Γ' (1956; pp. 866–894), pp. 892–893, fig. 28, from a late 4th-century tomb in Macedonia; M. Lang and M. Crosby, *The Athenian Agora*, X, *Weights, Measures, and Tokens*, Princeton 1964, C 24, p. 130, pl. 32, from the Agora.

[51] E.g., from Chertomlyk, see Artamanov, *Treasures*, p. 50, fig. 95.

[52] I. R. Metzger, "Funde aus dem Haus mit Mosaiken," *AK* 22, 1979 (pp. 14–20), pp. 14–15, pl. 5:1; Ducrey (footnote 50 above), p. 37.

[53] E. A. Gardner, *Naukratis* II, London 1888, p. 25, pl. XVI:10, 11. For plaster boukrania as sarcophagus ornaments see E. Breccia, *La Necropoli di Sciatbi*, Cairo 1912, no. 514, pp. 162–163, pl. 79; R. Pagenstecher, *Expedition Ernst von Sieglin*, II, *Die griechisch-ägyptische Sammlung Ernst von Sieglin*, I, *Malerei und Plastik* A, Leipzig 1923, nos. 11, 13, pp. 110–111. For boukrania on a Thracian tomb façade see P. Zazoff, C. Höcker, and L. Schneider, "Zur thrakischen Kunst im Frühhellenismus," *AA* (*JdI* 100) 1985 (pp. 595–643), p. 630, fig. 27.

[54] See footnote 2 above.

kind or another, do exist. But, curiously enough, there is something wrong with each one of them. No context for three of them (**106–108**), rather a model than a cast in one case (**108**), a positive for which there is no mold type in another (**106**), and fabrics unlike those usually found in Hellenistic times (**106, 109, 110**) together make up a thoroughly unsatisfactory lot.

V. THE REPERTORY IN CONTEXT

THE AGORA REPERTORY

Athenian relief molds keep, as we have seen, to an ancient and noble repertory, one that evolves little, as far as we can tell, as long as the molds lasted, and one that carries not much more than twenty-five different subjects, which can be summarized in tabular form:

Subject	Number of Pieces	Subject	Number of Pieces
Maenad	8–14	Griffins and Deer	4–5
Nike?	1	Lions and Horse	1
Kalathiskos Dancer?	2	Lion or Griffin and Bull	1
Kourete?	1	Griffin	2–3
Amazon	1	Lion	2
Nereid?	1	Panther	2
Ship	1–3	Predator and Prey	12–13
Triton	1–2	Bull and Person	1
Nike in Chariot	1–3	Bull	1
Chariot Group	7–11	Boar or Sow	2
Apobates	1	Fish	1
Banquet	4	Gorgoneion	6–10
Assembly of Gods?	1	Boukranion	1
Abduction	1	Indistinct	11
Shield Scene	1	Positives?	5–8
Human, indistinct	4		

The largest number of rectangular molds represents animal combats, usually two griffins bringing down a deer or two lions felling a bull, but with variations. The next largest shows a dancing maenad, the third a chariot group, the fourth a banquet, and scenes after that cannot be ranked since the numbers are too small for sensible interpretation. It may well be that more of the chariot scenes belong to Nike, Apobates, or Abduction scenes. The various ship and Triton molds may belong to a single representation. Most griffin, lion, and panther fragments probably belong to animal combats.

THE MISSING REPERTORY

We might note here the motifs and subjects that we would expect to find represented in Agora molds, since they form part of the 4th-century repertory as used in partly decorative contexts (discussed below under Subjects and Styles), but that, perhaps because of the incompleteness of our record, are missing. Those subjects we would expect to find in the Agora as well are already in two cases present either as molds or positives in the Kerameikos. The missing repertory includes the following:

Aphrodite on a Swan
An elegant motif in metalwork or painting, still within the Beauty-and-the-Beast circle of picturesque compositions elaborated or renewed in the 4th century.[55]

Nereid and Ketos, or Ketos alone
A mainstay of 4th-century funerary art.[56]

Nike or Eros Flying
They usually float diagonally within a rectangle; the type is particularly favored for arulae, where an additional variant shows a Nereid also in diagonal floating pose.[57] There is a mold fragment of the Flying Figure type in the Kerameikos.

Nike Sacrificing Bull
A particularly widespread type, in range and in time, especially in the later reworking of the repertory as part of the Neo-Attic complex, but already present in the 4th century.[58]

Scylla
Combining Beauty and the Beast in one person, and represented alone or as part of Odyssey scenes.[59]

[55] On bronze mirrors, Züchner, *Klappspiegel*, KS 1, pp. 5–7, pls. 1, 2 (last quarter of 5th century); KS 2, p. 7, pl. 5 (*ca.* 375). On Kerch vases, Schefold, *Untersuchungen*, no. 300, p. 35, pl. 49:1 and others listed on p. 153. On polychrome relief ware, Zervoudaki, "Reliefkeramik," no. 5, p. 21, pl. 19:3, 4. In terracotta, Besques, *Louvre* IV, i, D 3821, p. 91, pl. 87:a (disk from Taranto, 4th to 3rd century).

[56] In specifically funerary context, Lullies, *Tarent*, pls. 30, 31; Vaulina and Wasowicz, *Bois*, no. 12, pp. 87–94, pls. LXIII–LXXXIII; A. García y Bellido, "Archäologische Ausgrabungen und Forschungen in Spanien von 1939 bis 1940," *AA* (*JdI* 56) 1941 (cols. 201–225), cols. 211–214, fig. 15 (terracotta plaque from grave in Ibiza, 4th–3rd century); E. Buschor, *Griechische Vasen*, Munich 1969, p. 272, fig. 275 (Hadra vase). See also Artamanov, *Treasures*, pls. 256, 275 (gold plaque and ring from South Russian barrows); H. Hoffmann and V. von Claer, *Museum für Kunst und Gewerbe, Hamburg. Antiker Gold- und Silberschmuck*, Mainz 1968, no. 17, pp. 24–25 (gold plaques from Palaiokastro, late 2nd–1st century); Stella G. Miller, *Two Groups of Thessalian Gold* (*University of California Publications in Classical Studies* 18), Berkeley 1979, pl. 11 (rings). For the motif in 4th-century mosaic see, e.g., Ducrey (footnote 50 above), pl. 3 and Robinson, *Olynthus* V, pl. 11.

[57] On arulae: *RomaMedioRep*, nos. 56, 63, pp. 80, 84, pl. XIX; E. D. Van Buren, "Terracotta Arulae," *MAAR* 2, 1918 (pp. 15–51), pls. 19–20. On a terracotta antefix: *RomaMedioRep*, no. 481, p. 333, pl. XXII. A gold cut-out of a similar Nike ornamented a piece of wooden furniture in the antechamber of tomb II at Vergina (Andronikos, *Vergina*, p. 176, fig. 140). The figure is also found on Campana reliefs (Borbein, *Campanareliefs*, pl. 5), although an Augustan origin is posited for the type there (see G. M. A. Hanfmann, C. Vermeule, *et al.*, "A New Trajan," *AJA* 61, 1957 [pp. 223–253], p. 246).

[58] For a summary of the type and its interpretation see N. Kunisch, *Die Stiertötende Nike*, diss. Munich 1964. Borbein (*Campanareliefs*, pp. 43–48, pls. 9:4, 10) gives a discussion of the type from late 5th century through Hellenistic times and illustrates it on Campana reliefs (pls. 12–14, 16–20). On 4th-century mirrors: Züchner, *Klappspiegel*, KS 62, p. 47, fig. 124, KS 63, pp. 47–48, fig. 22.

[59] A selection of examples in various media: Lullies, *Tarent*, pl. 6:1, 2; Züchner, *Klappspiegel*, KS 78, p. 57, figs. 66 and 120; Wuilleumier (footnote 17 above), p. 113, pl. XIII:6 (terracotta disks from Apulia);

Muffled Dancers or Dancing Nymphs
A good Attic motif already present in minor arts in the 4th century and widely exported.[60]

Bellerophon, Pegasos, Chimaira
Together or separately, and found in pebble mosaics and in metalwork. The Black Sea Pegasos on a gold plaque from Kul Oba recalls the small Pegasos clay plaque from a 4th-century tomb in the Kerameikos.[61]

Ganymede and the Eagle
In one representation in metal the figure of Ganymede is particularly close to the Agora Maenad.[62]

Snake-footed Lady
Probably derived from a Black Sea myth and soon a standard decorative device.[63]

SUBJECTS AND STYLES
Looking back at the subjects selected by Agora mold makers, and by the craftsmen who chose the related subjects of the missing repertory, we note the curious limits of these repertories that keep firmly to a realm between heaven and earth. None of the molds bears the clearly identifiable image of a single divinity, such as we would expect to find on votive plaques, and there are few divinities altogether. On the other hand, no mold bears the clearly identifiable image of an ordinary human being such as a votary, or a participant in a genre scene—adorning of the bride, or a child playing—so common in the world of Kerch vases or that of terracottas.

R. Pagenstecher, *Die calenische Reliefkeramik* (*JdI-EH* VIII), Berlin 1909, no. 126, pp. 81–82, fig. 36 (with Odysseus); D. von Bothmer, "A Greek and Roman Treasury," *BMMA* 42, fasc. 1, 1984–1985 (pp. 5–72), no. 95, p. 55, and cover (gilt-silver emblem); P. Themeles, «Σκύλλα ἐρετρική», ᾿Αρχ᾿Εφ 1979 (1981), pp. 118–153 (mainly bronzes, but with much comparative material illustrated).

[60] J. N. Svoronos, *Das Athener Nationalmuseum*, Athens 1908, nos. 145–148, pp. 449–452, pls. LXXIII, LXXIV and Stucky (footnote 34 above), pp. 22–29, pls. 3, 5, 7, 15, 18 (stone reliefs); Artamanov, *Treasures*, pl. 234 (gold plaque); Züchner, *Klappspiegel*, KS 162, p. 98, fig. 97; Higgins (footnote 1 above), nos. 881, 882, 884–886, pp. 236–237, pls. 127, 128 (terracotta figurines).

[61] Kerameikos: U. Knigge, "Eridanos Nekropole II: Gräber hS 205–230," *AthMitt* 81, 1966 (pp. 112–135), p. 125, no. 225, pl. 76:7, Tomb hS 217, early 4th century, clay plaque KER 9422, with forequarters of winged horse, 10.3 × 9.5 × 1.3 cm. Kul Oba: Artamanov, *Treasures*, p. 77, pl. 252, H. 5.4 cm. For Pegasos in mosaics see Robinson, *Olynthus* V, pls. 12, 13; ῎Εργον 1976 (1977), pp. 168–169, figs. 145, 146 (Rhodes).

[62] Züchner, *Klappspiegel*, KS 86, p. 62, pl. 7; for others and a discussion of the motif, with bibliography, see R. Lunsingh-Sheurleer, "Ganymede Terracottas from Canosa," *BABesch* 58, 1983, pp. 83–90.

[63] E.g., "Scythians," where on p. 131 the passage from Herodotos (IV.9–10) and the motif from a gold horse frontlet from Tsimbalka (no. 69, p. 130, pl. 11) are conveniently confronted; Artamanov, *Treasures*, pl. 230; F. H. Marshall, *Catalogue of the Jewellery, Greek, Etruscan, and Roman, in the Departments of Antiquities, British Museum*, London 1911, no. 1610, p. 171, pl. XXVII, a 4th–3rd-century gold diadem. The winged central figure on a gold diadem from Ini, in Crete, has been interpreted as a kneeling goddess (G. Neumann, "Ein frühhellenistisches Golddiadem aus Kreta," *AthMitt* 80, 1965 [pp. 143–151], pp. 149–150), but may belong to the snake-footed lady type, who also appears on the cast of a helmet from Mit Rahinet (Egypt) which Neumann illustrates (*ibid.*, pl. 59:1).

Not only do mold makers select those subjects of mythology that fit between the world of gods and that of humans, a step towards secularization that had already been noted in other aspects of the 4th-century shift in ideas about the supernatural, notably the prologues of New Comedy, but they emphasize the impersonality by choosing subjects that exist as groups rather than individuals. Maenads, Amazons, Nereids, Nikai, heroes, Gorgons, and griffins share the same group anonymity and belong to the same category of supernatural beings of second rank. What seems unthinkable for anything Hellenistic is the absence of Erotes from the repertory of Agora molds. It may be due to the luck of archaeological recovery or possibly to the serious, even violent, quality of this particular repertory.

What we can discern of the style through the careless execution of most molds is at least consistent: if the subjects retreat into anonymity, the style makes up for it in animation. There is nothing cool about the way in which the anonymous beings are shown: Maenads quiver, Amazons strain, dancers pirouette, charioteers urge on horses, griffins tear out throats, and lions bite down on haunches, all with the liveliest intensity. From the point of view of composition, that movement and intensity are strengthened by the lack of those heraldic or antithetical compositions that would become the mainstay of the later Campana plaques. Finally, we might note in both choice of topic and style the occasional late 5th-century flavor to a late 4th-century subject, a phenomenon that can also be observed among some other 4th-century minor arts, particularly those from Western Greece.

Comparative Material

One of the most intriguing aspects of the Agora molds is the range of their closest iconographic and stylistic parallels, especially as concerns the characteristic animal combats. At first glance these parallels make up a motley and far-flung assemblage, but a second look reveals a well-integrated and closely interrelated group. From Greece itself, parallels include Attic stone reliefs of the late 5th and 4th centuries of course, but also metalwork, pebble mosaics, and the ornamentation and offerings found in early Hellenistic Macedonian tombs. From Italy, close comparisons can be made with Tarantine gilt-clay sarcophagus ornaments and late Etruscan stone sarcophagi, and more remote comparisons with Praenestine cistae, other Tarantine products, some Apulian vases, and Sicilian or Italian arulae. From the Black Sea, one finds close comparisons again with 4th-century metalwork from both the Ukraine and the Crimea and with the ornaments of wooden sarcophagi from Bosporan barrows, more remote ones with Kerch vases. From Egypt, some comparison with early Hellenistic sarcophagus and tomb decoration can also be drawn. We might note here the strong funerary orientation of most of the comparative material, while remembering that tombs give us most of what we know of the minor arts in this period.

Besides sharing a Greek artistic idiom and being made in the second half of the 4th century and perhaps the first half of the 3rd, what is it that ties this comparative material together?

The likeliest link, in an early Hellenistic world where Alexandria and other capitals in the Mediterranean are not yet challenging the position of Athens as an artistic and commercial center, is Atticism.

A brief review of this comparative material will point out its internal coherence. We will be looking not only at similarity of subjects but at the way these subjects are interpreted and combined, and at the place that the comparative material holds within the range of early Hellenistic art.

GREECE: STONE AND METALWORK

We need not follow in detail the obvious dependency of Agora molds on Attic stone reliefs, perhaps clearest in a local motif such as the Banqueting Hero.[64] Athenian coroplasts had an exceptionally rich gallery of votive, funerary, and architectural reliefs to draw from in Athens and Attica. Less obvious is the interaction with metalwork. Although Agora molds were not made for metal reliefs,[65] clay is usually very much involved with metalwork in Athenian workshops,[66] and it is indeed among examples of Greek metalwork, wherever found, that we can discern some of the strongest resemblances to these molds. The important material from the Black Sea is noted separately below (pp. 28–30, 31–32), but relationships with metalwork from the rest of the Greek world may make us want to reconsider the origin or date of some of the pieces.

Folding Mirrors

Züchner[67] describes and illustrates a number of bronze mirror covers with relief decorations related to Agora molds, e.g., his KS 55, Dancing Maenad, closest to the Agora Maenad. Its provenience is unknown, but it is in Leningrad, which gives it a chance of coming from one of the rich Black Sea tombs. Züchner ascribes it to an Ionian or Chalcidian workshop, but it now seems likelier to be Attic. KS 65, Nike, may be related to **15**, and KS 66, Nike in Biga, to **26–28**. As for KS 86, Ganymede, it is startingly similar to the Agora Maenad; both are perhaps derived from originals by the same (Kallimachean?) master.[68] KS 155 carries a Griffin and Deer related to Agora examples, while KS 98 bears a griffin engraved within the cover; Kalathiskos Dancers are also engraved inside KS 165. The gorgoneion illustrated in Züchner's fig. 75 is also in the manner of Agora molds.

Armor

The two pieces of armor from Siris and Palestrina (Fig. 1), often described and

---

[64] See pp. 9–11 above.

[65] See p. 39 below.

[66] For example, Zervoudaki, "Reliefkeramik," p. 76; E. R. Williams, "Ancient Clay Impressions from Greek Metalwork," *Hesperia* 45, 1976 (pp. 41–66), pp. 44–45, with bibliography; D. B. Thompson notes a bronze in the Ioaninna Museum virtually identical with a terracotta figurine found in the Agora ("A Dove for Dione," in *Hesperia*, Suppl. XX, *Studies in Athenian Architecture, Sculpture, and Topography Presented to Homer A. Thompson*, Princeton 1982, pp. 155–162).

[67] Züchner, *Klappspiegel*, KS 55, p. 43, fig. 16; KS 65, p. 49, fig. 56; KS 66, p. 49, pl. 18; KS 86, p. 62, pl. 7; KS 98, pp. 68–69, fig. 74; KS 165, p. 100, fig. 50; KS 155, p. 92 (illustrated in C. Jacopi, *Clara Rhodos* III, Rhodes 1929, p. 255, fig. 252).

[68] For a clay cast from Capua of a similar Ganymede and good pictures of both, M. Bonghi Jovino, "Una tabella capuana con ratto di Ganimede ed i suoi rapporti con l'arte tarantina," in *Hommages Renard* III (footnote 40 above), pp. 66–78, pls. XXVII, XXVIII, dated *ca.* 350–330.

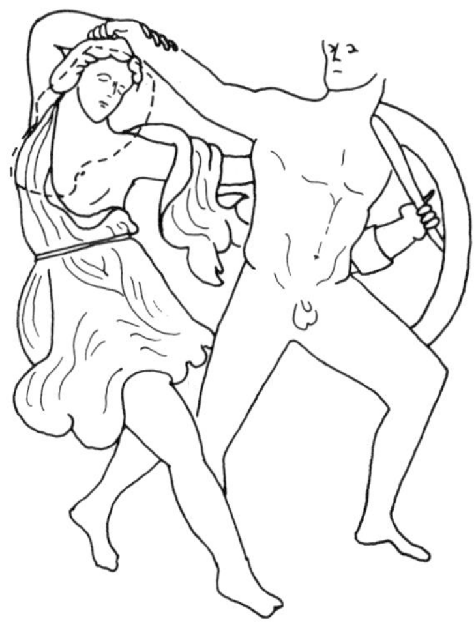

Fig. 1. Figures on bronze cheek piece from Palestrina. Broken line shows part of composition preserved on **19**

illustrated,[69] come perhaps closest to the Agora Amazon **19**, while a sculptured cuirass,[70] although later than most of the comparative material, may echo, with its splendid Arimasp and Griffins, some earlier piece of actual metalwork.

Vessels

The Derveni krater[71] provides close parallels for the Agora griffins, and the Maenad krater[72] more remote ones, although still related, for the Agora Maenad. Several curious details enliven the metal phialai with relief decoration and their imitations in clay published by Richter,[73] who dated the New York example in the late 5th century. An Agora metal impression published by Williams shows a reclining Silen close to the New York piece in both pose and style;[74] the Agora impression seems rightly dated in the second half of the 4th century, where the New York phiale could also fit. This would allow its bearded warrior riding to heaven in the company of Athena, Herakles, and Dionysos on Nike-driven chariots to be part of an apotheosis, not just a divinity's airing, and would allow the phiale to have been made in honor of a historical hero, either remote, like Leukippos of Metapontion,[75] or recent, like Philip II. He could probably not, unfortunately, be Demetrios Poliorketes, the obvious choice as abundantly deified in Athens, whose favorite deity was Dionysos and who would properly be represented as a contemporary *strategos*, but who was apparently clean-shaven[76] in contrast to the bearded hero on the phiale. These phialai, with Nikai related to those on Agora molds, were imitated, directly or

[69] Both illustrated in Wuilleumier (footnote 17 above), pl. XV, after which Figure 1 is drawn.

[70] See Flagge (footnote 39 above), figs. 55, 56; also a cuirass statue in the Villa Albani in Rome (*Einzelaufnahmen*, no. 3526; A. Hekler, "Beiträge zur Geschichte der antiken Panzerstatuen," *ÖJh* 19–20, 1919 [pp. 190–241], p. 225, fig. 151). Head of Hadrian now restored on statue may not belong (K. Fittschen and P. Zanker, *Katalog der römischen Porträts in den Capitolischen Museen und den anderen kommunalen Sammlungen der Stadt Rom*, I, *Kaiser- und Prinzenbildnisse*, Mainz 1985, p. 51, note 7b). Other cuirasses illustrated by Hekler also reflect motifs common in the Agora material.

[71] E. Gioure, Ὁ κρατήρας τοῦ Δερβενιοῦ, Athens 1978, pls. A, 39, 40.

[72] W. Züchner, *BerlWinckProg* XCVIII, *Der Berliner Mänadenkrater*, Berlin 1938.

[73] Richter, "Phiale." The phiale was later shown to be silvered tin; see D. E. Strong, *Greek and Roman Gold and Silver Plate*, London 1966, p. 89.

[74] Williams (footnote 66 above), no. 14, pp. 58–59, pl. 8 and Richter, "Phiale," p. 371, fig. 6. The relationship of the Agora piece to the one in New York was first pointed out by S. C. Stone, III at the library of the American School of Classical Studies in Athens in 1978.

[75] G. K. Jenkins, *Ancient Greek Coins*, London 1972, p. 190, no. 446. Dated *ca.* 330 B.C.

[76] E. T. Newell, *The Coinages of Demetrios Poliorketes*, London 1927, pls. VII–XVII.

indirectly, in Calenian Ware, an Italian relief ware generally dated in the 3rd century; this would also fit better with a date in the second half of the 4th century for the original. Agora molds with ships (and Tritons) such as **21–25** might in turn add to our idea of what the original phialai imitated in Calenian Odyssey bowls[77] looked like.

Ornaments

Most preserved ornaments come from Black Sea tombs, but we discern how closely the crafts were interconnected in something like the funerary diadems from Ini in Crete and Monte Cavalli in Sicily,[78] Ini with lively animals close to those on Agora molds, pebble mosaics, or contemporary tomb friezes both painted and sculptured, and Monte Cavalli with an equally contemporary ecstatic Thiasos.

GREECE: PEBBLE MOSAICS

That parallels with Agora molds should be found in pebble mosaics rather than paintings is not entirely due to the scarcity of the latter, since Macedonian and other tombs preserve a number of 4th-century and Hellenistic originals, in addition to imitations of early Hellenistic paintings reproduced on the walls of the Vesuvian cities. The relationship between mosaics and Agora molds appears instead due to the nature of the interrelated assemblage of which these molds form a part.

Just as the subjects of Agora molds belong between heaven and earth, the artifacts that carry these subjects belong between major and minor arts, in a curious middle position that the molds themselves help us to define. In major works of art—the Epidauros pediment, say, or the Derveni krater—the artist builds on the traditions of his time and uses the current climate of ideas, but he transcends both to create tradition or provoke ideas of his own. In the run of mass-produced minor arts—pottery, votives, jewelry—direct observation of the human world and a volatile following of fashion create a lively microcosm with its own distinct personality.

Between them stands a range of material that provides elegance for private use: tomb and house decoration, the ornamentation of sarcophagi and furniture, metalwork and mosaic, as well perhaps as textiles, from the few hints recovered.

This in-between group will become entirely decorative by the 1st century and solidify into the chill stylizations of Neo-Atticism. In the 4th century, however, the topics are still meaningful, chosen for auspiciousness or otherwise appropriate to the structure or object they embellish.

Pebble mosaics offer particularly close parallels to Agora molds in their choice of animal combats, animal confrontations, sea thiasoi, and chariot groups, and of course in the

---

[77] Pagenstecher (footnote 59 above), p. 81, fig. 36. Pagenstecher is, of course, painfully out of date; see now M. O. Jentel's comments on the related oil jugs in *Les gutti et les askoi à reliefs étrusques et apuliens*, Leiden 1976, especially pp. 31–33 for current dating of the gutti in the second half of the 4th and the early 3rd century.

[78] Ini: Neumann (footnote 63 above). Monte Cavalli: M. R. La Lamia, "Un diadema con raffigurazione del Thiasos dionisiaco," *ArchCl* 20, 1968 (pp. 58–75), pl. XXV. Animal friezes are also used on Boeotian Banqueting Hero late red-figure scenes, e.g. M. Collignon and L. Couve, *Vases peints du Musée National d'Athènes*, Athens 1904, p. 21, no. 1583, pl. XLVIII.

way these subjects are treated; this parallelism is also borne out by the floruit dates of pebble mosaics, second half of 4th century and first half of 3rd.[79]

GREEK: MACEDONIAN TOMBS

Macedonian tombs of the 4th and 3rd centuries provide an essential but often overlooked component of the history of Greek art during this period. Individual tomb paintings or a fine piece of metalwork may be illustrated over and over in handbooks, but a study that would consider the tombs as a whole (architecture, painting, offerings, and furnishings) is

---

[79] Pebble mosaics, using much the same repertory as the Agora molds, provide good comparisons, especially as concerns animal combats. For an overview, excellent illustrations, chronology, and bibliography, see D. Salzmann, *Untersuchungen zu den antiken Kieselmosaiken*, Berlin 1982. Some examples:

Athens: W. Höpfner, *Kerameikos*, X, *Die Pompeion und seine Nachfolgerbauten*, Berlin 1976, pp. 51–52, fig. 73 and frontispiece (griffins, animal combats; second quarter of 4th century); O. Alexandri, Δελτ 33, 1967, B' (1968), pp. 98–100, pls. 91, 92 (griffins attack stag; last quarter of 4th century).

Piraeus: M. K. Donaldson, "A Pebble Mosaic in Piraeus," *Hesperia* 34, 1965, pp. 77–88, pls. 23, 24 (a quadriga and charioteer; probably mid-4th century).

Eretria: Ducrey (footnote 50 above) and P. Ducrey, "La maison aux mosaïques," *UniLausanne* 22, April 1978, pp. 23–31, figs. 6–12 (I owe this last reference to H. A. Thompson), well-illustrated preliminary publications of a house with mosaics tentatively dated mid-4th century, exceptionally carefully executed and well preserved, that include griffins and Arimasps, lions attacking horses, and playful sphinxes and panthers.

Corinth: C. H. Morgan, "Excavations at Corinth, 1936–37," *AJA* 41, 1937 (pp. 539–552), p. 546, fig. 8, a pebble mosaic, broken and thrown into a pit, griffin and horse, dated late 5th but more likely mid-4th century (Salzmann, *op. cit.*, p. 96, gives a date in the second quarter of the 4th century); C. K. Williams, II ("Corinth 1975: Forum Southwest," *Hesperia* 45, 1976 [pp. 99–162], p. 114) in connection with the Centaur Bath pebble mosaic, notes the Theater House mosaic, with lion and horse, panther and deer(?) illustrated on pl. 24.

Sikyon: three mosaics with various motifs, including griffins, animal friezes, and gorgoneion, dating in the 4th century: A. K. Orlandos, «Ἀνασκαφὴ Σικυῶνος», Πρακτικά 1936 (1937; pp. 87–94), p. 94, fig. 8; *idem*, «Ἀνασκαφὴ Σικυῶνος 1938», Πρακτικά 1938 (1939; pp. 120–123), p. 122, fig. 3; K. Votsis, "Nouvelle mosaïque de Sicyon," *BCH* 100, 1976, pp. 575–588; D. Salzmann, "Ein wiedergewonnenes Kieselmosaik aus Sikyon," *AA* (*JdI* 94) 1979, pp. 290–306.

Olynthos: Robinson, *Olynthus* V, chap. I, where four mosaics have animal combats or threats: House A vi 1, a Nereid mosaic with panels that include two panthers and a deer, as well as one griffin (pls. 2, 9–11); House A vi 3, Bellerophon mosaic with a fine group of two griffins and a deer (pls. 3, 12); House B v 1, double sphinx mosaic with lion and deer (pls. 6, 15); House of Comedian, mosaic border with two griffins and a deer, lion facing a boar (pls. 8, 17). All 4th century.

Pella: D. Papaconstantinou-Diamantourou, *Pella* I, Athens 1971, pl. 13:a, fragment of a griffin-and-deer mosaic; for a sampling of the rich collection of Pella mosaics, P. Petsas, "Ten Years at Pella," *Archaeology* 17, 1964, pp. 74–84, dated late 4th to early 3rd century.

Alexandria: W. Daszewski, *Corpus of Mosaics from Egypt*, I, *Hellenistic and Early Roman Period*, Mainz 1985, nos. 1–3, pp. 101–111, pls. 1–4, 10–12 (last quarter of 4th century to early 3rd century), with a discussion of griffins and other animal combats in mosaics and other arts (pp. 56–62 and p. 110, notes 26 and 28).

Olbia: A. Vostchinina, "Mosaïques gréco-romaines trouvées en Union Soviétique," in *La mosaïque gréco-romaine* I (Colloque international du CNRS), Paris 1965 (pp. 315–324), pp. 318–319, fig. 5 (griffins: 3rd century).

Motya: V. Tusa, "Mozia dopo il 397 a. C.," *Mozia* III, Rome 1967, pp. 85–95, pls. XLIX, L, a pebble mosaic in the House of Mosaics, three panels with animal combats (griffin and horse, lion and bull, lion facing horse), dated by Salzmann, *op. cit.*, p. 97, to the 3rd century. This mosaic is particularly instructive, showing the local craftsman misinterpreting the Greek model and getting lost in the intricate pattern of tails and paws of the original. See also D. von Boeselager, *Antike Mosaiken in Sizilien. Hellenismus und römische Kaiserzeit 3. Jahrhundert v. Chr.—3. Jahrhundert n. Chr.*, Rome 1983, pp. 15–20, pls. 1–3.

still to come and would prove enlightening. At least five features of these tombs relate to Agora molds. We note, for example, the presence of figured *stucco reliefs*;[80] stucco would provide a possible answer for the lack of preserved positives made from Agora molds and is rare in figured form (see pp. 35–36 below). *Painted* animal or animal confrontation friezes[81] that feature griffins of the proper type can also be found in these tombs. The use of elaborate *gilt-clay ornaments* (part of the funerary make-believe that may have some significance for Agora molds; see pp. 36, 40–42 below), which can include griffins, such as those from Alatini, Derveni, Sedes, and elsewhere in Macedonia, now in the Thessaloniki Museum,[82] adds to the comparison.

It is clear that the important Macedonian material, by taking away the curious isolation of Tarantine gilt-clay ornaments, especially those featuring animal combats, allows us to recognize that it is chiefly the luck of preservation and excavation, and the wealth of a particular tomb, that dictate whether archaeologists find metal, gilt-wood, gilt-stucco, or gilt-clay ornaments in tombs of the 4th and 3rd centuries in Egypt, South Italy, the Crimea, Macedonia, and perhaps Attica itself.

Also notable is the use in Macedonian tombs of boxes, coffins, or couches decorated with *ivory and bone ornament*, among which we count griffins.[83] Although the wood sculpture that would accompany them is gone, Black Sea coffins and Etruscan stone versions[84] can give us some idea of the arrangements. Finally, we note the fine *metalwork*, such as that coming from the complex of tombs at Derveni, a complex, again, that should be studied as a whole, in particular the fine krater with griffins so close to those in the Agora.[85]

ITALY: TARANTINE GILT CLAY

The close connection between Athens and Taras in the second half of the 4th century

[80] P. M. Petsas, Ὁ τάφος τῶν Λευκαδίων, Athens 1966, pls. 27–29.

[81] K. A. Rhomaios, Ὁ Μακεδονικὸς τάφος τῆς Βεργίνας, Athens 1951 (with griffin, painted on throne in the tomb), p. 41, pl. γ'; Andronikos, *Vergina*, pp. 87, 89, figs. 46, 48, with painted frieze of lion-griffins.

[82] Katerina Rhomiopoulou, Director of the Museum in Thessaloniki, very kindly allowed me to inspect some of this material, both on view and in storerooms. Reclining figures, dancers, amazonomachies, and animal combats echo, but do not duplicate, Tarantine material, and the pieces tend to be larger. In many cases, the clay is discolored with burning, and it is possible that the gilt-clay pieces ornamented a bier burnt on the pyre. See also Besques, *Louvre* III, pp. 41–43, pls. 50, 51 (gilt and other reliefs from Topsin and Kavakli in eastern Macedonia, which include imitation jewelry) and footnote 148 below.

[83] K. Rhomiopoulou, "A New Monumental Chamber Tomb with Paintings of the Hellenistic Period near Lefkadia (Western Macedonia)," *AAA* 6, 1973, pp. 87–92, figs. 3–5; Kotzias (footnote 50 above), pp. 886–888, figs. 21, 22, XII, XIII (Sedes, Macedonia). The material from the Sedes tomb includes characteristic gilt-clay ornaments (pp. 892–893, fig. 28), as well as ivory fragments from what must have been a box with a wood-and-ivory relief of an Amazon- or Arimasp-and-griffin combat (*ibid.*). The tomb also contained small repoussé gold plaques (*ibid.*, pp. 882–883, fig. 16) related, in kind and motif, to those plaques and other objects found in Bosporan barrows. Compare, e.g., the three dancing nymphs on Sedes plaques and on wooden boxes from a Taman Peninsula burial illustrated in Vaulina and Wasowicz, *Bois*, no. 4, p. 70, fig. 20; these Attic nymphs we later find, of course, on Neo-Attic reliefs, e.g. Fuchs, *Vorbilder*, pp. 20–41. Ivory appliqués from the couch in Tomb II at Vergina include confronted animals; see Andronikos, *Vergina*, p. 122, fig. 75 for reconstruction of the couch, and p. 133, fig. 89 for a feline.

[84] See footnotes 90 and 109 below.

[85] C. Makaronas, «Τάφοι παρὰ τὸ Δερβένι Θεσσαλονίκης», Δελτ 18, 1963, Β' 2 (1965), pp. 193–196, pls. 230–234; Gioure (footnote 71 above).

has often been noted but not properly explained as yet. The present study will not bring the awaited explanation, but by reinforcing the connection and comparing it to that with Athens' great overseas market of the time, the Bosporan Kingdom, it may prompt further exploration of the commercial ties, perhaps related to the South Italian grain trade, that manifest themselves in the Atticism of Tarantine products.

Lullies has done the essential work on Tarantine gilt-clay ornaments in three studies written between 1958 and 1977.[86] To summarize some of his conclusions: Tarantine gilt-clay reliefs, moldmade in single molds, cut out and gilded with 95% pure gold, were made to ornament wooden sarcophagi, to which they were fastened with nails driven through pre-pierced holes. Wooden sarcophagi were much used in the Greek world; although few have survived, mainly in Egypt and South Russia, traces of them, sometimes only nails or decoration, are often reported, including examples from Attica. The Tarantine gilt-clay ornaments should date between 350 and 320. They include three main kinds of scenes: relaxed persons in idyllic settings, either the heroized dead of an idealized Dionysiac afterlife or supernatural members of the Thiasos; combats of Arimasps and griffins or animal combats often involving griffins; and finally, either single animals or Sea Thiasos personages. In addition, a few Amazons-and-Greeks, Amazons-and-Griffins, or Lapiths-and-Centaurs battle groups are occasionally found. Dionysiac afterlife on a sarcophagus speaks for itself, the Sea Thiasos would assume its psychopompic role in funerary contexts, and the single animals may be apotropaic guardians. Animal combats and Griffins and Arimasps have been variously interpreted, but opinion in general favors the unexpected and inevitable, yet perhaps also liberating, power of death.

The likeness between Tarantine reliefs and Athenian molds is unmistakable, especially in animal combats. Discrepancy in size, partly diverging repertories, and greater elaboration in Athens preclude either Athens taking Tarantine reliefs as models, or Athenian molds serving to make Tarantine reliefs, but a connection, with Athens apparently the leader, remains.

Other Atticizing Tarantine products include animal-headed rhyta, especially those with relief decorations on the neck, often featuring griffins,[87] also much of its soft limestone funerary sculpture.[88] It is also in Taras that clay banquet reliefs abound;[89] they are rare elsewhere outside Athens, if we interpret clay molds as meaning clay reliefs in Athens.

---

[86] R. Lullies, "Vergoldete Terrakotta-Appliken aus Tarent," a brief introduction in *AA* (*JdI* 73) 1958, pp. 143–155; Lullies, *Tarent*, a major presentation of the material; and Lullies, "Addenda," a richly dense update with important bibliography 1962–1977, which will not be repeated here. H. Hoffmann, in his review of Lullies, *Tarent* (*AJA* 68, 1964, pp. 315–316), stresses the Atticism of 4th-century Tarantine art and assumes Attic models for the gilt-clay reliefs. It may be that the Agora molds provide these models or at least echoes of them; they at least reinforce the Atticism noted by Hoffmann. See also Besques, *Louvre* IV, i, p. 97, pl. 92:b–f; C. Delplace, "A propos de nouvelles appliqués en terre cuite dorée représentant des griffons trouvées à Tarente," *BInstHistBelgRom* 39, 1968, pp. 31–46; E. Berger, *Antike Kunstwerke aus der Sammlung Ludwig*, II, *Terrakotten und Bronzen*, Basel 1982, nos. 129–130, pp. 75–77.

[87] See Hoffmann (footnote 41 above), p. 119 for some possible meanings of griffins and animal combat.

[88] L. Bernabò Brea, "I rilievi Tarantini in pietra tenera," *RivIstArch*, n.s. 1, 1952, pp. 5–241, esp. pp. 29–45, 199–235, with a discussion of funerary animals, including griffins, and of the Marine Thiasos, and Carter (footnote 35 above), pp. 17–20.

[89] See footnote 25 above.

ITALY: ETRUSCAN SARCOPHAGI

Herbig in 1952 published a number of Etruscan stone sarcophagi of Hellenistic date, of which a group, often imitating wooden sarcophagi with carved panels and mostly dating from the second half of the 4th century, not only carry the same motifs as many Agora molds but indicate how they could have been used.[90] We find on these sarcophagi single dancing figures (that correspond to the Agora vertical molds) carved on the narrow framing panels of the long sides and animal or human combats on the broad central frieze of those sides. A gorgoneion or another animal combat or animal occupies the narrow sides. In addition, a number of other sarcophagi carry related motifs, such as members of the Sea Thiasos.[91] It may well be through some medium such as casts from Agora molds, or Attic wooden sarcophagi, that animal combats and other Greek motifs, occasionally misinterpreted or reinterpreted (Nike into Etruscan Fury) by the Etruscan stone carvers, were transmitted to Etruria.

ITALY: PRAENESTINE CISTAE

Hill in 1969 drew attention to the abundance of griffins engraved on the lids of Praenestine cistae, chiefly of the 3rd century;[92] she noted the Italian craftsman's eclectic and sometimes apparently thoughtless use of the griffin as little more than decorative subsidiary pattern along with other animals and floral designs and doubted whether griffins retain on cistae the funerary significance they held on earlier objects in Italy. Praenestine griffins may be Atticizing at second remove, that is, through Tarantine or Apulian artifacts.

ITALY: APULIAN VASES

Apulian vases in ornate style of the second half of the 4th century also offer some parallels to Agora molds, but relatively remote ones, perhaps just because the pottery is inspired by Attic models rather than made in Attic workshops. It is the general style that recalls Agora molds in such pieces as the krater from Ruvo with an amazonomachy.[93]

---

[90] The following are among the closest parallels between Etruscan sarcophagi and Agora molds. Herbig, no. 6, pp. 14–15, pls. 37, 38, in Boston: head, two lions attack bull; feet, two griffins attack horse; long sides, Amazonomachy and battle scene. Herbig, no. 50, p. 32, pls. 11, 12, in Copenhagen: both long sides, at corners, Etruscan winged demons; center, lion and griffin attack bull. Herbig, no. 84, pp. 47–48, pl. 8, in Rome: corners, winged dancing figures; all four sides, varied and indistinct animal combats. Herbig, no. 98, pp. 53–54, pls. 13, 14, in Tarquinia: front, lion and griffin attack boar, panther; back, lion and griffin attack deer, panther; both narrow sides, gorgoneion. Herbig, no. 99, p. 54, pl. 14, in Tarquinia: corners, winged dancing figures; long sides, lion and griffin attack boar, two lions attack horse; narrow sides, gorgoneion. Herbig, no. 100, pp. 54–55, pls. 15, 16, in Tarquinia: corners, winged dancing figures; long sides, lion and lioness or panther attack deer; narrow side, two seated sphinxes face each other. F. Matz ("Chronologische Bemerkungen zu einigen Deckelfiguren etruskischer Sarkophage," *MarbWinckProg* 1973 [pp. 13–36], pp. 17–20) places the Boston sarcophagus, Herbig, no. 6, close to 310 B.C.

[91] Herbig, pls. 25, 46, 49, 59, 68–71, 78–84, 108–110.

[92] D. K. Hill, "Griffins and Praenestine Metalwork," in *Hommages Renard* III (footnote 40 above), pp. 296–303.

[93] Borda (footnote 21 above), fig. 37, dated *ca.* 330–320.

Schneider-Herrmann[94] notes that the earliest Griffins and Arimasps on Apulian vases occur *ca.* 360–350 and that it is in the 4th century that griffins join the Dionysiac Thiasos.

ITALY AND SICILY: ARULAE

A general updating of arulae, sturdy altar- or table-shaped clay artifacts, often decorated in relief on one or more faces, is long overdue; their study has proceeded in uneasy
and disjointed fashion. Van Buren[95] in 1918 made a good attempt at setting the material in
order, but the study is now, of course, very much out of date. Jastrow in 1941 and 1946 used
the reliefs on arulae for her important study of the way in which clay workshops use casts
from their first molds to make second molds and of the shrinkage and blurring that occur in
the process.[96] Orlandini in 1959 gathered the earlier bibliography in his publication of
arulae from the area of Gela.[97] Other articles tend to be simply records of excavations,[98]
brief iconographical studies,[99] or notices of museum acquisitions or collections.[100] Arulae
may have been used as portable altars or offering tables but should not be confused with
miniature clay altars, which are made differently and tend to be much smaller.[101] Mean-
while, one notes the recovery of arulae from cemeteries (although usually outside graves),

[94] G. Schneider-Herrmann, "Zur Grypomachie auf apulischen Vasenbildern," *BABesch* 50, 1975, pp. 271–
272; see also K. Schauenburg, "Arimaspen in Unteritalien," *RA* 1982, pp. 249–262.

[95] Van Buren (footnote 57 above).

[96] E. Jastrow, "Abformung und Typenwandel in der antiken Tonplastik," *OpusArch* 2, 1939–41, pp. 1–28;
eadem, "Two Terracotta Reliefs in American Museums," *AJA* 50, 1946, pp. 67–80. The relationship of
arulae and Etruscan urns is briefly examined in another technical study: L. B. van der Meer, "Archetype—
Transmitting Model—Prototype. Studies of Etruscan Urns from Volterra, I," *BABesch* 50, 1975,
pp. 179–186.

[97] P. Orlandini, "Arule arcaiche a rilievo nel Museo Nazionale di Gela," *RömMitt* 66, 1959, pp. 97–103.

[98] E.g., A. de Franciscis, *NSc*, ser. 8, 11, 1957 (pp. 184–190), pp. 184–186, figs. 1–8, Archaic arulae from
Monasterace Marina; E. De Miro, *NSc*, ser. 8, 12, 1958 (pp. 232–287), p. 277, fig. 46, Archaic arula from
Heraclea Minoa; F. G. Lo Porto, *NSc*, ser. 8, 20, 1966 (pp. 136–231), pp. 153–156, figs. 13–16, Archaic
arulae from Metapontum; M. N. Pagliardi, *NSc*, ser. 8, 26, 1972, *Supplement, Sibari* 3 (pp. 52–143), no. 213,
pp. 115–116, figs. 122, 123, Archaic arula from Sybaris; J. Du Plat Taylor, "Motya, a Phoenician Trading
Settlement in Sicily," *Archaeology* 17, 1964 (pp. 91–100), p. 97, fig. 10, arula from Motya; N. Bonacasa *et al.*,
Himera, II, *Campagne di Scavo 1966–73*, Rome 1976, pls. 29, 51, 52, 71 (the piece with two griffins and prey,
pl. 71, is particularly interesting for its possible relationship with Agora molds; it is dated second half of the
5th century [p. 445]).

[99] E.g., P. Devambez, "Une 'arula' sicilienne au Louvre," *MonPiot* 58, 1972, pp. 1–23; T. Fischer-Hansen,
"To Siciliske Arulae," *Meddedelser fra Ny Carlsberg Glyptotek* 30, 1973, pp. 61–88; *idem*, "Terrakottakunst
fra Sicilien," *Meddedelser fra Ny Carlsberg Glyptotek* 31, 1974, pp. 22–58.

[100] E.g., B. M. Kingsley, *The Terracottas of the Tarantine Greeks*, San Simeon 1976, no. 36.

[101] P. Wuilleumier, "Brûle-parfums en terre cuite," *Mélanges d'archéologie et d'histoire* 46, 1929, pp. 43–76
and more recently, Siebert (footnote 21 above), p. 240; C. E. Vafopoulou, "An Unpublished Arula in the
Ashmolean Museum," *JHS* 102, 1982, pp. 229–232. For examples in Athens see D. B. Thompson, "Three
Centuries of Hellenistic Terracottas II C. The Satyr Cistern," *Hesperia* 31, 1962 (pp. 244–262) [reprinted,
Hellenistic Pottery and Terracottas, Princeton 1987], nos. 19, 20, pp. 256–260, 262, pls. 90, 91. For Corinth
see O. Broneer, "The Corinthian Altar Painter," *Hesperia* 16, 1947, pp. 214–223; *idem*, "Terracotta Altars
from Corinth," *Hesperia* 19, 1950, pp. 370–375; *Corinth* XII, nos. 883–887, 889–891, 894, pp. 130–131,
pls. 65, 66. For Pergamon see E. Töpperwein, *Terrakotten von Pergamon*, Berlin 1976, nos. 601–606,
pp. 144–145, 242–243, pls. 86, 87. For South Italy see Besques, *Louvre* IV, i, pls. 84, 85, pp. 90–91.

sanctuaries, households, and, since they are solid little structures, from varied fills where they have survived.

Arulae have a floruit in the 6th century B.C. and are more often found outside the mainland, in Sicily and South Italy in particular. Motifs used on arulae, with great emphasis on animal combats, fit the Agora molds, although a bit uneasily, since many arulae favorites, e.g. Herakles, are lacking on Athenian molds. This could, of course, be due to the chance of excavation and what particular Athenian workshop dump ended up as one of the stoa building fills.

There are 5th- and 4th-century arulae, although in lesser number than during their 6th-century acme, and even Hellenistic ones, and it is among these late examples that we find occasional strong resemblances to Agora molds.[102] Of particular importance are the arulae or antepagmenta from Apulian Gioia del Colle: in an important article, Scarfi published the site of Monte Sannace near Gioia del Colle, excavated between 1957 and 1961, which gives us much-needed material for the knowledge of an Apulian city of the 4th and 3rd century, even though only a small part of the site was excavated.[103] Two sets of arula-like objects with griffins attacking horses very much in the manner of Agora molds and dating from the mid-3rd century give us the possibility of an architectural use for some of the reliefs and provide another link between Athens and South Italy.

BLACK SEA: METALWORK

The curiously close parallels between Agora molds, especially the animal combats, and the metalwork found in a number of barrows with rich burials dating from the second half of the 4th and perhaps the beginning of the 3rd century in both the Ukraine and the Bosporan Kingdom might prompt a reappraisal of the notable Atticism of much of the Black Sea material, which has too often been studied piecemeal.[104]

In the Ukraine, three barrows in particular offer close parallels: Chertomlyk, Tolstaya Mogila, and Solokha, on the banks of the great bend of the Dneiper.[105] On either side of the

[102] Post-Archaic arulae are beginning to attract attention; three groups of them may throw some light on Agora molds. Settis (footnote 36 above) publishes a group of unusual and elaborate arulae from Medma, dated to the late 5th century but possibly in part later, with scenes from tragedy and myth. D. Ricciotti ("Arule," in *RomaMedioRep*, pp. 72–96), discussing arulae from Rome, suggests that since so many arulae were found in tombs, they may have something to do with the *corredo funebre*; note the molds, no. 52 (p. 78, pl. 17), Griffin and Arimasp, end of the 4th century, and no. 88 (p. 96, pl. 22), Maenad with tympanon, no date. On the arulae themselves, we see griffins, maenads, and Nereids, but none close enough to the Agora examples to argue a direct relationship. From Metapontum: Letta (footnote 25 above), pp. 145–151.

[103] B. M. Scarfi, "Gioia del Colle," *NSc*, ser. 8, 16, 1962 (pp. 1–286), p. 134, fig. 129, fragment of arula-like "clay antepagmentum" with a moldmade relief, griffin attacking horse, found on the paved area in front of the imposing building constructed *ca.* mid-3rd century over five monumental tombs destroyed then; p. 256, fig. 218, arula-like clay "architectural elements", with moldmade reliefs, two griffins attack horse, within a wave, palmette, dentil, and rinceau frame (apparently added in the mold because the central motif, as a result of a [or several] secondary archetype[s], no longer filled the frame). From House II.9, the best house in the area, one piece found just beside the threshold, others in the house cistern. Dated 3rd century.

[104] An overview of the material can be found in two well-illustrated works with bibliographies: "Scythians" and Artamanov, *Treasures*.

[105] Chertomlyk: the griffins on the famous silver amphora (Artamanov, *Treasures*, pl. 170) and on a gold gorytos, scabbard, and gold plaques (*ibid.*, p. 50, fig. 93, pls. 181, 183, 185, and "Scythians," no. 68, p. 109,

Kerch straits, three more: Kul Oba on the Crimaean side, Great Bliznitza on the Taman peninsula, and Seven Brothers (Barrow 3) on the lower Kuban left bank;[106] there are also sporadic finds elsewhere.[107] In addition to close parallels to specific objects, the material in these tombs, apart from some easily discernible Scythian objects, belongs very much to the inner circle of the assemblage of which Agora molds are a part. The same repertory with Animal Combats, Griffins and Arimasps, Sea Thiasos, Dionysiac Thiasos, and single animals is used very much the same way. The chief difference is that the barrows from the Black Sea tend to feature these motifs in precious materials and with superior workmanship.

BLACK SEA: BOSPORAN SARCOPHAGI

In an important work, Vaulina and Wasowicz[108] examine Bosporan wooden sarcophagi, making full use of context and studies in other fields. Most of these sarcophagi were found in the region immediately on both sides of the straits of Kerch, a group of them to be associated with the Bosporan Kingdom under the Spartocids, dating as they do from the 4th and early 3rd centuries. It may be that the dates could come down a decade or two, but this will need careful restudy of all material from Bosporan barrows in connection with its Macedonian and Attic counterparts.

Vaulina and Wasowicz publish preserved fragments of sarcophagi, with details of their construction and ornamentation. They point out the abundance of wood objects of different kinds in Bosporan tombs along with the more usually preserved ceramics; the construction of sarcophagi with tenons, pegs, and glue rather than nails; the use of luxury woods from Eastern Mediterranean trees, not local flora, for different parts of sarcophagi (cypress and cedar for planks, yew in sculpture, juniper and boxwood for turned moldings); the bright, not to say gaudy, appearance of the sarcophagi, with extensive polychromy, gilt moldings, and ornaments on red or pink backgrounds, wood and ivory encrustation, amber and glass centers to Ionic column volutes, patterned cloth or fur also used as decoration, and the finishing touch of painted lead akroteria. Architectural decoration is favored, with animal combats coming next. Finally the authors review the evidence for sarcophagi having been made in the Eastern Mediterranean, the close relations between Athens and the Bosporan Kingdom in the 4th century, and the strong possibility of a number of sarcophagi being

---

pl. 10) are perhaps the closest of all to those on Agora molds, and there is a gorgoneion ornament related to Agora gorgoneia (Artamanov, *Treasures*, p. 50, fig. 95). Tolstaya Mogila: griffins on a gold scabbard and on a superb gold collar are also close ("Scythians," nos. 170, 171, p. 126, pls. 30–32). Solokha: gorytos with griffin and lion attacking deer (Artamanov, *Treasures*, pl. 161).

[106] Kul Oba: bracelet and silver vase with Animal Combats (Artamanov, *Treasures*, pls. 236–238, 242, 245, 246); see also the painted sarcophagus (footnote 109 below). Great Bliznitza: sarcophagus with griffin and deer, Kalathiskos Dancer, and gorgoneion gold ornaments, gold headdress decorated with Griffins and Arimasps (*ibid.*, p. 77, fig. 148, pls. 266, 284, 285, 291–294). Seven Brothers: griffin sword hilt and ring with leopard and deer (*ibid.*, pls. 132, 137).

[107] E.g., Vani: K. S. Gorbunova, "Archaeological Investigations on the Northern Shore of the Black Sea in the Territory of the Soviet Union, 1965–1970," *JHS-AR* 1971–72 (pp. 48–59), p. 59, fig. 22, gold brooch with two lions attacking ibex. Duvanli: I. Venedikov and T. Gerassimov, *Trakivskogo Izkusstvo*, Sofia 1973, pls. 170–172, phiale with Apobates Race, also in Strong (footnote 73 above), pl. 15:b.

[108] Vaulina and Wasowicz, *Bois*, with full bibliography.

made in Attic workshops. They note that the series of sarcophagi ends after the second half
of the 3rd century, not to start again until the beginning of the 1st.[109]

Again the simple listing of a few sarcophagi with motifs related to Agora molds is not
enough to convey the closeness of the relationship between many of these wooden objects
from Russia and other Attic or Atticizing pieces in metal, stone, or clay. Pose, arrangement,
and choice of figures all suggest interrelated workshops in Athens with the same models
interpreted in different materials.

BLACK SEA: KERCH VASES

Kerch vases, that is, Attic vases of the mid-4th and especially those of the second half of
the 4th century, exported in considerable quantity to the Bosporan Kingdom and provided
with themes (Arimasps, Amazons, griffins) probably meant to appeal to Bosporan buyers,
naturally provide parallels with Agora molds.[110] Nikai driving Chariots, Nereids, and the
Dionysiac Thiasos appear in addition to eastern motifs. But there is a quality of softness and
airiness in these vases that is unlike the rest of the interrelated assemblage: great numbers of
floating Erotes, bridal festivities, and Athenian festivals uncharacteristic of molds, metalwork, or mosaic.

The possible implications of the variety and luxury of Attic and Atticizing objects on the
northern shores of the Black Sea are briefly discussed below (pp. 31–32).

EGYPT: TOMB AND SARCOPHAGUS ORNAMENTATION

Sarcophagi in Naukratis were decorated with painted and gilt-clay ornaments, and
stucco ornaments (both painted and in relief) decorated both sarcophagi and tombs elsewhere in early Hellenistic Egypt.[111] One may also point to griffins and Sea Thiasoi on
Hadra vases, ash urns made, it seems, in Crete, but primarily for the Alexandrian market.[112] But comparisons with Egyptian material are not so close as those with Italy or the
Black Sea.

[109] Of particular interest for Agora molds are Vaulina and Wasowicz, *Bois*, no. 1, pp. 45–51, pls. I–VII, the
great Kul Oba painted sarcophagus, with Nike in Chariot, Abduction, Hunt, and Animal Frieze with griffins;
no. 4, pp. 68–71, pls. XL, XLI, Taman peninsula, of "Attic" type, with griffin and deer; no. 8, pp. 82–84,
pls. XLIX–LIV, Great Bliznitza Tomb I, with griffin and deer; and no. 12, pp. 87–94, pls. LXIII–
LXXXIII, from near Anapa, with Sea Thiasos. See also P. Pinelli and A. Wasowicz, *Musée du Louvre.
Catalogue des bois et stucs grecs et romains provenant de Kertch*, Paris 1986, no. 2, pp. 38–40, with griffins
and bull.

[110] E.g., Schefold, *Untersuchungen*, no. 228, pl. 21, which not only shows a Nike in Chariot but in shape
recalls the krater on the Agora Banquet relief **43**. Schefold's no. 392 (pl. 22:2), Theseus and Bull, might relate
to Agora **80**. J. M. Bohac (*Kercske Vazy*, Prague 1958, pl. 52) illustrates a griffin crouching with one paw up,
close to both metal and Agora molds like **74**; see also Zervoudaki, "Reliefkeramik," 4th-century Attic relief
ware sharing subject matter with the Kerch vases and the Agora molds.

[111] E.g., C. Watzinger, *Griechische Holzsarcophage aus der Zeit Alexanders des Grossen*, Leipzig 1905,
no. 8, pp. 32–33, from Memphis, stucco and clay decoration; Gardner (footnote 53 above), pl. XVI, pp. 24–34,
sarcophagus ornaments, gilt and painted, clay and plaster.

[112] E.g., Daszewski (footnote 79 above), pl. 12:a; A. Enklaar, "Les hydries de Hadra II: Formes et ateliers,"
BABesch 61, 1986 (pp. 41–63), p. 47, fig. 7; Buschor (footnote 56 above). For production of Hadras in Crete
see P. J. Callaghan and R. E. Jones, "Hadra Hydriae and Central Crete: A Fabric Analysis," *BSA* 80, 1985,
pp. 1–17.

THE ATTIC REPERTORY AND BLACK SEA TRADE

A brief review of material comparable to the Agora molds in style and subjects shows that a repertory of elegant motifs, used partly for decoration, especially of costly structures and objects for private use, was common to much of the Greek world during the second half of the 4th century. This material, sometimes derived from major Attic works of art, often features animal combats and confrontations, as well as combats involving griffins fighting other animals or else Amazons or Arimasps. The most splendid examples of this repertory were recovered from sites along the shores of the Black Sea and the most numerous examples from South Italy; yet the place of origin does seem to have been Athens.

The close relationship during most of the 4th century between the Bosporan Kingdom, under the middle Spartocids, and Athens had already been stressed by Minns.[113] It is emphasized by inscriptions, such as the one honoring Spartokos (*IG* II², 653), by bronze statues of Crimaean dynasts in the Athenian Agora (Deinarchos, 1.43), and by the speech of Demosthenes (xx.31–35) stressing the importance of Bosporan good will for the wheat supply of Athens, especially in times of scarcity in the city.[114] This close relationship may begin to provide clues to explain aspects of the repertory of both Agora molds and related objects elsewhere in the Greek world.

It would be tempting to associate works of art executed for the Crimaean dynasts, either in Athens or for export, with the models of those Agora molds concerned with animal combats featuring griffins. It would be tempting as well to connect the desire on the part of skilled Athenian craftsmen to please the tastes of wealthy customers from the Black Sea with the new popularity of themes involving griffins and their traditional adversaries in the 4th century. Greek craftsmen, looking for appropriate myths to set in the foreigners' homeland, might have turned to Herodotos recounting Scythian myths, that of the Griffins and Arimasps or of the Snake-footed Lady (*Histories* iv.9–10, 13). It might thus have come about that the evocative and decorative griffins appealed in turn to other customers of the manufactured products of Athens, those from Italy. It could be for that reason that Tarantine or Etruscan sarcophagi became decorated with griffins or that metalwork in Crete bore a Snake-footed Lady,[115] copies of those richer artifacts, precious woods inlaid with ivory and decorated with gilt wood or metal, fine vessels, weapons, and headgear that were shipped to the Ukraine or the Crimea.

---

[113] E. A. Minns, *Scythians and Greeks: A Survey of Ancient History and Archaeology on the North Coast of the Euxine from the Danube to the Caucasus*, Cambridge 1913, echoed, after more material became available for study, by later scholars, e.g., W. Blavatsky, "Le processus de développement historique et le rôle des états antiques situés au nord de la Mer Noire," *XI Congrès International des Sciences Historiques, Stockholm 1960, Rapports*, II, *Antiquité*, Uppsala 1960, pp. 98–116, or C. M. Danoff, *s.v.* "Pontos Euxeinos" in *RE*, Suppl. IX, 1962 (cols. 866–1175), cols. 1062–1151.

[114] J. McK. Camp II, "Drought and Famine in the 4th Century," in *Hesperia*, Suppl. XX (footnote 66 above), pp. 9–17; *idem, The Water Supply of Ancient Athens from 3000 to 86 B.C.*, diss. Princeton University 1978. Dr. Camp generously allowed me to consult the latter work in manuscript during the summer of 1978 and discussed with me the strong evidence he has gathered for a serious famine in Athens in the third quarter of the 4th century.

[115] See footnotes 63, 86, and 90 above.

The role of Macedonia as another customer for the best that Athenian metalworking establishments had to offer and its relationship with Scythia in turn remain to be clarified. Discoveries of unlooted tombs in the 1960's and 1970's, such as at Derveni or Vergina, have joined material such as the jewelry from Amphipolis and will help this clarification.[116]

But as concerns Athens, it may be that the Agora molds remind us that in order to visualize the range of Athenian artistic production in the 4th century we should not confine ourselves to stone and clay. We know of great 4th-century Athenian architectural innovations and sculptural complexes, and we know as well the uneven quality of 4th-century pottery; but we should flesh out this picture (that owes too much to the chance of archaeological preservation) not only with the paintings that texts report to have been executed at the time, and with their echoes in mosaic or tomb painting, but with the intricately worked and inlaid wood, the elaborately delicate or aggressively lively metalwork, the bold and baroque stucco or painted clay that we recover from other parts of the Greek or Greek-influenced world.

VI. USE

Since we do not have the objects made from Athenian molds, we must be particularly careful about assigning a use to them. It might be best first to consider what we know of moldmade reliefs in the Greek world. Moldmade reliefs, of clay for the most part, although we cannot entirely discount metal hammered into molds, plaster, and even dough or other edibles, fall into a number of easily recognizable categories, none of which the Agora molds absolutely fit.

Votive plaques or tablets

Sizable stone reliefs, metal plaques, or painted wooden tablets which may indeed have been the most numerous, even though the most perishable, could all be used for votive dedications. So too, of course, could clay tablets, painted or moldmade with representations in relief. Clay relief plaques are known from a great many sanctuaries all over the Greek world, perhaps the best known group being those recovered from a sanctuary in Lokri.[117]

[116] Derveni tombs: Makaronas (footnote 85 above); *The Search for Alexander*, New York 1980, nos. 123–139, pp. 162–171, pls. 13, 19–21. Vergina tombs: Andronikos, *Vergina*, pp. 55–235. Amphipolis jewelry: *The Search for Alexander*, nos. 88–90, pp. 148–149, pls. 12, 13; see reports by D. Lazarides in Πρακτικά 1956, pp. 141–142, pl. 48; 1957, pp. 70–72, pl. 21; 1958, pp. 81–83, pls. 56–58; 1960, pp. 67–73, pls. 47, 48, 51; 1961, pp. 63–67, pl. 31.

[117] A sampler of painted and relief votive clay plaques from various periods and areas of the Greek world follows:

Aigina and general: Boardman, "Votive Plaques."

Athens, Akropolis: Brouskari (footnote 19 above), pp. 41–42, figs. 59–67, 69–71. B. Graef and E. Langlotz, *Die antiken Vasen von der Akropolis zu Athen*, Berlin 1925–1933, I, nos. 286, 287, p. 28, pl. 10; no. 414, p. 43, pl. 14; nos. 2493–2592, pp. 242–253, pls. 101–111; II, nos. 1037–1051, pp. 93–95, pls. 80–82. For plaques from the Shrine of Nymphe see Brouskari, *op. cit.*, pp. 84–85; I. Meliades, «Ἀνασκαφὴ νοτίως τῆς Ἀκροπόλεως», Πρακτικά 1957, pp. 23–26, pl. 2.

Athens, Agora: Boardman, "Votive Plaques," p. 197.

Votive plaques could be dedicated both to gods and to heroes, and we find representations of them on vase paintings and even on votive tablets themselves. Depending on the sanctuary and on the size and importance of the tablet, they would be set up on bases about the shrine, hung on sacred trees near by, or more commonly nailed to or hung on pegs from the walls of the sanctuary.[118]

Votive plaques, and relief clay plaques in particular, share some common characteristics besides the suspension hole with which they are usually provided. They tend to show the local divinity, often seated to denote habitation in the sanctuary, or groups of divinities, and votaries bringing gifts. Some appropriate moment in the mythology of the particular deity or expression of his power can be shown, and illustrations of moments in the festival of the particular sanctuary or of the athletic events at games given for that festival are also canonical. Apart from Banquet reliefs, a possible Assembly of Gods, and, stretching a point, the Kalathiskos Dancer and the Apobates, Agora molds are iconographically unsuitable for votives; this is particularly so in the case of animal combats, which may indeed form part of the furnishings of a heroön or sanctuary but are seldom dedicated as votive tablets.[119]

Brauron: P. G. Themelis, *Brauron: Führer durch das Heiligtum und das Museum*, Athens 1971, pp. 76–81, painted relief plaques.

Corinth: A. N. Stillwell and J. L. Benson, *Corinth*, XV, iii, *The Potters' Quarter, The Pottery*, Princeton 1984, nos. 1320–1357, pp. 239–245, pls. 55, 56, 112, 113, 122, painted, 7th–6th centuries.

Corinth (Penteskouphia): H. A. Geagan, "Mythological Themes in the Plaques from Penteskouphia," *AA* (*JdI* 85) 1970, pp. 31–48, painted, mostly 6th century.

Amyklai: C. Chestou, «'Ανασκαφὴ ἐν 'Αμύκλαις», Πρακτικά 1956, pp. 211–212 and pls. 104, 105, 5th-century relief plaques.

Olynthos: e.g., D. M. Robinson, *Excavations at Olynthus*, IV, *The Terra-Cottas at Olynthus Found in 1928*, Baltimore/London 1931, no. 358, pp. 65–66, pl. 37, relief, late 5th century.

Crete: e.g., H. W. Catling, "The Knossos Area 1974–76," *JHS-AR* 1976–77 (pp. 3–23), pp. 20–21, figs. 48–50. A. Lebessi, "Sanctuary of Hermes and Aphrodite near Kato Syme Viannou," *AAA* 6, 1973 (pp. 104–114), p. 114, relief plaques of Protogeometric through 6th-century date, described but not illustrated. *BCH* 85, 1961, p. 897, 5th-century plaques from the Arkouda cave. Forster, "Plaques."

Taras: relief votive plaques to a number of heroes, the Dioskouroi in particular, published in a number of places, e.g. N. Breitenstein, *Danish National Museum, Catalogue of Terracottas, Cypriote, Greek, Etrusco-Italian and Roman*, Copenhagen 1941, pp. 43–45, nos. 382–398, pls. 46, 47.

Lokri: H. Prückner, *Die Lokrischen Tonreliefs*, Mainz 1968, where Lokri plaques are dated in the second quarter of the 5th century; they are mostly found in the sanctuary of Persephone where they came as votives. From the point of view of Agora molds, pl. 4:4, a fragment now in Taranto that shows a piece of furniture with relief panels, reminds us of carved wood and its possible clay imitations, not only in sarcophagi but also in furniture.

Lipari: L. Bernabò Brea and M. Cavalier, *Il Castello di Lipari e il Museo Archeologico Eoliano*, Palermo 1977, pp. 133–135, figs. 146–148, 150, 151, votive relief plaques of the late 4th to early 3rd century from the sanctuary of Demeter and Kore at Terreno Maggiore.

Troy: D. B. Thompson, *Troy*, Suppl. Monograph III, *The Terracotta Figurines of the Hellenistic Period*, Princeton 1963, nos. 103–128, pp. 108–116, pls. 27, 28, reliefs of the horseman hero, 3rd–1st centuries.

Orta Köy: Besques, *Louvre* III, D 723–D 736, pp. 112–114, pls. 140–142, reliefs, late 3rd and 2nd centuries.

[118] For ways in which plaques were set up or hung in sanctuaries, see Boardman, "Votive Plaques," pp. 187–189.

[119] Some examples follow.

Samothrace: E. Conze *et al.*, *Neue archäologische Untersuchungen auf Samothrake* II, Vienna 1880,

Architectural Revetments

Terracotta painted or relief plaques for the protection of wooden-framed buildings, used in continuous or interrupted friezes or occasionally for other kinds of revetments (sima, antepagmentum), have a long history in the Greek world, with a strong floruit in the 6th century, after which stone often replaces clay. There are three areas in particular where relief plaques were much in use: the Greek cities of Anatolia; Sicily and Southern Italy; and the Etrusco-Italic region.[120] A fourth, the mainland itself, also has its own traditions but seems to have made less use of clay.[121]

The repertory of 6th-century Etrusco-Italic plaques, those that show the most figured decoration, fits in remarkably well with that of Agora molds: chariots, banquets, animals. And it is in the Etrusco-Italic area that clay plaques were used longest, almost merging into the following 1st-century Campana plaque development.[122] But if plaques from Agora molds were intended for architectural use, on the outside of buildings like all Greek plaques

---

pl. 49, anta capital of Propylaion of Ptolemy II, *ca.* 285–280, with two griffins attacking a deer, motif close to Agora molds with less careful detail.

Paros: two reliefs, probably from a heroön, in Paros, one with a banquet and the other with a lion attacking a bull, cf. Hölscher (footnote 46 above), pp. 31–36, pl. 5.

Thasos: C. Picard, "Trapézophore sculpté d'un sanctuaire Thasien," *MonPiot* 40, 1944, pp. 107–134, pl. 10, with two griffins attacking a deer. The piece is dated in Roman Imperial times, but it is not impossible that it constitutes a Roman reworking and readaptation of a Hellenistic piece; there is a strong contrast between a small frieze of humans in Roman style and the great animal combat taking up most of the space.

Some clay votive plaques with griffins were used in Archaic times, e.g., in Praisos (Forster, "Plaques," pp. 255–256, fig. 19) and Smyrna (Boardman, "Votive Plaques," p. 199, 7th century).

[120] Good bibliography and review of topic by A. Andrén, *Architectural Terracottas from Etrusco-Italic Temples*, Lund 1940, pp. LXXI–CCXLIII and *idem*, *s.v.* "Terracotta" in *EAA* VII, Rome 1966, pp. 732–743. We might note a few regional studies:

Anatolia: Å. Åkerström (*Die Architektonischen Terrakotten Kleinasiens*, Lund 1966) suggests a Corinthian origin in the second half of the 7th century for such building decorations and stresses a floruit in Anatolia in the second half of the 6th century.

Sicily and South Italy: E. D. Van Buren, *Archaic Fictile Revetments in Sicily and Magna Graecia*, London 1923, still with useful illustrations.

Etrusco-Italic: A. Andrén, "Osservazioni sulle terrecotte architettoniche etrusco-italiche," *OpusRom* 8, 1974, pp. 1–16. Andrén thinks terracotta revetments must have reached Italy before the mid-6th-century date often advanced. E. D. Van Buren, *Figurative Terra-cotta Revetments in Etruria and Latium in the VI. and V. Centuries B.C.*, London 1921 is out of date but has useful illustrations. S. Stopponi, *Case e palazzi d'Etruria*, Milan 1985, with bibliography.

[121] For an overview of Archaic material see N. Winter, *A Handbook of Greek Architectural Terracottas*, I, *The Archaic Period*, forthcoming. For a recent study, limited to the Corinthian system, see J. Heiden, *Korinthische Dachziegel. Zur Entwicklung der korinthischen Dächer*, Frankfort/New York 1987. Good basic bibliography to 1966 appears in Andrén, *EAA* VII (footnote 120 above), but without K. A. Rhomaios, Κέραμοι τῆς Καλυδῶνος, Athens 1951, which includes a painted sima (pp. 94–97), with Nikai racing chariots. R. Nicholls, "Architectural Terracotta Sculpture from the Agora," *Hesperia* 39, 1970, pp. 115–138, belongs more to sculpture than to revetment, but G. Steinhauer (Δελτ 27, 1972, Β′ 1 (1977), pp. 245–246, pl. 182) publishes a remarkable set of Laconian clay metopes in relief, walking hoplites and riders, dated to the beginning of the 6th century. For a thorough study of 5th- and 4th-century Attic material, see G. Hübner, "Dachterrakotten aus dem Kerameikos von Athen. Ein Beitrag zur Bauornamentik des 5. und 4. Jhs. v. Chr.," *AthMitt* 88, 1973, pp. 67–143, pls. 57–76.

[122] Borbein, *Campanareliefs*, p. 13 and § 5, pp. 20–24.

known so far, or on the inside on the analogy either of painted decorations or of the Augustan Campana reliefs (a promising clue appears in the mid-4th-century House of the Mosaics at Eretria, where a gorgoneion in clay was recovered from one of the mosaic rooms where it had apparently been used as decoration[123]), it is difficult to believe that no plaques, be it only workshop rejects if the entire production was meant for export, should have been recovered in Athens.

Stucco Reliefs

It has been suggested that Agora molds could have served for plaster or stucco reliefs;[124] this deserves consideration. Hellenistic stucco reliefs are usually treated as an appendage of the more abundant and elaborate Roman ones, as by Mielsch,[125] whose work, largely complete by 1970, was partly superseded by Ling's important article[126] on pre-Augustan Italian stucco. To summarize some of the points made by Ling: the Pompeian "First" or "Masonry" style may have been invented in Athens in the first half of the 4th century; figured decoration came from a blend of the Greek tradition of masonry-style stucco and the Egyptian tradition of modeling and casting figures in plaster, the blending of both traditions taking place some time after the founding of Alexandria; figured decoration is rare in houses before the 2nd century.[127] We should add, however, the tomb in Leukadia with a freehand-modeled stucco frieze, dated by Petsas about 300,[128] to Ling's full list of references to Priene, Pergamon, and Alexandria, including the use of plaster medallions and figures as decoration for sarcophagi. The evidence for moldmade stucco reliefs of the kind that would be produced by Agora molds is scanty,[129] and if the Athenian molds were intended for stucco reliefs it is unusual not to find associated with them similar molds for the floral and architectural motifs used in greater quantity than figured ones in preserved stucco decoration. The Agora molds with their deep border and self-contained designs going to the edge of the frame would also seem ill suited to the loose, shallow, spacious style of stucco reliefs.

Comparison of the Athenian molds with the later stuccoes, especially those of the 1st century,[130] proves deceptive: as with Campana reliefs,[131] at first glance such mannerisms as the tiptoe stances and the presence of griffins encourage us to look more closely, but Italian

[123] See footnote 52 above.

[124] The suggestion was made, e.g., by R. Nicholls, recorded in Jameson (footnote 1 above); also by J. Binder, private communication, winter 1978, suggesting the resulting plaques of painted plaster might have been used in household shrines.

[125] H. Mielsch, *Römische Stuckreliefs* (*RömMitt-EH* XXI), Heidelberg 1975.

[126] R. Ling, "Stucco Decoration in Pre-Augustan Italy," *BSR* 40, 1972, pp. 11–57, with full bibliography of earlier material.

[127] Cf. in Delos, J. Marcadé, "A propos des statuettes hellénistiques en aragonite du Musée de Délos," *BCH* 76, 1952 (pp. 96–135), pp. 109–113, figs. 8–11.

[128] Petsas (footnote 80 above).

[129] Ling ([footnote 126 above], p. 18, note 45) lists some Alexandrian moldmade reliefs, but these are too attenuated and stylized to be close.

[130] E.g., those from the Casa Farnesina, *ca.* 20 B.C., well illustrated in I. Bragantini, A. M. Dolciotti, *et al.*, *Museo Nazionale Romano*, II, i, *Le pitture. Le decorazione della villa romana della Farnesina*, Rome 1982, figs. 52–55, 57, pls. 71–82, 110–121, 192–202. Wadsworth (footnote 12 above), pls. 1–9.

[131] Borbein, *Campanareliefs.*

stuccoes shine as yet another facet of the Neo-Attic complex: the attenuated figures, delicate decorativeness, and sharp and shallow relief of the plaster belong to a world far different from that of the energetic and lively scenes on Agora molds. It yet remains that Augustan stuccoes, like other Neo-Attic forms of decorative art, use in large part the Attic repertory composed or renewed during the 4th century.

Theophrastos (*On Stones*, 64–67) speaks of *gypsos*, meaning both gypsum plaster and lime plaster, as used in fastening stone together, that is as mortar, and also as useful for making impressions, but does not mention it as used in the decoration of buildings, which should mean that this use of *gypsos* was at least not widespread by his time. Later, Pliny (*Natural History* xxxv.153) talks of plaster molds as an invention of Lysistratos, brother of Lysippos, in the 4th century. Neither testimony allows us to accept or reject the notion of figured stucco reliefs in buildings of the second half of the 4th century, but taken together, they tend to the negative.

We should also note in connection with either clay or plaster reliefs used to decorate houses the preponderance among Agora molds of otherworldly themes, including Hero Banquets, which were more suited, one would think, to funerary use, although one must also remember that some of these otherworldly themes such as Animal Combats or Nereids on Ketoi appear in pebble mosaics inside houses or baths as well as in tomb paintings or in sarcophagus decoration.

Arulae

Arulae have been discussed above (pp. 27–28) in connection with comparative material. They bear moldmade reliefs that are self-contained and fit into a rectangle, use many of the motifs found on Agora molds, and would therefore make excellent candidates for the products of these molds. Against the attribution of Agora molds to arulae stand the dimensions of the largest vertical (usually dancer) Athenian molds, larger than known arulae, the lack of a local tradition of arulae going back to Archaic times in Athens, and the unlikelihood of Italy or Sicily importing their arulae from Athens just when they tried to do everything else ceramic at home. None of these arguments in itself would be enough, but the chief one remains that there is not one arula that can be traced directly to an Agora mold, despite the obvious relationship between the two series.

Sarcophagus Decoration

Three main bodies of moldmade clay reliefs used to decorate sarcophagi or tomb furniture and utensils come from different times and parts of the Greek world: the 5th-century Melian reliefs, the 4th-century Tarantine gilt reliefs, and the Macedonian gilt reliefs; we should associate with them the 4th-century Bosporan wood, metal, and ivory sarcophagus reliefs.[132] Some of the clay reliefs are plaques, but most take the form of semi-plaque or cut-through reliefs, with each figure cut away from the background. They are often gilt and obviously stood for the bronze, gold, ivory, or boxwood panels and figures that would have been used for richer sarcophagi.

[132] Melian reliefs: P. Jacobstal, *Die melischen Reliefs*, Berlin 1931. Tarantine gilt reliefs: see footnote 86 above. Macedonian gilt reliefs: see footnote 83 above. South Russian sarcophagi: see footnote 109 above.

In style, subjects, and use of space (both vertical and horizontal compositions) and in the contrast of stately motifs stressing otherworldly themes with careless execution, the sarcophagus decorations, both in clay and in other materials (wood, stone, paint) stand closest to the Agora molds. But the clay decorations so far recovered are smaller than those that would have been produced by the run of Agora molds, and again, there is no single representation that can be traced to a specific mold, despite the general likeness.

Campana Plaques

These clay reliefs were made to decorate the inside of walls of sanctuaries, houses, and built tombs; since their floruit falls in Augustan times, they need to be considered as part of the entire Neo-Attic complex.[133] Neo-Attic style, at its best encouraging the ample serenities of the Ara Pacis or setting tables at Boscoreale with the double coolness of leaf pattern and silver sheen, at its worst could be positively institutional in its insistence on refinement, cleanliness, and unrelenting graciousness.

Stone reliefs, metalwork (especially tableware in silver), cameo glass, Arretine ware, Augustan stuccoes, and Campana clay reliefs all contribute to the Neo-Attic complex: their repertories intertwine. The style favors plant decoration, lightly poised figures, and heraldic compositions. The Neo-Attic detachment often commented on, that deepens into frigidity with the worst pieces and changes to an airy and welcoming timelessness in the best, is achieved with much space, a stress on the decorative, stylized movement, and sharp edges. The contrast with contemporary portraiture is startling and clearly reveals the Roman, and later, attitude that sees art as pleasant but not important, a relaxing and elegant background for those who can afford it and who take care of more serious business. Fuchs[134] rightly stressed Neo-Atticism's eclectic and disdainful quality: a secularization of thought perhaps more felt because of the frequency of divine or at least supernatural subjects, Nikai and Nereids, Kouretes, and Erotes. Just that precedence of pattern over meaning, that cool appraisal of the supernatural as picturesque, of the wings of power as decorative, of monsters as fine for the mantelpiece, are found in Ovid's *Metamorphoses*.

Two works, by Von Rohden and Winnefeld in 1911 and Borbein in 1968,[135] provide a good survey of Campana reliefs, so called after their principal collector in the 19th century. To summarize some of the points noted by Borbein: It is only in Italy that Campana reliefs serve as building decoration, and within Italy only from the Alps down to the region of Naples, with a concentration around Rome. Campana reliefs are used to decorate shrines, especially minor ones, but are more often used in villas, baths, theaters, even luxury ships

---

[133] Fuchs (*Vorbilder*) explores Neo-Attic art and in his summary (pp. 193–197) shows that it reached for sources in art of the late 5th, late 4th, and second half of the 2nd century, pointing out how secularized and decorative this art had become, with form much more important than content. C. Börker ("Neuattisches und pergamenisches an den Ara Pacis-Ranken," *JdI* 88, 1973, pp. 283–317) writes further of the mixed ancestry of Neo-Attic (Italian, Pergamene, and Attic), finding the Ara Pacis both the end and acme of late Hellenistic decoration.

[134] See footnote 133 above.

[135] Von Rohden-Winnefeld; Borbein, *Campanareliefs*. For a more recent study see S. Tortorella, "Le lastre Campana: Problemi di produzione e di iconografia," in *L'Art décoratif à Rome à la fin de la République et au début du Principat*, Rome 1981, pp. 61–99.

(Nemi), but above all in columbaria and tombs (inside); these plaques replace Etrusco-Italic architectural decoration in the mid-1st century. Campana plaques are a specifically Roman phenomenon, picking old and new figured and floral motifs not only from outside Etruscan tradition but from the entire Hellenistic world and blending them into a new mixture. These reliefs begin in the mid-1st century, have a floruit in the first quarter of the 1st century after Christ, and end by the mid-2nd century. Since Borbein's work, well-preserved Campana plaques with bright color still visible have been recovered from the Roman sanctuary of Apollo on the Palatine.[136]

At first glance, the size (up to 76 × 62 cm.), the sturdy rectangular composition, the use of similar motifs, and the simple fact that Campana plaques are clay reliefs made from clay molds makes them appear the logical descendants of, and explanation for, Agora molds. But it becomes clear upon further study that like the rest of the Neo-Attic complex they are a new creation of the 1st century, using the products of Agora molds, if they survived, or their models in more permanent materials, as well as models from other parts of the Hellenistic world and the Hellenistic centuries, as Borbein noted, to recompose a decorative form that belongs to its own time. Campana reliefs do not in fact provide us with a solution to the question of material and use for the products of Agora molds, those poor battered fragments and clumsy miniaturizations that nevertheless retain the drive and hot blood of the 4th century: ancestral, but not parental, to the Campana plaques.

Relief Wares

Moldmade reliefs, either instead of painted decoration or combined with it, have often been used on Greek pottery; for an overview of the succession of different relief wares in Greece, the basic work remains that of Courby,[137] which is otherwise out of date. More recent studies tend to be specialized.[138] From a look at the different relief wares of 4th-century and Hellenistic date, it becomes clear that Agora molds do not fit in with the late Hellenistic group of Megarian or Pergamene bowls, except for remotely sharing some motifs such as Nikai in chariots. Fourth- and 3rd-century medallion reliefs studied by Jentel offer better comparison, for instance in animal combats,[139] and other comparisons should emerge with the forthcoming publication of Jentel's studies on other contemporary relief

---

[136] Illustrated in color in G. Carettoni, "Nuova serie di grandi lastre fittili 'Campana'," *BdA* 58, 1973, pp. 75–87. A varied group of plaques including one (no. 16, p. 16, fig. 13) with a griffin-and-bull combat is published by H. Mielsch in *Römische Architekturterrakotten und Wandmalereien im Akademischen Kunstmuseum Bonn*, Berlin 1971.

[137] F. Courby, *Les vases grecs à relief*, Paris 1922.

[138] E.g., W. Schwabacher, "Hellenistische Reliefkeramik im Kerameikos," *AJA* 45, 1941, pp. 182–228; U. Hausmann, *Hellenistische Reliefbecher aus attischen und böotischen Werkstätten*, Stuttgart 1959; A. Greifenhagen, *Beiträge zur antiken Reliefkeramik*, Berlin 1963; J. Schäfer, *Hellenistische Keramik aus Pergamon*, Berlin 1968, pp. 64–100; Zervoudaki, "Reliefkeramik"; G. R. Edwards, *Corinth*, VII, iii, *Corinthian Hellenistic Pottery*, Princeton 1975, pp. 151–189; A. Hochuli-Gysel, *Kleinasiatische glasierte Reliefkeramik* (*Acta Bernensia* VII), Bern 1977; A. Laumonier, *Exploration archéologique de Délos*, XXXI, *La céramique hellénistique à reliefs. 1. Ateliers "ioniens"*, Paris 1977; Siebert (footnote 21 above); U. Sinn, *Die homerischen Becher: hellenistische Reliefkeramik aus Makedonien* (*AthMitt*, Beiheft VII), Berlin 1979; Rotroff, *Agora* XXII (footnote 4 above); T. Dohrn, "Schwarzgefirniste Plakettenvasen," *RömMitt* 92, 1985, pp. 77–106.

[139] Jentel (footnote 77 above), AP I, no. 48:a, p. 237, fig. 134.

wares. Fourth-century relief wares do share much of the repertory of the rest of the interrelated group but not more than mosaic or metal and perhaps less. It is clear at any rate
that Agora molds were not meant to produce reliefs for vases.

Moldmade Reliefs in Other Materials

The question of whether Agora molds could be intended for metal reliefs is not an idle
one; although the relief molds show no trace of having been used to cast metal,[140] reliefs
executed in repoussé, with the aid of a shallow mold (that is, hammered into a mold), with
details hand chased afterwards, existed in quantity in the Greek world, and we have large
numbers of these for the period of the late 4th and early 3rd centuries which correspond
with many of the Agora molds. Neumann[141] illustrates one mold, and the diadem he studies
must have been made over such a crisp and shallow mold. Small gold plaques made from the
same mold have been found in different barrows of the Bosporan region and the Ukraine,
and that this technique extended to larger objects is shown by the fact that the quivers from
one of the unlooted Macedonian tombs of Vergina and the Karagoeudashkh barrow are
apparently from the same mold.[142] In addition to occasional luxury objects found not only in
the Black Sea area but also in Greece, such as gold-covered quivers, more usual funerary
diadems, and small gold plaques often meant to ornament clothing,[143] there were small
metal plaques, about playing-card size, apparently used as ex-votos much as their modern
counterparts are.[144]

Three obstacles would seem, however, to make Agora molds unsuitable for metal reliefs: first, the high rims, which would impede hammering and be useless for the final relief
in metal; second, the size of both molds and the resulting metal reliefs, larger than any
known for the period; and finally, the coarseness of the clay and a carelessness of execution
thoroughly uncharacteristic of metalwork.

Edibles

One might also consider whether Agora molds could have been used for impermanent
materials, such as cakes, that texts tell us were often shaped in various forms. But there are

[140] For the appearance of molds used to cast metal, see C. C. Mattusch, "Bronze- and Ironworking in the
Area of the Athenian Agora," *Hesperia* 46, 1977, pp. 340–379.

[141] Neumann (footnote 63 above), pl. 59:1.

[142] P. Amandry was the first to note the similarity; see M. Andronikos, «Βεργίνα. Οἱ βασιλικοὶ τάφοι τῆς
Μεγάλης Τούμβας», *AAA* 10, 1977 (pp. 1–72), p. 66, note 11. See also Andronikos, *Vergina*, p. 181; A. P.
Mantsevitch, "On the Discovery of a Royal Tomb in Macedonia," *Soobshcheniia Gosudarstvennogo ordena
Lenina Ermitazha* 44, 1979, pp. 49–51 (in Russian, with English abstract); *idem*, "Discovery of a Royal Tomb
in Northern Greece (Ancient Macedonia)," *Vestnik drevnei istorii* 153, 1980, pp. 153–167 (in Russian, with
English abstract). The South Russian piece is also illustrated in Minns (footnote 113 above), pp. 220–221,
figs. 124, 125.

[143] E.g., from tombs in and near Thessaloniki, Kotzias (footnote 50 above), p. 883, fig. 16 (Sedes) and Δελτ
20, 1965, Β′ 2 (1968), p. 411, pls. 462, 463 (Stauropolis); from Thessaly, *Treasures of Ancient Macedonia*,
Thessaloniki [1978], nos. 22–29, pp. 35–36, pl. 5 (Katerini).

[144] *Ibid.*, nos. 434–457, pp. 101, 104–106, pls. 60, 62; A. K. Babritsas, «Ἀνασκαφὴ Μεσεμβρίας Θράκης»,
Πρακτικά 1973 (1975; pp. 70–82), pp. 77–79, pls. 92–96, from Mesembria. Katerina Rhomiopoulou, Director of the Museum in Thessaloniki, generously mentioned these in a personal communication, spring 1978.

two main ways to handle such shaping: either a close-grained dough is stamped with a hard mold in shallow intaglio, or a soft dough is hand shaped into a representation. Before the advent of sugar and chocolate few other edibles could be shaped in relief (e.g., almond paste, sesame sweets), and Agora molds of porous clay would be awkward and unlike what other ages and regions have used as cake stamps or cake molds.[145] Exceptions might include the pig and fish molds that could indeed have been used for food.

Moldmade Reliefs and Agora Molds

This brief review of the main series of moldmade reliefs in the Greek world (votive, architectural in clay and stucco, arula, sarcophagus, Campana, utensil, metal, and the hypothetical edibles) offers no immediate solution. Agora molds partake of the nature of votive, arula, architectural, and sarcophagus reliefs without belonging entirely to any of them as recovered so far, and we constantly run up against the absence of reliefs made from the Athenian molds, which should be present as workshop debris alongside the molds even if the entire relief production went for export.

Athenian Molds and Athens

While Agora molds share in a repertory that spread to most of the Greek world, that repertory is largely Attic, and if we cannot find the reliefs elsewhere, the molds must have been made and used in Athens; they look inexpensive and common enough to have served local customers without much to spend. It may be in the Athenian way of life in the late 4th century that we might find clues for the use of Agora molds. The most sensible way to use them would be to make clay reliefs with them. What would result would be raw-clay plaques of sturdy construction using a noble repertory common in the 4th century for areas where art and decoration mix, especially in funerary contexts.[146] This opens a number of possibilities.

A funeral is a family rite of passage, a ceremony, almost a festival requiring special activities, clothing, foods, and expenses. As with all festivals, both happy and sad, there is an area for the expression of feelings, helped by a body of customary actions and sayings, and

---

[145] E.g., J. Montandon, *Le livre du pain: histoire et gastronomie*, Lausanne 1974, bread and cake molds illustrated on pp. 18, 36, 61. For ancient bread stamps see W. Deonna, *Exploration archéologique de Délos*, XVIII, *Le mobilier délien*, Paris 1938, nos. 622–629, 631, pp. 230–233, pl. LXXVI (with discussion and bibliography); R. Pagenstecher, *Expedition Ernst von Sieglin. Die griechisch-ägyptische Sammlung Ernst von Sieglin*, II, iii, *Die Gefässe in Stein und Ton, Knochenschnitzereien*, Leipzig 1913, pp. 166–167, pls. 49–52; R. Zahn, "Thongeschirr," pp. 394–468 in T. Wiegand and H. Schrader, edd., *Priene*, Berlin 1904, pp. 465–468, figs. 573, 574; Besques, *Louvre* IV, i, pp. 103, 105, pls. 100:a–c, 104:a–c.

[146] The heroic repertory being re-used in the 4th century in a funerary context after serving gods or heroes in the 6th has been noted, e.g., by Karouzou ([footnote 42 above] particularly pp. 12–15) discussing a griffin-protome cauldron of the 4th century. Another griffin cauldron is discussed by F. Willemsen in "Zu den Lakedämoniergräbern im Kerameikos," *AthMitt* 92, 1977 (pp. 117–157), particularly pp. 148–150, where he dates this cauldron to the end of the 5th century; this date is possible because of, among other things, the spiky collar instead of a short ruff on the griffins' necks. See also P. Devambez, *Bas relief de Téos*, Paris 1962, concerning Amazons and animal combats, and H. Luschey, "Zur Wiederkehr archaischer Bildzeichen in der attischen Grabmalkunst des 4. Jahrhunderts v. Chr.," *Festschrift Bernhard Schweitzer* (*Neue Beiträge zur klassischen Altertumswissenschaft*), Stuttgart 1954, pp. 243–255. See also pp. 9–11 above.

an area for potlatch, that is for gathering reputation and renown by impressing the community with a display, or better, an expense, of wealth. This potlatch element was strong in ancient Greece, and in Athens in particular, where sumptuary laws tried more than once to curb it.[147] Funerals are not alone in inciting to potlatch: anyone who has experienced an American Christmas or a Greek Easter will recall the onerous efforts made, especially among the poor, to achieve the ephemeral and superfluous chocolate egg or glittering tree. Superfluous at least in the vision of human life as the exclusive pursuit of survival: food, shelter, sex, *y tiempo para gastarlos*. But human life has always been incongruous, with enormous amounts of time, money, and energy devoted to tinsel and bunting. Bunting and tinsel, because of a third element of festivals, make-believe, which mitigates the difference between rich and poor, allowing more of the community to participate in ceremonies. Santa Claus' costume is not really red velvet and ermine, glass chips sparkle in the foil crowns of divinities in Indian processions, and paper limousines burn in Chinese funerals. Since appearance and formula will consecrate and embody anything that has one foot in the supernatural world, make-believe is much used in funerary ceremonial.

Funerary make-believe can take many forms, from professional mourners to veneered coffins. In Greek antiquity it mostly took the ordinary form of substitution of materials or quantities in offerings: the false-bodied lekythos holding only the few drops of oil needed for an initial libation, gilt-clay beads or studs, crowns or reliefs substituting on bier, couch, and cerements for metal ones, paint mimicking relief and encrustation.[148] In this way, families

---

[147] Cicero (*Laws*, ii.26) notes sumptuary laws of Solon and adds, "Somewhat later it was promulgated by law that no one should build a tomb it would take ten men more than three days to build, nor to ornament it with stucco (*opere tectorio*), nor to set what they call herms upon it." And later, Demetrios of Phaleron in turn forbade that anything should be set over the tumulus except "a *columella* of no more than three cubits, or a *mensa* or a *labellum*. . . ."

[148] Examples of clay or plaster made to look like costlier materials may be found in various parts of the Greek world.

Attica: e.g., in the Kerameikos Museum, from Grave 10, Precinct V, dated *ca.* 430–420, a number of gilt-clay disks and rosettes; also from Grave hS 196, gilt-clay rosettes (B. Schlörb-Vierneisel, "Eridanos-Nekropole," *AthMitt* 81, 1966 (pp. 1–135), no. 144:3, p. 85, pl. 55:2).

Macedonia: see footnotes 82 and 83 above.

Hellenistic Egypt: see footnote 111 above.

Cyprus: gilt-clay alabastra and gilt-clay, paste, and metal wreaths, as well as raw-clay statues, in the pyre of Nikokreon, V. Karageorghis, *Salamis in Cyprus*, London 1969, pp. 153–155, pls. 88, XIII, XIV.

Italy: e.g., D. K. Hill, "Terra-Cotta Reliefs from Praeneste," *StEtr* 45, 1977, pp. 169–171 with bibliography, for clay attachments to funerary furniture; for the gilt-clay couch fittings, used into Roman times, e.g., M. Fortunati Zuccàla, "Nuove appliques fittili dalla necropoli romana di Gropello Cairoli," *Acme* 29, 1976, pp. 301–303. For gilt-clay imitation jewelry from South Italy see Besques, *Louvre IV*, i, pp. 100–101, pls. 95, 96. And of course the Tarantine gilt-clay sarcophagus decoration: see footnote 86 above. For chests and boxes with the metal panels and decorations that clay imitates, see, for example, E. Pernice, *Die hellenistische Kunst in Pompeji*, V, *Hellenistische Tische, Zistermündungen, Beckenuntersätze, Altäre und Truhen*, Berlin/Leipzig 1932, pp. 76–94, pls. 46–58.

For some general comment on imitation jewelry and examples in museum collections see R. A. Lunsingh-Scheurleer, "Terracotta 'Imitation' Jewelry," *BABesch* 57, 1982, pp. 192–199; also I. Blanck, "Griechische Goldschmuckimitationen des 4. Jahrhunderts v. Chr.," *AW* 1976, fasc. 3, pp. 19–27; I. Kriseleit, "Griechischer Schmuck aus vergoldertem Ton," in *Forschungen und Berichte, Staatliche Museen zu Berlin*

with moderate incomes could keep up the show of wealth and express the stylized grief essential to both their feelings and their standing in the community.

Athens, as Kurtz and Boardman have noted[149] "yields the fullest series of vases and other clay artifacts made especially for the grave. There is little to match them elsewhere." The passage, in a general chapter on grave offerings, stressed the 8th century, but the funerary ceramic industry continued in Athens, with lekythoi, animal-headed rhyta, and perhaps gilt-clay decorated disks meant only for tombs. The Agora molds would fit particularly well in the funerary world of early Hellenistic Athens. Their size, shape, and motifs would fit them for use on sarcophagi, couches, and funerary caskets: single metopes, tall narrow panels to cover the wide corner supports, box lids, or narrow friezes. But although it is conceivable that painted raw-clay plaques may have substituted for carved wood or ivory panels for the space of a funeral, and logical that none should have survived, it is difficult to accept an entire set of artifacts none of which should have survived—even though it is almost entirely from representations on vases and a few texts that we can reconstruct, for example, the flourishing box and basket industry of ancient Athens.

Raw clay was of course a material in common and abundant use in the Greek world. Above a stone socle, it made up, as mud brick, the common run of fortification and virtually all house walls. It was also used in major sculpture, not only in Hellenized Afghanistan, where stuccoed raw-clay statues were the rule,[150] but as was discovered through the chance of their having been baked by the heat of a huge funerary pyre, for late 4th-century statuary closer to Athens, in Cyprus, as well.[151] Raw clay, once whitewashed or even lightly stuccoed, and painted, looks of course like baked clay, is much less expensive, and can last a generation or two as we see in countries that still use mud-brick houses, provided it is maintained (whitewashed) occasionally and protected by a roof or overhang from direct rainfall.

Agora reliefs could therefore have been ancestral to Campana plaques as raw-clay plaques on mud-brick walls, both wall and relief whitewashed and the relief picked out with paint, either in private houses or in small shrines or heroa. But since their repertory is used so often elsewhere for funerary purposes, it would be sensible to include a possible funerary use for Agora reliefs in Athens as well. In the 6th century, painted clay plaques (baked clay) were used in funerary contexts,[152] the plaques perhaps decorating plastered mud-brick built

---

XVIII, Berlin 1977, pp. 13–20; M. Maas, "Ein Terrakottaschmuckfund aus dem Zeitalter Alexanders d. Gr.," *AthMitt* 100, 1985, pp. 309–326; Marshall (footnote 63 above), nos. 2130–2171, 2190–2192, pp. 243–249, pl. XLII.

[149] D. C. Kurtz and J. Boardman, *Greek Burial Customs*, London 1971, p. 213.

[150] Raw clay for statues, e.g., Z. Tarzi, "Hadda à la lumière des trois dernières campagnes de fouilles de Tapa-é-Shotor," *CRAI* 1976 (pp. 381–410), pp. 386–404, figs. 2–17; for a curious occurrence of a raw-clay mold, P. Bernard, "Fouilles d'Aï Khanoum (Afghanistan), campagnes de 1972 et 1973," *CRAI* 1974 (pp. 280–308), p. 302, fig. 14 on p. 304.

[151] Karageorghis (footnote 148 above), pp. 155–162, pls. 92–95 and XI–XVI: traces of 16 large raw-clay statues used in the pyre of king Nikokreon and his family at the end of the 4th century. Note also Pliny, *Natural History* xxxv.155, which relates that Chalcosthenes made works in Athens of unbaked clay.

[152] Kurtz and Boardman (footnote 149 above), p. 83: "it is generally thought that these plaques . . . were set into the plaster walls of the built tomb. . . ." See also M. Robertson, *A History of Greek Art*, Cambridge 1975, p. 131 and notes 125 and 126 on p. 637.

tombs. A mud-brick structure, either a built tomb, tomb enclosure, or bench- or table-shaped tomb monument, continued in use in Athens, among other forms of monuments, down to Roman times.[153] These inexpensive mud-brick or clay-and-rubble structures, often stuccoed, would make good candidates for raw-clay or even plaster plaques that would imitate more expensive decoration. At the time of the appearance of Agora molds in Agora deposits, the last quarter of the 4th century, Demetrios of Phaleron had proclaimed his sumptuary laws restricting the kind of Athenian funeral monuments and the money that could be spent upon them.[154] The *mensa*, most probably the table or bench structure, could be decorated at very little cost with the kind of plaques that would be produced from Agora molds, which coincide, of course, with the virtual absence of large stone funerary reliefs in Athens. Agora reliefs, moldmade, would not allow the personalization of stone reliefs, and craftsmen would fall back on the funerary repertory already in use for export.

VII. CONCLUSION

A hundred-odd fragments of clay molds. Not a large, nor a distinguished set of objects, but an important one. Important both because of its date and of its repertory. The existence of clay relief molds in such a variety of sizes in late 4th-century Athens presupposes a thorough, almost a tired, familiarity with the repertory they illustrate, since these molds are not equivalent to haute couture but to off-the-rack, not to paintings but to prints. The repertory in turn, with its emphasis on animal combats featuring griffins, presupposes that Athens had a considerable griffin market, and not only in pottery. Agora molds would thus join not only Kerch vases but Atticizing metalwork, wood, and written testimony concerning the grain trade to suggest a ready market in the Black Sea during the second half (possibly the last two-thirds) of the 4th century and into the 3rd for Athenian luxury products.

Such a market would go far in turn to explain the rise of the Greek animal style of the 4th century, not the specifically Persian motifs more readily ascribable to Alexander's conquests and the new Hellenistic entrepreneurs who followed these conquests[155] but the curious earlier combination of far-off themes with down-home style that produced the slightly incongruous but impeccably decorative Snake-footed Lady, the Arimasps and Griffins, and the Griffins and Wild Horses.

This style, perhaps prompted by generous but alien customers from South Russia (who must sometimes have been as bewildered by the *interpretatio graeca* of their myths as they were pleased by the craftsmen's virtuosity), became welcome in most of the Greek world. With perhaps one difference: while on the best of metalwork recovered from Black Sea tombs

---

[153] K. Kübler, "Der attische Grabbau," *MdI* 2, 1949, pp. 7–22. The clay and mud-brick structures are also noted in subsequent Kerameikos publication of cemeteries; e.g. *idem*, *Kerameikos*, VII, i, *Die Nekropole der Mitte des 6. bis Ende des 5. Jahrhunderts*, Berlin 1976, pp. 185–187.

[154] See footnote 147 above.

[155] M. Maas, *Die Prohedrie des Dionysostheaters in Athen*, Munich 1972.

animal combats may be the main, or at least a co-equal, representation on a given artifact, they are more often relegated to subsidiary and partly ornamental use in the Mediterranean.

If we deduce a strong industry for metalwork and other luxury products, fed with Black Sea gold and grain, in 4th-century Athens, this would allow us better to understand the link between bodies of artifacts far removed from one another yet curiously related. Scholars studying minor arts at the edges of the Greek world have often wanted to trace their origins back to one of the ancient centers of Greek manufacture; it may be that Agora molds will be of help.

Agora molds would also suggest that if the rich tombs and well-furnished houses of Athens during the 4th century, when we know that the city was active artistically and commercially, have been legislated or looted past recovery, we should look at the assemblage of 4th- and 3rd-century Athenian exports to help reconstruct some of the brilliance that challenged Alexandria and Pergamon to emulate and later to surpass Athens. Agora molds would then take their place among the archaeologically recoverable remnants of a richer range of Attic crafts and industries.

For the later Neo-Attic complex, Agora molds reinforce the Attic component of an eclectic repertory and establish a lineage going back at least to the 4th century for clay or possibly stucco reliefs ancestral to Campana plaques and perhaps also to Republican figured stuccoes. But it is for the 4th and 3rd centuries that Athenian relief molds, fragmentary and clumsy in themselves, bring us more than another lot of the miscellaneous clay pieces that careful archaeologists conscientiously append to catalogues of small finds. They provide significant witnesses to the far-reaching vitality of early Hellenistic craftsmanship in Athens.

CATALOGUE

Catalogue entries include the Agora number, then context, preservation, size, and fabric, followed by a brief description. Every piece is illustrated in the Plates. The following conventions are used throughout the catalogue:

Agora number

Headed with T for Terracotta (except for two pieces originally catalogued under A for Architecture and two others under MC for Miscellaneous Clay), this is the inventory master number that appears on the Agora catalogue card and gives access to other information. A concordance (p. 73) relates Agora number to present catalogue.

Context

Numbered context groups, e.g. N 20:6, besides being noted in catalogue entries, are briefly described and separately listed, with the molds belonging to them, in Appendix 2. Looser contexts are noted in catalogue entries. Area numbers refer to the standard Agora plan grid (Plan).

Size

Size is given in centimeters. Only height, H., or maximum dimension, max. dim., and thickness, T., are noted. To help visualization, estimated sizes for what would be the complete mold are also given where possible.

Fabric

To describe Attic clay, which can range from cream to dark brick in tones of buff, beige, or tan with a flush of red or pink, the old "rb" or "pb" (for reddish or pinkish buff) of the Agora cards has been retained. Since the molds, except where noted, are uniform in fabric, it seemed pointless to describe minutely slight differences in color due to firing. See above, pp. 2–3, for other notes on fabric; in catalogue entries, since all objects are made of clay, the word "clay" is implied but not repeated in every entry.

Description

Casts were made from all molds in preparation for publication, all but one in Attic clay (because of its large size, **53** had to be cast in plaster). It is important, where possible, to make clay and not plaster or plasticine casts from ancient molds, since the soft clay shrinks on partial drying and falls easily out of the mold without injuring or staining it. While all *technical* indications, such as "chipped on top" or "slip inside and out" refer to the mold, all *iconographical* indications, such as "moving right" or "below paw on left" refer to the cast, since this carries the actual representation.

Illustrations

The most informative photograph has been selected for each object, usually the cast, but sometimes the mold or both, whichever makes the often sadly fragmentary piece clearest. [Preliminary reconstructions of fragmentary pieces are reproduced from the author's sketchbook on Plates 27–34.]

1.   Dancing Maenad   Pls. 1, 27

T 3386; area H 14, context probably mid-2nd century. Part of upper edge preserved; H. 8.2, T. 2.5 at rim. Hard dark pb clay, some fine grit; buff slip inside.

Miniature. Preserves part of maenad dancing left, from head to hips. Body twists so that shoulders are seen from the back, hips in profile; head thrown back, left arm raised and bent, bent right arm holds thyrsos. Body framed in swirls of opened peplos hanging from shoulders.

2.   Dancing Maenad   Pls. 1, 27

T 388; H–K 12–14 (MSBF), second half of 4th to first quarter of 2nd century. Lower fourth preserved; H. 6.1, T. 2.7, est. size of cast 15.5 × 8.5. Hard pb with grog and grit; relatively fine, buff slip inside and on rim.

Miniature. Feet and swirling drapery of maenad dancing left.

3.   Dancing Maenad   Pls. 1, 2, 27

T 3023; area A–D 16–23, no context. Part of left and top edges preserved; H. 5.5, T. 3.5. Coarse pb to light brick with grog and grit; thin pb slip inside and on rim.

Fragment from top of representation: face of thrown-back head of maenad moving left and head of thyrsos, probably with ribbon tie beneath, to right.

4.   Dancing Maenad   Pls. 2, 27

T 1612; N 20:6, 3rd into early 2nd century. Broken all around; max. dim. 14. Dark pb with grog and grit, buff slip; inside stained, from early plasticine cast or from oiling to take plaster cast.

Curve of back of maenad dancing left, with some of the drapery flying out behind her, hair falling over her right shoulder and her elbow. Two finger grooves on back of mold, perhaps forming a nu.

5.   Dancing Maenad   Pls. 2, 27

T 3119; J 11:1, to fourth quarter of 4th century. Broken all around; max. dim. 9.7, T. 3.3. Coarse pb with grit and grog; buff slip.

Swirl of drapery from opposite lower thigh and knee of maenad dancing left.

6.   Dancing Maenad   Pls. 1, 3, 27

T 3045; area Q–R 10–12, to second quarter of 2nd century. Part of bottom and right edges preserved; H. 31, T. 3.5–4.5. Standard coarse pb to light brick with grog and grit, two main layers; buff slip inside and out. Finger grooves on back, perpendicular to direction of representation.

Legs of maenad dancing left, among drapery swirls. Particularly large mold.
Hesperia 20, 1951, p. 53, pl. 26:c.

7.   Dancing Maenad   Pls. 1, 3, 27

T 3476 a–c, e; A 16:3, last quarter of 4th century? a) lower left corner preserved; H. 22.6. b) right edge preserved; H. 16.4. c) broken all around; H. 18. e) edge preserved; H. 12, T. 3.1–4.6. Pb to light buff with coarse particles of grog and grit; buff slip inside and on rim.

Three non-joining fragments preserve (a) foot, drapery, end of thyrsos; (b) part of left arm, breast, torso, and drapery; (c) legs, of a maenad dancing left, similar to **1–6** above. Standard fabric, middle size; e is an edge fragment, from this or a similar mold. For T 3476 d, see **17** below.

8.   Dancing Maenad   Pls. 4, 27

T 3443; area K–D 15, to mid-2nd century. Part of right edge preserved; H. 9, T. 2.4. Very hard, fine pb to brick; dark pb slip.

Part of body (waist to thighs) and swirl of drapery in front, of maenad dancing left.

9.   Dancing Maenad?   Pls. 4, 27

T 3120; J 11:1, to fourth quarter of 4th century. Broken all around; max. dim. 9.9, T. 2.7. Coarse, streaky pb to brick with grit and grog; pb slip inside.

Two legs and drapery; figure moves right: Maenad?

10.   Dancing Maenad?   Pls, 1, 4, 27

T 2830; C 20:2, with material of the 4th through 2nd century. Broken all around; max. dim. 12, T. 2.5. Pb to light brick with grit and grog; buff slip inside and out.

Two legs and drapery of figure moving right: Maenad?

11. Dancing Maenad? Pls. 4, 27

T 3361; H–K 12–14 (MSBF), second half of 4th to first quarter of 2nd century. Part of left edge preserved; H. 10.4, T. 4.5 at edge. Coarse pb from buff to violet tinged; buff slip inside and on rim.

Swirl of drapery and part of arm: from Maenad?

12. Dancing Maenad? Pls. 4, 27

T 3389; area O–R 7–9, in a general context of the 4th century. Part of left edge preserved; max. dim. 12, T. 3.8. Coarse pb with grit and grog; buff slip inside.

Swirl of drapery, perhaps from Dancing Maenad; curves would also allow this to be part of a floral decoration.

13. Dancing Maenad? Pls. 4, 27

T 389; H–K 12–14 (MSBF), second half of 4th to first quarter of 2nd century. Part of top edge preserved; max. dim. 13, T. 3.9. Pb to light brick, baked very hard but without grog or grit; buff slip inside and out.

Limp left hand, perhaps of Dancing Maenad.

14. Dancing Maenad? Pl. 4

T 3228; area J 13 in a Hellenistic context. Broken all around; max. dim. 13.5, T. 3. Coarse, hard pb to brick; buff slip inside, self-slip outside.

Person (woman?) with drapery fastened over left shoulder but opening and swirling around body. Kin to standard Maenad?

15. Dancing Figure: Nike? Pl. 5

T 4164; R 13:11, general context of third quarter of 4th century. Lower center part with bottom edge preserved; H. 8.8, T. 2–3. Coarse pb; thin pb slip or self-slip inside and on rim.

Two bare feet and ankles in tiptoe dancing motion to right. Perhaps Dancing Maenad, but left foot forward and drapery line around calf rather than ankle suggest a figure like the Nikai on late Republican stucco reliefs; see pp. 35–36 above.

16. Kalathiskos Dancer? Pl. 5

T 1287; area K 10, in an early Roman context. Broken all around; max. dim. 12.2, T. 3.5. Rela-

tively fine, very hard pb, fired buff to brick; buff slip inside. Part of finger grooves on back.

Part of skirt, apparently Kalathiskos Dancer, but possibly Kourete.

17. Kalathiskos Dancer? Pl. 5

T 3476 d; A 16:3, last quarter of 4th century? Part of right edge preserved; H. 14.3, T. 3.2. Pb with small particles of grit and grog, burnt in parts red to dark gray; buff slip inside, self-slip outside?

Person in short light skirt, in violent motion. Kalathiskos Dancer, Amazon, or Kourete, but no greaves, and drapery looks as if in motion from pirouette: most likely Kalathiskos Dancer. Faint grass pattern on background.

18. Kourete? Pl. 6

T 3788; area G 16, no context. Lower right corner preserved; H. 26.5, T. 2.5–3.9. Coarse pb to brick; buff slip inside and on rim.

Two legs bent in dancing motion; greaves visible. Perhaps dancing Kourete.

19. Amazon Fig. 1, Pl. 6

T 2986; P–R 6–12 (SABF), second half of 4th to mid-2nd century. Broken all around; max. dim. 22, T. 5. Very coarse pb with grit and grog; buff slip inside, self-slip outside. Battered mold.

Woman, head to mid-torso, wearing chiton leaving left breast bare; right arm lifted high, left arm down, turns head to look over left shoulder. Edge of shield(?) visible over left shoulder. Possibly from Amazon-and-Greek group in which Greek pulls Amazon by the hair.

20. Nereid? Pl. 7

T 3118; J 11:1, to fourth quarter of 4th century. Broken all around; max. dim. 21, T. 5.5. Coarse pb; buff slip inside.

Torso and part of left arm of woman with torso facing front in thin drapery slipping off shoulder, possibly Nereid or Aphrodite.

21. Ship Pls. 7, 28

A 99; area C 14, no context. Broken all around; H. 10.5, T. 3.1. Clay in two distinct layers: fine, greenish buff inside and coarse pb with grit, partly fired to a purplish tinge, outside, both very hard.

Prow of ship, with eye; beginning of upper ram indicated, thus warship. Part of terminal housing of deck and beginning of outrigger for upper row of oars; delicate rinceau and egg-and-dart moldings on wales below outrigger. Ship moves left.

22.   Ship   Pls. 7, 28

T 3121; J 11:1, to fourth quarter of 4th century. Broken all around; max. dim. 12.7, T. 3.1. Clay as **21**.

Bank of oars. Scale, clay, and technique are so close to the preceding that this may be a non-joining fragment from the same mold.

23.   Ship   Pls. 7, 28

T 3660; area H 14, context of second half of 2nd century. Broken all around; H. 6, T. 3.5. Inner layer of fine buff, outer layer of coarse reddish to purplish clay, possibly the same as the two preceding examples of ship molds.

Four young men (*thranitai*), nude, rowing, seen between the cambered stanchions supporting the upper deck. Ship moves left.

24.   Ship with Triton or Ketos   Pls. 7, 28

T 3187; H–K 12–14 (MSBF), second half of 4th to first quarter of 2nd century. Part of bottom edge preserved; H. 17.6, T. 3.5. Coarse brick; dark pb slip inside and on rim.

Bank of oars with oarthresh and snaky curve of spiny-backed sea monster below.

25.   Triton   Pl. 7

T 3198; area I 12, in a Hellenistic context. Broken all around; H. 12, T. 1.3. Represents inner layer only, from which outer layer has apparently broken off; coarse brick, buff slip.

Possibly from mold **24**, or the same representation. Triton with oar(?) in crook of left arm, right arm raised perhaps in hailing or welcoming gesture; part of ridged object (drapery of Nereid?) in front of him. Triton faces and moves left.

26.   Nike driving Chariot   Pls. 8, 33

T 377; H–K 12–14 (MSBF), second half of 4th to first quarter of 2nd century. Broken all around;

max. dim. 14, T. 2.7. Hard, gritty pb, sand tempered; thin slip or self-slip.

Nike: torso with part of arms and wings, arms stretched before her towards horse, part of whose mane and left ear are visible. Apparently driving chariot left. Wings of Nike, mane of horse detailed.

27.   Nike driving Chariot?   Pls. 8, 33

T 1925; area G 3 in a Late Roman context. Part of left edge preserved; H. 12.8, T. 4.5, est. size 21 × 27. Coarse pb with grog and grit; thin self-slip.

Nike, chin to hips, facing left, bent forward, arms extended in front of her. Wind pulls chiton back, wing arches behind her. Perhaps driving chariot, but could possibly be sacrificing bull.

28.   Nike driving Chariot?   Pls. 8, 33

T 2595; area M 20, no context. Part of upper edge preserved; H. 12.7, T. 5.5. Coarse pb with grit and grog.

Head and part of torso or upper arm of female figure which seems to be facing and bending left but turning head back; object or wing to right of figure. Possibly Nike driving chariot.

29.   Chariot Group   Pls. 8, 33

T 3155; area Q 10 in a chiefly 4th-century context with earlier material. Part of right and bottom edges preserved; H. 7, T. 2.6, est. size 10 × 15. Relatively gritty pb with some grog; thin buff slip or self-slip.

Miniature. Person in chariot: lower torso and legs in long drapery; a hand may hold on to chariot rail. Chariot wheel, part of tail and right hind leg of horse running right.

30.   Chariot Group   Pls. 8, 33

T 1621; N 20:7, to first and early second quarters of 2nd century. Part of left and upper edges preserved; H. 7.4, T. 1.8, est. size 10 × 15. Very hard, reddish clay, relatively fine.

Miniature. Part of three prancing horses to right, heads, necks, part of forelegs, with harness indicated. Delicate work, recalls metal impression.

31.   Chariot Group   Pls. 9, 33

T 3008; area D 12, no context. Part of lower edge preserved; H. 6, T. 2.7, est. size 10 × 15.

Relatively gritty pb, not so coarse as that used for larger molds.

Dog running right below legs of prancing chariot horses.

32.   Chariot Group   Pls. 9, 33

T 3360; H–K 12–14 (MSBF), second half of 4th to first quarter of 2nd century. Part of left edge preserved; H. 17, T. 3. Coarse pb with grit and grog; thick slip inside.

Person in long drapery (charioteer's tunic or Nike's chiton) driving chariot to left; representation hard to make out because of accidental heavy scored line across mold. Part of lower half of person, some of chariot including upper part of wheel rim, and hindquarters of horse with tail sweeping across chariot.

33.   Chariot Group   Pls. 9, 33

T 981; area K 15, no context. Part of lower edge preserved; H. 15, T. 4.3. Coarse pb to reddish, with grog and grit; buff slip inside. Finger grooves on back.

Far chariot wheel, part of hind legs and belly of horse moving left.

34.   Chariot Group   Pls. 9, 33

T 617; area J 20, no context. Part of lower edge preserved; H. 12.5, T. 5.4. Coarse pinkish with grog and grit; thin pale buff slip inside.

Wheel of chariot, part of left hind leg of horse moving left.

35.   Chariot Group   Pls. 9, 33

T 2948; area D 17, Hellenistic to early Roman context. Broken all around; max. dim. 14, T. 3.6. Coarse pinkish with grog outer layer and one or two inner layers of fine buff clay.

Neck and back of horse with short mane; reins leading to hands of person who, from the position, is probably driving a chariot rather than riding the horse.

36.   Chariot Group?   Pls. 9, 33

T 453; J 12:2, to early 3rd century after Christ. Broken all around; max. dim 7.7, T. 2.7. Pb with grog and grit.

Legs of horses moving left, probably from a chariot group.

37.   Chariot Group?   Pls. 9, 33

MC 14; H–K 12–14 (MSBF), second half of 4th to first quarter of 2nd century. Broken all around; H. 19.5, T. 2.5–4. Hard, gritty pb with traces of burnt-out temper, also some sand, but less grog and grit than usual; buff slip. Back shows traces of having rested on what may have been a rough mat.

Legs of four(?) horses prancing left towards palmette and rinceau pattern.

38.   Chariot Group?   Pls. 10, 33

T 2596; area M 20, no context. Broken all around; max. dim. 12, T. 4. Coarse pb with fine grog and some grit; thick slip inside.

Legs of horses, probably from chariot group but possibly from group of riders, prancing left towards curved lines, probably palmette or rinceau.

39.   Chariot Group?   Pls. 10, 33

T 3416; O 16:4, to late 4th or early 3rd century. Part of lower edge preserved; H. 7, T. 2.5. Slightly gritty pb, hard, with buff slip; bottom inside edge picked out in streaky black glaze.

Small mold, probably about 25 cm. wide, with prancing horse to right: belly, part of all four legs visible; perhaps from a chariot group.

40.   Apobates Group   Pl. 10

T 3373; area I 15, Hellenistic context. Broken all around; max. dim. 15.5, T. 5. Pb clay in two layers: outer coarse with large pieces of grog and grit, inner finer; buff slip or self-slip.

Upper part of Apobates, nude except for helmet and shield. Torso facing, head turned left, arm extended to chariot rail across body of charioteer who wears his professional long tunic, with long embroidered or gartered sleeve. Part of horse's mane visible at extreme left; group moves left.

41.   Banquet   Pls. 10, 29

T 883 a and c; E 14:1, in a context of the 3rd century with some later material. The two fragments are apparently from the same archetype but represent different molds. a) part of bottom edge of panel preserved; H. 17.7, T. 2.8. Dark pb baked very hard, some grit; worn buff slip. c) broken all around; H. 8.2, T. 2.8. Dark pb with orange tinge, sand and chaff tempered? Possible self-slip.

a) couch on which two men recline; the one on the right holds a phiale. A three-legged table, with cake and fruit, stands in front of the couch, and a serving boy, nude, moves left and appears to be placing something on the table. c) fragment from the same archetype, preserving a smaller portion of the same scene.

42.   Banquet   Pls. 11, 32

T 883 b; E 14:1, in a context of the 3rd century with some later material. Part of bottom edge preserved; H. 14, T. 3.1–3.8. Dark pb, sand and chaff tempered? Buff slip inside and out. Mended in antiquity with lead clamps.

Part of couch between two chairs with footstools. A three-legged table with cakes and fruit upon it stands in front of the couch. Central cake is flat and round, with radiating lines on top; on either side a piece of fruit or a pyramidal cake. Drapery, perhaps from seated women, visible just above footstool. Part of a scene like that shown on **41**?

43.   Banquet   Pls. 11, 32

T 653 a and b; G 13:4, context of third quarter of 4th to second quarter of 3rd century. a) part of lower edge preserved; H. 10, T. 4. Relatively coarse pb to light brick, little grog and grit; buff slip inside. b) corner; max. dim. 13.2. Hard pb, probably not same fabric as a.

a) lower part of a banquet scene: on a low stand, a large krater; on the left, a footstool with feet and drapery, probably a woman seated beside couch; on the right, another footstool, possibly part of a foot upon it. b) deep corner from a mold or an architectural fragment, featureless, probably unrelated to a; not illustrated.

44.   Banquet   Pls. 11, 31

T 2349; area M 20, no context. Broken all around; max. dim. 13, T. 3.2. Hard, relatively fine pb to light brick; pb slip outside, self-slip inside?

Part of couch and possibly of man's torso or large cushion over folded thin cushion above it. In front of couch, a table with two pyramidal cakes and a piece of fruit; also on the table, a ribbed bowl, and visible above it, the right arm and hand of a serving boy pouring from a trefoil-mouth oinochoe into the bowl.

45.   Assembly of Gods?   Pl. 12

T 421; H–K 12–14 (MSBF), second half of 4th to first quarter of 2nd century.
T 3033; area N 7, no context. Two joining fragments. Part of top edge preserved; H. 15.3, T. 3.6, 4.3 at rim.
Coarse pb with grog and grit; pb slip inside.

Bearded, seated god with bare torso at right, goddess with branch or grain at left, both partly preserved to waist.

46.   Abduction   Pl. 12

T 3774; area N 16 in a 3rd-century context. Most of upper half including parts of top and both side edges preserved; H. 12, T. 2.5, est. size 10 × 15. Coarse pb to brick, with large particles of grog and grit; thin buff slip or self-slip inside and on rim.

Miniature. Man wearing a chlamys that billows around him, carrying off a woman whose drapery has fallen to her waist and over her left arm. He has short curly hair and is beardless; her hair is dressed in a thick, indistinct chignon or possibly a sakkos. Both are shown almost full face, the man's arms crossed about the woman's waist, his body braced to carry her. She looks back to right and spreads her arms wide in alarm.

47.   Scene with shield   Pl. 12

T 3048; area K–N 19–21, no context. Lower left corner preserved; H. 18, T. 4.7. Coarse pb with grit and grog, partly fired dark brick; sandy pb slip.

Circular shield, seen in profile, leaning against edge of representation, bottom of rim resting on ground, apparently decorated with a satyr head; what may be a rock with drapery thrown over it to left of shield.

48.   Person holding object?   Pl. 13

T 337; I 16:1, mixed 5th- and 4th-century context. Broken all around; max. dim. 9.5. Sandy, dark pb to brick; dark pb slip inside.

Possibly torso, drapery, and arm holding sword or tripod leg.

49.   Person and pattern   Pl. 13

T 1392 a and b; area L 18, in mostly 4th-century context. a) part of right edge preserved; H. 15, T. 4.8. Standard coarse pb, light brick at core, buff at edges; light buff slip inside. b) different mold, right edge preserved; max. dim. 14, T. inside 4.8. Coarse, even, dark reddish buff with large particles of grog and grit.

a) person in fluttering drapery, ivy leaf border. b) rinceau and object.

50. Person and pattern Pl. 13

T 2985; P–R 6–12 (SABF), second half of 4th to mid-2nd century. Part of curved edge preserved at left; max. dim. 14, T. 3–5. Dark pb, very coarse clay with grog and grit; buff slip inside and on rim.

Within an egg-and-dart border intaglio on cast, a woman moving, perhaps fleeing, to right turns head back.

51. Person reclining or fallen? Pl. 13

T 3233; M–N 15:1 (SSIIBF), to early third quarter of 2nd century. Part of bottom and right edges preserved; max. dim. 8, T. 2.5. Fine, hard pb, self-slip?

Miniature. Legs wearing trousers, left bent, right stretched out parallel with bottom edge. Perhaps a fallen Arimasp or Persian?

52. Two Griffins attacking a Deer Pls. 14, 30

T 3151; area N 12, in a Roman context. Part of inner top edge preserved; H. 8, T. 1.6, est. size 10 × 15 or 16. Two layers of clay, light brick and buff, both relatively fine but gritty.

From upper central part of scene: griffin on right bites the deer's throat, griffin on left has felled the deer by springing on its back and bends down to bite its flank. Head of deer and right-hand griffin, neck and part of wings of left-hand griffin preserved.

53. Two Griffins attacking a Deer Pls. 14, 30

T 376 + T 3362; H–K 12–14 (MSBF), second half of 4th to first quarter of 2nd century. Joining fragments together preserve part of both top and bottom edges; H. 37, T. 5.5, est. size of representation without allowing for shrinkage 35 × 60 or 65. Dark pb to light brick; thick (2 mm.), fine buff slip brushed inside and out. Clay gritty and hard, but no large particles of grog or grit.

Restored as two griffins attacking a deer on the analogy of this piece with the one preceding and the two following. The deer has fallen; **53** preserves most of its hindquarters, left hind leg bent under body, right stretched back with griffin's left hind paw clamped upon it. Griffin's hindquarters and part of wing preserved.

54. Two Griffins attacking a Deer Pls. 15, 30

T 2142; area H 19, no context. Broken all around; max. dim. 12.5, T. 4.5. Coarse pb with light buff slip.

From center of scene: part of head of deer, beak of right-hand griffin, crested neck of griffin on left.

55. Two Griffins attacking a Deer Pls. 15, 30

T 3156; area R 8, in a late 4th- to 3rd-century context. Broken all around; max. dim. 16. Coarse pb with sand, grog, grit, and chaff; light buff slip.

Small fragment from a large mold: center of the scene. Neck of deer, neck, jowl, beak, and forepaw of griffin on right, part of crested neck of griffin on left with deer's antlers cutting across it. Same subject and about the same scale as **53** but apparently from a slightly different archetype.

56. Two Griffins attacking a Deer? Pls. 15, 30

T 628 a and b; area E 12, late Hellenistic context. a) part of left and bottom edges; H. 13.5, T. 3.5. b) part of right edge; H. 8.2, T. 3.5. These two non-joining fragments are part of the same piece; est. size 18 × 27. Coarse pb with grog and grit; thin buff slip. Mold mended in antiquity with lead rivets partially preserved in a.

a) griffin (or possibly lion) rearing up, facing left, and front leg of deer being attacked. b) part of back and wing of left-hand griffin.

57. Griffin Pl. 15

T 2070; F 19:1 in a 5th-century (after Christ) context. Part of left edge preserved; H. 20, T. at edge 4.5. Coarse clay, with sand, grog, and grit, fired unevenly pinkish to pb to buff, built up in two main layers; buff slip brushed on inside and more lightly outside. Faint impression of coarse mat, or just split reeds or twigs, on back.

Tail, part of left hind leg and wing of griffin moving left, tail up, probably to attack.

H. S. Robinson, *The Athenian Agora*, V, *Pottery of the Roman Period*, Princeton 1959, p. 80, under L 62.

58. Griffin   Pl. 15

T 508; J 12:3, late 4th-to-mid-3rd-century context. Broken all around; max. dim. 13.2, T. 3.3.
Coarse pb with grog and grit; thick buff slip
inside.

Part of back and wing of griffin moving left. Possibly
right-hand griffin from a group like that in **52**.

59. Griffin   Pls. 15, 30

T 3564; area J–L 15–19, no context. Part of
curved edge preserved; max. dim. 10.4, T. 5. Very
coarse rb to light brick with large particles of grog,
some grit and sand; thick buff slip inside, thin or
self-slip outside.

No rim on this heavy curved mold. Part of a large-
scale griffin head to right, brow, part of eye, spiny
crest, and start of laid-back ear.

60.   Two Lions attacking Horse   Pl. 15

T 3494; A 19:5, to last quarter of 4th century?
Part of top and right edges preserved; H. 5.6, T.
2.6, est. size 8 × 15. Relatively coarse, hard pb
with fine grit; fine pb slip inside.

Miniature. Two lions springing upon a horse; the
lion on the left springs for its throat, hindquarters
raised, head down. Part of the head and hind legs are
missing. Part of the mane and head of the lion on the
right, which has probably sprung onto the horse's
back, felling it, are visible. The horse is down, head
thrown back in agony.

61.   Griffins or Lions attacking Bull   Pls. 16, 34

T 1965; area H 19, no relevant context. H. 17, T.
3.7.
T 2047; area E 19, no relevant context. H. 10, T.
3.7.

Two non-joining fragments apparently from the
same piece on the basis of fabric, size, and subject;
est. size ca. 23 × 36. Coarse pb with large particles
of grog and grit; pb to buff slip.

T 1965 preserves the start of the left foreleg, part of
the ribs, and most of the hind legs of a predator
which has sprung on the back of a bull, felling it.
There should be a matching predator on the other
side. T 2047 preserves the hind hooves, belly curve,
and left foreleg of the fallen bull.

62.   Lion or Griffin attacking   Pl. 16

T 3237; H–K 12–14 (MSBF), second half of 4th

to first quarter of 2nd century. Part of bottom edge
preserved; H. 30.5, T. at rim 5.4, est. size
ca. 40 × 70. Coarse pb to light-brick clay with
sand, grit, and grog; worn buff slip exposing
sandy surface.

Perhaps the largest mold so far found in the Agora
excavations. From lower left corner of mold. Hind
legs of lion springing left and down to attack animal;
tail lashes around legs. Rocky ground below.

63.   Lion or Griffin attacking   Pl. 16

T 3003; area D 16 in a 4th- and 3rd-century context. Preserves part of right edge; H. at edge 15,
T. 4.5, est. size ca. 20 × 38. Coarse pb with large
particles of grog and some grit; buff slip, almost
entirely worn, brushed on inside.

Part of lion or griffin springing right and down,
hindquarters raised, right hind paw resting on rocky
ground, forequarters crouched. Mold preserves start
of right foreleg, ribs, most of hindquarters, and tail.

64.   Lion or Griffin attacking Herbivore   Pl. 16

T 2989; P–R 6–12 (SABF), second half of 4th to
mid-2nd century. Part of bottom edge preserved;
H. 12.7, T. 5 at edge. Coarse pb fired partly light
brick to pale purplish with grog and grit; fine buff
slip.

Paw of predator, probably lion, against bent foreleg
of herbivore. Small fragment from one of the large
molds, possibly ca. 40 × 60.

65.   Lion or Griffin attacking Animal?   Pl. 16

T 3415; area Q 17, no context. Lower right corner
preserved; H. 16, T. 3.9. Coarse rb to pb with grit
and grog; buff slip brushed inside, self-slip outside? Finger grooves on back.

Lion or griffin moving right as if to attack animal.
Part of hind legs and of tail preserved; right hind
paw rests on rock or ledge.

66.   Lion or Griffin   Pl. 17

T 3236; area I 14, MSBF with later material.
Lower left corner preserved; H. 12, T. 4.2–3.3,
est. size ca. 15 × 30. Hard, gritty, fine pb applied
in layers; sand-tempered? Pb thin slip or self-slip
inside and out.

Lion(?) moving left crouches on bent forepaws; left
elbow touches ground at left, body arches up from it,
hindquarters raised, tail curved behind. Spring of

forepaw, curve of ribs, most of hindquarters preserved. Mold very crisp, probably new when broken and discarded.

67. Lion(?) attacking Pl. 17

T 769; area L 11, no context. Part of bottom edge preserved; H. 10, T. 3. Coarse pb with grog; buff slip inside. Est. size *ca.* 13 × 28 if there were two predators.

From a small mold, showing a predator, probably a lion (more robust than a griffin) attacking left, crouched on forelegs, hindquarters raised. The fragment preserves the curve of ribs and belly, most of hind legs, and tail.

68. Lion(?) attacking Pl. 17

T 1553; area M 18, in a Hellenistic context. Upper right corner preserved; H. 9.2, T. 3.5. Hard, gritty, fine brick to pb; buff slip inside and out.

Raised hindquarters of a lion(?) moving to right and down.

69. Predator and Prey Pl. 17

T 1975; U 26:1, 3rd and early 2nd centuries. Broken all around; max. dim. 10, T. 3. Coarse pb with grog and grit; buff slip inside.

Hind paw of predator facing right on bent foreleg of herbivore.

70. Predator Pl. 17

T 3287; M–N 15:1 (SSIIBF), to early third quarter of 2nd century. Broken all around; max. dim. 17, T. 3.3. Coarse pb, baked almost purplish at core, with grit and grog; thick buff slip.

Preserves curve of ribs and belly and start of hind legs of predator; probably lion or griffin, moving left.

71. Predator Pl. 18

MC 13; H–K 12–14 (MSBF), second half of 4th to first quarter of 2nd century. Upper left corner preserved; H. 9.8, T. 5 at rim. Coarse pb with grog and grit; thin buff slip inside.

Hindquarters of predator moving left and down.

72. Predator Pl. 18

T 1842; O 20:3, 3rd century. Broken all around; max. dim. 19.5, T. 4. Coarse pb with grayish tinge, sand, grog, and grit.

Rib cage, curve of belly, and start of hind leg, with

tail curving behind, of predator; another object or animal behind it.

73. Predator Pl. 18

T 4167; area D 17. Part of lower center of mold with bottom edge preserved; H. 16.3, T. 3.2. Clay in two distinct layers: inner fine, dark pb with purplish cast; outer coarse, light yellowish with much grog; thin buff slip or self-slip inside.

Hind legs and tail of predator moving left; part of front legs or part of other animal to left of tail. Probably from Animal Combat.

74. Predator? Pl. 18

T 1654; area N–Q 17–19, no context. Part of bottom right corner preserved; H. 7.5, T. 3.7. Pb coarse clay with much grog; worn pb slip inside.

Left foreleg of predator, crouching to left; right foreleg or neck behind.

75. Lion Pl. 18

T 3043; P–R 6–12 (SABF), second half of 4th to mid-2nd century. Left third of mold preserved; H. 18, T. 4.6. Hard, extremely coarse pb clay, baked to purplish in part, with sand, grog, and grit; apparently no slip inside.

Hindquarters of lion moving left.

76. Lion Pl. 19

T 1860; area R 18, Roman context. Upper right corner preserved; H. 6.8, T. 2.7, est. size 10 × 13. Unusual fabric: smooth, fine, hard pb, traces of dilute red-glaze wash inside and out.

Head of lion walking left. Apparently not part of an animal combat scene and outside the tradition of large relief molds; more likely a mold of the 5th or early 4th century for a small votive plaque.

77. Panther Pl. 19

T 1862; area T 22, late Roman context. Part of top edge preserved; H. 10, T. 5.5. Coarse pb to light brick with grit and grog; buff slip inside.

Panther moving left, head facing, mouth open in snarl.

78. Panther Pl. 19

T 2380; area C 19, in a Hellenistic context. Part of curved right edge preserved; max. dim. 11.3, T. at edge 3.5. Unusual fabric: pb fired unevenly from light brick to light buff, floury, a little sandy, but no grit or grog.

Panther, head and neck, facing, with curved background behind. Not for a relief plaque? Fresh, crisp mold.

79.   Bull and person   Pl. 19

T 2197 a and b; area B 22, with late Hellenistic material. a) part of right edge; H. 16.2, T. 3.3. b) a corner; max. dim. 14. Unusual fabric: fine pb clay such as that used for terracotta figurines, with buff slip, in two layers; the inner one follows the contours of the archetype; the outer was used as reinforcement.

a) head of bull grasped at horn by person's hand. b) uncertain representation. Possibly Herakles or Theseus with bull, but it could possibly represent a bull led to sacrifice or being sacrificed by a Nike.

80.   Bull   Pl. 19

T 3417; area Q 17, late Roman context. Part of bottom and curved right edges preserved; H. 17.5, T. 5. Pb to light brick with grit and grog; light buff slip inside and out.

Curve of neck, and forelegs, of bull walking left. Finished with curved edge, perhaps to accommodate architectural feature.

81.   Boar or Sow   Pl. 20

T 2024; area E 18, no context. Right side with part of top and bottom preserved; H. 16.5, T. 4.5, est. size *ca.* 13 × 18. Clay unevenly fired yellowish to pb, with some grog and grit; very hard.

From a small mold, with the representation apparently freshened by hand in the mold. Pig walking left, probably alone on plaque since upper edge shows little room above its back. Possibly for a votive plaque.

82.   Boar or Sow   Pl. 20

T 3984; area Q–S 17–20, no context. Upper left corner preserved; H. 10.2, T. 3.2. Coarse, heavy, dark pb to light reddish; thin slip or self-slip inside.

Preserves part of forehead, eye, and snout of pig facing right.

83.   Fish   Pl. 20

T 136; area F–H 13–16, no context. About half of mold preserved; H. 14, T. 3.5. Very sandy, coarse pb to light brown.

Oval-shaped mold, perhaps a food mold, showing fish with roe or on a bed of vegetables.

84.   Gorgoneion   Pl. 21

T 405 + T 429; H–K 12–14 (MSBF), second half of 4th to first quarter of 2nd century. Two joining fragments. Part of right edge preserved; max. dim. 15.5, T. 3, est. diam. 20. Unusual fabric: very fine, hard, dark pb to reddish clay; self-slip inside and out?

Gorgoneion with tongue resting on lower lip, upper teeth just visible, short hair streaming out. Iris does not touch lower lid, pupil indicated. Close to T 4098, gorgoneion mold from U 13:1, well dating to *ca.* 380, not illustrated. **84** is probably earlier than the standard relief molds catalogued here.

85.   Gorgoneion   Pl. 21

T 2918; area D 17; max. dim. 18.5.
T 2920; area D 17; max. dim. 13.5.
T 2925 a and b; D 17:4, to first quarter of 1st century. T 2925 a, max. dim. 12; T 2925 b, max. dim. 10.7, T. 3.7.
Est. diam. 36–38. Pb to light brick, with fine grit and sand, fired very hard; pb thick slip inside.

Four fragments, similar in scale and fabric, three from the rim and one (T 2920) from the center of a large gorgoneion with hanging tongue, visible teeth, and disheveled hair around which snakes writhe.

86.   Gorgoneion   Pl. 21

T 3340; area A–D 14–17, no context. Part of lower edge preserved; max. dim. 19.5, T. 4, est. diam. 26. Unusual fabric: reddish buff clay fired very hard, only slightly gritty.

Mouth, chin, part of right cheek and lock of hair from a gorgoneion with hanging tongue.

87.   Gorgoneion   Pl. 21

T 3786; area G 14, no context. Part of left edge preserved; max. dim. 19, T. 6.2, est. diam. 38–40. Coarse pb with grit and grog, possibly partly chaff tempered; buff slip inside.

Some hair and part of the cheek from a large gorgoneion.

88. Gorgoneion Pl. 21

T 2177; G 14:2, 4th to 2nd century. Part of left edge preserved; max. dim. 10.6, T. 6, est. diam. 35. Coarse pb fired to a purplish tinge at core, large particles of grog and grit.

Streaming hair from gorgoneion.

89. Gorgoneion Pl. 21

T 2829; C 20:2, with material of 4th to 2nd century. Part of top edge preserved; max. dim. 13.1, T. 3.8, est. diam. 26–27. Relatively fine clay, fired buff to light brick, faintly gritty but without large particles; buff slip inside and out.

Central parting and streaming hair from top of gorgoneion.

90. Gorgoneion(?) Pl. 22

T 2981; area Q 8–9, with Hellenistic material. Part of one edge preserved; max. dim. 8, T. 4.2, est. diam. 30–31. Coarse clay fired pale buff throughout; buff slip inside.

Preserves part of curling snake with scales or spots indicated.

91. Gorgoneion(?) Pl. 22

T 3324; N 16:2, third quarter of 4th century? Preserves part of curving edge; max. dim. 10, T. 4.5. Coarse pb with grog and grit, fired brick at core; thick buff slip inside, self-slip outside.

Probably part of the cheek of a gorgoneion.

92. Gorgoneion(?) Pl. 22

T 3109; J 11:1, to last quarter of 4th century. Part of curved edge preserved; max. dim. 9, T. 2. Relatively coarse, dark pb to light brick, with small particles of grit; buff slip inside and on rim.

Scallops, curved shapes, and convex curve, perhaps a gorgoneion or part of a griffin or ketos.

93. Gorgoneion(?) Pl. 22

T 3256; area I 12, with Hellenistic material. Part of curved edge preserved; max. dim. 8.4, T. 3.6. Coarse pb with grit and grog; worn pb slip inside.

Probably preserves part of a snake from a gorgoneion.

94. Boukranion Pl. 22

T 2965; area P–R 7–13, no context. Part of top and left-hand edges preserved; max. dim. 9, T. 4.3. Very coarse pb with much grog, fired almost purplish; thin, pale buff slip inside, self-slip outside.

One horn and part of the forehead of a boukranion; mold follows shape of object.

95. Uncertain Pl. 22

T 3061; area O 7, no context. Part of one edge preserved; max. dim. 13.5, T. 4. Very coarse pb to light brick with large particles of grit and grog; pb slip inside.

Uncertain: animal tail or flower tendril.

96. Uncertain Pl. 22

T 3418; area P 17, Roman context. Part of one edge preserved; max. dim. 12, T. 4.5. Sandy pb to brick at core; worn buff slip inside.

Small fragment from large mold. Grooved oval and diagonal ridge, uncertain.

97. Uncertain Pl. 23

T 3313; area I 12, in a context of 4th century. Part of one edge preserved; max. dim. 12, T. 3.8. Coarse pb fired almost purplish; buff slip inside.

Small fragment from large mold. Two sets of curves linked with a straight line; possibly part of thyrsos head, stem, and ribbon tie (see **3** above).

98. Uncertain Pl. 23

T 3787; area G 14, no context. Part of one edge preserved; max. dim. 8.8, T. 1.5. Pb to light buff, hard but not coarse; buff slip inside.

Convex curve, uncertain.

99. Uncertain Pl. 23

T 3657; area I–J 14–15, context mostly end of 4th century with later intrusions. Broken all around; max. dim. 11, T. 4.2. Coarse pb with grit and grog; sandy pb slip inside.

Sharp curves: floral ornament or tail of fish or ketos?

100. Uncertain Pl. 23

T 2353; area C 17, no context. Part of curved edge

preserved; max. dim. 12, T. 2.8. Coarse reddish buff; buff slip inside.

Curves: palmette? Animal?

101.   Uncertain   Pl. 23

T 266; area P 17, with late 5th- and 4th-century material. Part of one edge preserved; max. dim. 9, T. 2. Coarse pb; buff slip.

Flying drapery?

102.   Uncertain   Pl. 23

T 1595; G 5:2, in a late Roman context. Broken all around; max. dim. 7.9, T. 2.4. Sandy coarse pb to light brick.

Rinceau or palmette?

103.   Fragment: mold or positive   Pl. 23

T 330; area H 17, Roman context; max. dim. 6.8, T. 2.2. Coarse, light pb with large particles of grit and grog; plaster or mortar with small stones on back.

S-curve could belong to a snake, animal tail, or an intaglio rinceau on a positive. One edge seems finished.

104.   Fragment: mold or positive   Pl. 23

T 3050; N 20:3, to 1st century after Christ. Broken all around; max. dim. 5.6, T. 2. Sandy, dark pb with some grit but not standard fabric; pb to light brick slip. Uneven back with fingermarks.

Bead and reel and large ovolo. Could be either mold or positive.

105.   Fragment: mold or positive   Pl. 24

T 1963; S 21:1, context of 1st centuries before and after Christ. Part of one edge preserved; max. dim. 11.5, T. 4.5. Sandy pb with orange tinge, some grit.

Uncertain, much worn.

106.   Positive: Man striding   Pl. 24

T 3083; area P–Q 14, with late Roman material.

Part of bottom edge preserved; H. 13.3, T. 4.4. Very coarse clay fired brick to dark red; traces of plaster or whitewash on both front and back but not on breaks.

Lower half of nude man, striding right, perhaps from battle scene.

107.   Positive: Horses   Pl. 24

T 574; area H 13, no context. Broken all around; max. dim. 8.8, T. 2.5. Very sandy, reddish buff clay.

Forelegs of a horse moving left on a curving background, perhaps the body of another horse.

108.   Positive: Lion or Griffin attacking   Pl. 24
            Horse

T 1059; area F 6–7, no context. Part of bottom edge preserved; H. 9.5, T. 3.5. Standard coarse pb with grog and grit; buff slip on front. Back rough; cracked in places and retouched by hand, or even entirely handmade.

Predator bringing down horse. The fragment preserves the right front paw of the lion clamped on the horse's right foreleg. The hand working or extensive retouching suggest this piece was an archetype or secondary positive.

109.   Positive: Gorgoneion   Pl. 24

A 1204; C 20:2, with material of 4th to 2nd century. Part of bottom edge preserved; H. 15.6, T. 4.5, est. diam. 31–32. Very coarse, pb clay with large particles of grog and grit; buff slip on modeled side. Back and edges rough.

Nose, mouth, and chin of gorgoneion.

110.   Positive: Gorgoneion   Pl. 24

T 2765; C 20:2, with material of 4th to 2nd century. Part of one edge preserved; max. dim. 8, T. 4.6. Very coarse pb; buff slip.

Hair from gorgoneion, possibly part of **109**.

APPENDIX 1: THE FOOD OF THE HEROES

[The author prepared a study of this question, which she presented, among other places, at an illustrated "After Tea Talk" entitled "Classical Cake" at the American School of Classical Studies at Athens in 1978. Her manuscript, in which she added bibliographical references, is published here with a minimum of editing. See Dentzer, *Banquet*, pp. 519–520 for a recent discussion of these cakes.—Ed.]

Any study of ancient material is bound to illuminate a corner of antiquity; the most curious of these illuminations deriving from the study of the Agora molds concerns the food served to heroes on banquet reliefs and leads us in turn to consider revising the accepted meaning of one Greek and one Latin word, and the translations of several passages.

Festive meals in classical Greece ended with δεύτεραι τράπεζαι, "Second Tables". Debris from the main courses was cleared away and the guests' hands washed, then wine and dessert courses were brought in.[1] For these τραγήματα, "Nibbles", ἐπιφορήματα, "Brought Afters", or ἐπιδορπίσματα, "After Dinners", three main kinds of food were served: what we would call appetizers (hard-boiled eggs, small roasted birds, cheeses and such); fruit, dried fruit, and nuts; and cakes. We know this largely because of Athenaeus, who drew from now largely lost works, especially Athenian comedies of the 5th and 4th centuries; it was chiefly in comedy that food was thought a fit subject for literature.

Among the cakes served at dessert courses, one in particular stands out: the πλακοῦς, usually referred to in the accusative and therefore better known as πλακοῦντα, which is what we will call it. *Plakounta* came to mean cake in general, whence πλακουντοποιός, "cake maker", φιλοπλάκουντος, "cake lover", and even ἀπλάκουντος, "cakeless". A variety of passages quoted by Athenaeus stresses the superiority of the original plakounta over other pastries of classical Greece.[2] Its irresistibility is brought out by the 4th-century writer of parodies, Matron, quoted by Athenaeus (IV.137b–c): the poet describes eating an elaborate meal; by the time the Second Tables are served, he is no longer hungry and turns up his nose at the Nibbles, but

> When [he] saw the golden, sweet, huge, round, thick-swollen
> child of Demeter, a baked plakounta . . .[3]

he found a spot for it. "Child of Demeter" would apply, of course, to anything wheaten. Plakountas made in Athens or in Samos were particularly renowned and exported in

---

[1] For "Second Tables", the discussion in Athenaeus, *Deipnosophistae* XIV.640a–643e; D. Tolles, *The Banquet Libations of the Greeks*, Ann Arbor 1943, *passim*. I should like to acknowledge here the friendly assistance I received in Athens from Mrs. M. de la Motte and the staff of the Goulandris Museum of Natural History; Mrs. M. N. Drouliskos of the British Council Library; Dr. Vasilios Rozos of Athens University; and Dr. J. Binder, who unselfishly shared her knowledge of ancient and modern Athens. The American School of Classical Studies at Athens, where this brief study was written, as always provided the most generous hospitality.

[2] Athenaeus, XIV.640c, Philippides; 640d, Diphilos; 642f, Alexis. Alcibiades sends a plakounta to Socrates: 643f, Antipater.

[3] ὡς δὲ ἴδον ξανθόν, γλυκερόν, μέγαν, ἔγκυκλον, ἁδρὸν
Δήμητρος παῖδ' ὀπτὸν ἐπεισελθόντα πλακοῦντα. . . .

individual containers.[4] But what this cake of cakes looked like, what it was, and how it was made have so far remained obscure, despite a number of clues.

First, the name: πλακοῦς, contracted, as Athenaeus (XIV.644b) learnedly notes, from πλακόεις (like σησαμοῦς, "full of sesame", from σησαμόεις) and therefore really an adjective, with ἄρτος, "loaf", understood to follow. Πλακόεις, everybody agrees, from πλάξ, a word that can mean anything broad and flat and which we recognize in English words related to it: plank, plaice and fluke, plaque, flake, flagstone, all going back to an ancient Indo-European root *pla-k*, expressing the idea of a flat sheet.[5] *Plakounta* is usually translated "flat-cake". Why "flat-cake" instead of "cake rich in plaques", since the -*oeis* adjective form usually means "full of, rich in"? Perhaps because scholars found it difficult to visualize a cake rich in plaques or in flagstones; but it could certainly be rich in flakes, *flaky*. Was it in fact flat or flaky? We can try to find out from preserved descriptions and recipes.

The crucial descriptive passage is again quoted by Athenaeus (X.449b–c) in a section on riddles, from the 4th-century B.C. comic poet Antiphanes:

> Do you want me to say: "The stream from humming bee commingled
> with the clot that flows from bleating goats, nesting
> in a broad receptacle of the virgin daughter of pure Demeter,
> and cuddling itself in ten thousand thin-textured veils,"
> or just plain "plakounta"?[6]

The riddle is from an Attic play, not an Alexandrian fantasy, and therefore more elaborate than subtle. In fact it clearly lists the three components of a plakounta: cheese-and-honey, dough, and "ten thousand veils", footnoted by C. B. Gulick, the translator of Athenaeus for the Loeb Library edition, as "spices", which seems farfetched.

Another passage describing a related cake, the ἄμυλος, comes from the *Banquet* of Philoxenus, quoted by Athenaeus (XIV.643a–b):

> . . . and in the middle of them
> there was set up a delight for mortals, sweet white marrow
>   muffling up its face in thin draperies like spiderwebs,
> ashamed that someone might see
> it had to leave the sheep-flock
> dry among the dry back-flowing springs of Aristaeus.[7]

---

[4] Athenaeus, III.101d, Archestratos; XIV.644c, Sopater; IV.130d, Hippolochos.

[5] *Pla-k* and its derivatives: J. Pokorny, *Indogermanisches etymologisches Wörterbuch*, Bern/Munich I, 1959, p. 831.

[6] . . . ξουθῆς μελίσσης νάμασιν δὲ συμμιγῆ
μηκάδων αἰγῶν ἀπόρρουν θρόμβον, ἐγκαθειμένον
εἰς πλατὺ στέγαστρον ἁγνῆς παρθένου Δηοῦς κόρης,
λεπτοσυνθέτοις τρυφῶντα μυρίοις καλύμμασιν,
ἢ σαφῶς πλακοῦντα φράζω σοι;

[7] . . . ταῖσι δ' ἐν μέσαις
ἐγκαθιδρύθη μέγα χάρμα βροτοῖς, λευκὸς μυελὸς γλυκερός, λεπτοῖς

In other words, sheep's-milk cheese and honey (Aristaeus, the bee-keeping hero), and spiderweb draperies instead of thin-textured veils, no crust.

What a plakounta looked like is described—backwards—in a work *On Plants* by the 4th-century B.C. writer Phanias, once more quoted by Athenaeus, in a section on vegetables (II.58d–e):

> The seed-pod of the domesticated mallow [possibly the small *Malva moschata* or else *M. sylvestris*] is called *plakous* from the following: its ribbed structure is like the base of a plakounta, and there is a central knob in the middle of the plakounta-like swelling.[8]

A round cake, then, with a ribbed base and a convex top with a knob in the middle. This passage was found of extreme obscurity by learned translators who failed to go outside their studies to look at the fruit of any number of related mallows, from *Malva sylvestris* to hollyhocks. All these fruits look like particularly neat, ribbed cakes with a knob on top (Fig. 2). If taken from the plant, leaving the knob behind, they look like the shells of sea-urchins, which is what Phanias goes on to say.

For another indication of shape and contents, we turn to Italy in the 2nd century B.C., when Marcus Porcius Cato, the Censor, wrote his dour *de agri cultura*. This extraordinary work preserves for us not a literary text but the back pages of a farmer's almanac: full of canny recipes, good addresses, and useful tricks in pest control, dosing the beasts, and clothing slaves cheaply. It includes a recipe for *placenta*, both name and cake derived, scholars agree, from plakounta.

Cato (LXXVI) first lists ingredients in cookbook style: flour for the dough, flour and groats for the *tracta*. *Tracta* remain vague for dictionaries and translators; let us simply note here a distinction between dough and *tracta*. He then gives step-by-step instructions.

1. Make the *tracta*, wipe them with an oiled cloth, spread them out to dry on a basket.
2. Knead dough, pre-heat hearth and the clay tile that will serve as an oven.
3. Mix pre-soaked and drained fresh sweet cheese, kneaded and pressed through a sieve, with good honey, set aside.
4. Spread dough over oiled bayleaves on a clean foot-wide board, over it place a layer of *tracta*, cover with the cheese-and-honey filling, add another layer of *tracta*, another of

---

ἀράχνας ἐναλιγκίοισι πέπλοις
συγκαλύπτων ὄψιν αἰσχύνας ὕπο, μὴ κατίδῃ τις
μηλογενὲς πῶυ λιπόντ' ἀνάγκαις
ξηρὸν ἐν ξηραῖς 'Αρισταίου παλιρρύτοισι παγαῖς. . . .

[8] τῆς ἡμέρου μαλάχης ὁ σπερματικὸς τύπος καλεῖται πλακοῦς, ἐμφερὴς ὢν αὐτῷ· τὸ μὲν γὰρ κτενῶδες ἀνάλογον καθάπερ ἡ τοῦ πλακοῦντος κρηπίς, κατὰ μέσον δὲ τοῦ πλακουντικοῦ ὄγκου τὸ κέντρον ὀμφαλικόν.

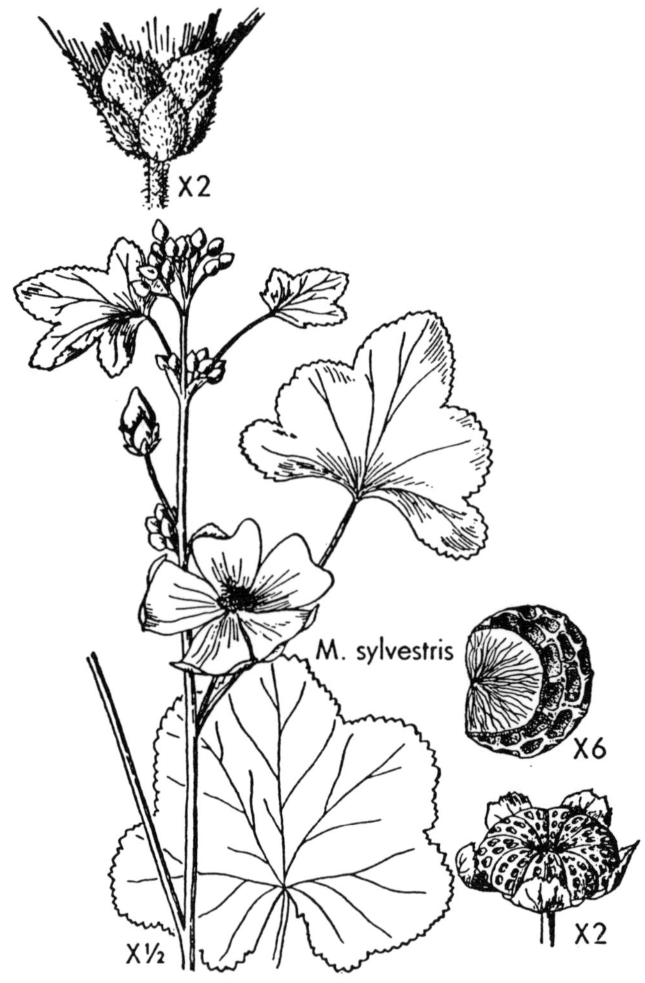

FIG. 2. *Malva sylvestris* (Henry A. Gleason, *The New Britton and Brown Illustrated Flora of the Northeast-ern United States and Adjacent Canada* II, New York/London 1968, fig. on p. 526)

       filling, continue alternating until all filling is used up, fin-
       ish with a layer of *tracta*, fold crust up.
  5. Bake slowly, checking two or three times for doneness.
       Brush with honey.

This recipe confirms the three components of plakounta: filling, crust, and *tracta* here in-stead of ten thousand veils; it adds the fact of layering.

In pursuit of *tracta*, which W. D. Hooper and H. B. Ash, the Loeb translators of Cato in 1934, footnoted as "seemingly bits of pastry", and R. Goujard, who translated Cato into French in 1975 for the Budé series, sees as *feuilles de pâte*, sheets of dough, we go on to Apicius' *On Cookery*. This collection of recipes attributed to a famous Roman gourmet of Augustan times really includes parts of several later Greek and Roman cookbooks. The work has no section on cakes; it does, however, mention *tracta*, always crumbled and always used to thicken a liquid. In a section that deals with the *minutal*, a highly spiced fricassee, each of seven recipes (IV.3.1–7) ends with "crumble in *tracta* and thicken" with a word connoting both binding and thickening (*tractam confringes et ex ea obligas*). Among scattered other uses we find *tracta* crumbled in simmering milk for mush and that mush combined with eggs and spices for a custard (V.1.3 and VII.13.5). J. André, who translated Apicius into French in 1974 for the Budé series, gives *pâte*, dough, for *tracta*, even though other terms, like *subacta*, kneaded, and *lagana*, oil-and-flour dough,[9] are used for dough elsewhere in the same work. Apicius' manual recommends a variety of thickening agents besides *tracta*, most often wheat starch but also bread and eggs or egg whites.

We may now consider a translation for the "ten thousand veils" and for *tracta* and test it with experiments. Let us then assume that both veils and *tracta* mean *phyllo* or *strudel*, thin sheets of dough pulled to translucent fineness, and used partly dried, the mainstay of modern Greek pastrymaking. Plakounta would thus become Napoleon pie: layers of *phyllo* alternating with filling, held in a crust. Its descendants, or descendants of its crustless cousin, could then be recognized in the modern Greek *galaktoboureko* and *bougatsa*, and even the humble *tiropita*, described in the 1978 menu of a restaurant in Delphi as "cheese flake cake". This would translate again into ancient Greek as τυρῶντα πλακοῦντα (ἄρτον) and reminds us in turn of the dedication poem of the 3rd century by Theodoridas (*Palatine Anthology* VI.155):

> Of the same age the four-year-old boy Krobylos
> And the hair this son of Hegisidikos cut off
> For Phoibos, god of music and dance.
> He also gave a fierce rooster
> And a fat, cheese-bearing plakounta.
> Apollo, make Krobylos grow up to be a man;
> Keep your hands over his house and holdings.[10]

A curious confirmation of this identification comes from a French novel of Romanian village life at the turn of the century, Panait Istrati's *Codine* (Paris 1926). Istrati describes the childhood joys of watching the village baker prepare the chief Romanian delicacy, *platchynta*. The baker, or *platchyntar* (close to the Latin *placentarius*), has set the yeast going at nine, kneaded the dough at midnight, and now at four in the morning begins the platchynta itself. On the big board six feet square he first separates the dough into lumps; each lump is kneaded into a ball, brushed with fat, and set aside. For each individual platchynta, the baker picks up a ball in each hand, flattens them to the size of plates, brushes them with fat

---

[9] A bread baked in Greece on the first day of Lent is still called *langana*.

[10] Ἅλικες αἵ τε κόμαι καὶ ὁ Κρωβύλος, ᾶς ἀπὸ Φοίβῳ
>   πέξατο μολπαστᾷ κῶρος ὁ τετραετής·
> αἰχμητὰν δ' ἐπέθυσεν ἀλέκτορα καὶ πλακόεντα
>   παῖς Ἡγησιδίκου πίονα τυροφόρον.
> Ὤπολλον, θείης τὸν Κρωβύλον εἰς τέλος ἄνδρα
>   οἴκου καὶ κτεάνων χεῖρας ὕπερθεν ἔχειν.

again, and sticks them together. The disk is then pulled and set whirling over the baker's head, to slap back on the board thinner and broader each time until it is paper-thin, translucent, and covers more than three feet square. The baker then folds it eightfold as his helper spreads a filling of cottage cheese, beaten eggs, and sugar between each fold. Ends are tucked in, and the finished platchynta is ready for baking. No crust, and the additional eggs—but still close to Cato's cake.

Experiments bring additional support: First, phyllo is made not by rolling out but by pulling or drawing out sheets of dough, and this process neatly fits the name *tracta*, drawn or pulled; in fact it explains the name. Second, Cato's recipe makes a fine cake with a ribbed base and a tendency to swell in the middle, as Matron noted. Finally, dried, crumbled phyllo thickens a liquid remarkably fast without changing its taste. Crumbled dough ends up lumpy and floury, breadcrumbs grainy, but phyllo flakes dissolve smoothly. Crumbled in simmering milk they make a suitably bland thick cream or mush.

Thus we can reconstruct a cake of phyllo sheets, honey-cheese filling, and crust, the plakounta, now better translated "flaky cake" or "layered cake", more like the French *feuilleté* with its connotation of leaves or sheets rather than short flakes. This was adopted by the Romans as *placenta*, the sheets or *tracta* being used also in other cakes described by Cato, as well as in other cookery. If we now compare a mallow pod and an experimental plakounta, the similarities will encourage us to try to find other comparisons in ancient Greek art.

This is not a simple task, since ancient Greeks are seldom represented actually eating. There are a few traditional scenes—Achilles dining at Troy with the body of Hektor under his couch, Herakles banqueting in heaven, Dionysos and his followers reveling[11]—but of all the scenes painted on 5th-century B.C. vases to celebrate the joyous symposium, that dinner, drinking, and entertainment party, hardly any celebrate the dining stage. Sacrifices, which usually of course involved an outdoor roast and picnic, are also shown in painting and sculpture, but the two stages most often seen are the arrival at the shrine, with the sacrificial animal still alive and the rest of the picnic decorously carried in a covered hamper, or the immediate preparations, with the participants reverently gathered at the altar. Occasionally, we see the roasting actually in progress and more rarely the gift to a divinity of bloodless offerings, usually a basket of fruit and cakes.[12]

---

[11] The following examples illustrate the traditional banquet scenes: Achilles, e.g., J. Boardman, *Athenian Red Figure Vases: The Archaic Period*, London 1975, fig. 248. Herakles, e.g., *idem, Athenian Black Figure Vases*, London 1974, figs. 161:1 and 161:2; and in sculpture, the relief from Amphipolis in Ἔργον 1977 (1978), pp. 43–44. For the Dionysiac symposium, see for example P. E. Arias and M. Hirmer, *A History of 1000 Years of Greek Vase Painting*, London 1962, pl. XXI; K. Schauenburg, "Silene beim Symposion," *JdI* 88, 1973 (pp. 1–26), p. 11 and fig. 10, a cup in the American Academy in Rome with two of the ribbed cakes discussed in this study; and G. M. A. Richter, *Red-figured Athenian Vases in the Metropolitan Museum of Art*, New Haven/London 1936, pl. 152, no. 153, also with a ribbed cake. For some of the few symposia with food visible, see Boardman, *Black Figure*, fig. 36; *idem, Red Figure*, fig. 25; Arias and Hirmer, *op. cit.*, pl. IX and fig. 106; and J. Charbonneaux, R. Martin, and F. Villard, *Classical Greek Art*, New York 1972, fig. 376.

[12] Scenes of sacrifice: Arrival at the shrine, e.g., N. Alfieri and P. E. Arias, *Spina, Guida al Museo*

Virtually the only exception is found in banquet reliefs.[13] These reliefs apparently began as gifts to divinities and to heroes and went on to become used as memorials to the ordinary dead, who could be thought of as attaining blessed or hero status in the afterworld, characterized by the happy banquet. R. N. Thönges-Stringaris notes that the table, when laden, invariably bears a restricted repertory of formally arranged fruit and cakes, which she believes do not represent an ordinary meal but rather specific offerings. But a different interpretation might be that these fruits and cakes represent, in stylized fashion, the "Second Tables", the sated and relaxed stage of dinner at which wine-drinking, almost always a feature of banquet reliefs, began.

This restricted repertory includes fruit—especially pomegranates but also figs and grapes, sometimes apples—occasionally eggs, always cakes. Cakes of two main kinds: firm little pyramids and large ribbed cakes with a central knob. The pyramids are no trouble, since we find πυραμίδες of roasted wheat soaked in honey among the cakes carefully listed by Athenaeus (xiv.647c). The heavy looking, knobbed and ribbed cakes are obviously what Phanias described and would make excellent candidates for plakounta had not some scholars already tentatively identified them with ὀμφαλωτὰ πόπανα, knobbed cakes, which ancient literature mentions as used in sacrifices.

What were these *popana* and why does the encyclopaedic Athenaeus never mention them? Following up most recorded uses of the word in ancient Greek literature, papyri, and inscriptions[14] we find that *popanon* (the singular) rivals *plakounta* in meaning simply "cake" and is related to the Greek verb to cook or bake, rather like "cake" and "cooking" in English. Late, and therefore often unreliable, lexicographers defined *popana* as small cakes (*placentia*), flat, round, and thin, used in sacrifices. We often find this association of *popana* and sacrifices in the sources. The crucial descriptive passage, however, occurs in Polybius, in a section about early Roman cavalry (*Histories*, vi.25.7):

> They had oxhide shields like knobbed *popana*, the kind used
> in sacrifices.[15]

Archeologico in Ferrara, Florence 1960, pl. LXI; J. N. Svoronos, *Das athener Nationalmuseum*, Athens 1908, pl. vol. I, pl. XXXVI:3 (N.M. 1333), pl. XXXVII:6 (N.M. 1429), and pl. vol. II, pl. CLXXXIII, top left (N.M. 1016); U. Hausmann, *Griechische Weihreliefs*, Berlin 1960, figs. 4, 40. Preparation for sacrifice, *ibid.*, fig. 55; on vases, e.g., G. A. Reisner, C. S. Fisher, and D. G. Lyon, *Harvard Excavations at Samaria, 1908–1910* II, Cambridge, Mass. 1924, pl. 70; C. Lenormant and J. de Witte, *Élite des monuments céramographiques*, Paris 1844–1861, II, pls. CV, CVI. The roasting stage: e.g., Boardman, *Red Figure* (footnote 11, p. 62 above), fig. 340; E. Gerhard, *Auserlesene griechische Vasenbilder* III, Berlin 1847, pl. 155; Lenormant and de Witte, *op. cit.*, pls. CVII, CVIII; M. Wegner, *Das Musikleben der Griechen*, Berlin 1949, pl. 27:a; and H. Metzger, *Recherches sur l'imagerie athénienne*, Paris 1965, chap. VII and pl. XLVII. Bringing clearly represented fruit and cake, e.g., Svoronos, *op. cit.*, pl. vol. I, pl. XXXVI:4 (N.M. 1335).

[13] See footnote 25, p. 9 above.

[14] Partial lists of usage in LSJ[9] and H. Stephanus, *Thesaurus graecae linguae, s.v.* πόπανον; G. Herzog-Hauser, *popanon, RE* XXII, i, 1953, cols. 49–50; and the *Oxford Latin Dictionary, s.v. popanum*.

[15] τόν γε μὴν θυρεὸν εἶχον ἐκ βοείου δέρματος, τοῖς ὀμφαλωτοῖς ποπάνοις παραπλήσιων τοῖς ἐπὶ τὰς θυσίας ἐπιτιθεμένοις. . . .

Indeed the knob seems to be important in sacrificial cakes, at least around Athens. Attic inscriptions,[16] ranging from the 4th century B.C. to the 1st century after Christ and prescribing offerings in various cults, call for "three *popana*" (Sokolowski, no. 21), or just "three single-knobbed" with *popana* understood (Sokolowski, nos. 23, 24) as an ordinary offering. One inscription calls for a "twelve-knobbed *popanon* made with one *choenix* [*ca.* 1,090 cc.] of flour" (πόπανον χοινικιαῖον δωδεκόνφαλον, Sokolowski, no. 52), which recalls the many Biblical prescriptions governing cake offerings, such as Leviticus 23:17:

> You shall bring from your dwellings two loaves of bread . . .
> made of two tenths of an ephah, they shall be of fine flour, they
> shall be baked with leaven, as first fruits of the Lord.

The inscription that specifies twelve knobs even calls for them to be upright (ὀρθονφαλον) or flattened (καθήμενον), according to the divinity to whom the offering is made. This is so intriguing that we search ancient representations of sacrifices for twelve-knobbed cakes, but with little success, except in the clay models of offering trays laden with cakes recovered from the Sanctuary of Demeter and Kore at Corinth, where multi-knobbed cakes indeed appear among a bewildering range of cakes and other foodstuffs.[17]

Other archaeologists prefer, for the knobbed cakes, plain-looking buns arranged in one or two concentric circles around a central knob. These have the merit of looking easy to handle and carry about, the sort of all-purpose bread-dough cake one can well visualize placed on humble altars along with a few fruits, and it has also been found in religious contexts;[18] but the votive and banquet reliefs of Athens show the large ribbed cake. A

[16] These inscriptions have been gathered in F. Sokolowski, *Lois sacrées des cités grecques*, Paris 1969, where *popana* or *monomphala* are mentioned in nos. 21, 23, 24, 38, and 52, from Attica; also possibly no. 169, from Kos; *idem, Lois sacrées des cités grecques, Supplément*, Paris 1962, no. 80, from Samos.

[17] The ribbed, knobbed cakes are found on vases as well as reliefs, e.g., Boardman, *Black Figure* (footnote 11, p. 62 above), fig. 36, cup; Schauenberg, *loc. cit.* (footnote 11, p. 62 above), krater; N. Zapheiropoulos, «Δύο πρώϊμοι Ἀττικαὶ λήκυθοι», Ἀρχ᾽Ἐφ 1950–1951, pp. 149–163, fig. 1 and pl. 1, lekythos; G. Van Hoorn, *Choes and Anthesteria*, Leiden 1951, figs. 10, 24, 80, 334, 467, 522, choes, to note only the clearest examples; *ibid.*, figs. 223, 224, plastic lekythoi, where the secondary cakes around the main one might be interpreted as multiple knobs; D. Robinson *et al., A Catalogue of the Greek Vases in the Royal Ontario Museum of Archaeology, Toronto*, Toronto 1930, no. 389, pp. 193–194, pl. LXIX, a Campanian amphora. But the best candidates for multiple-knobbed cakes, along with other contents of the mystic chest of the Eleusinian mysteries (as listed in a fine burst of indignation by Clement of Alexandria, *Exhortation to the Greeks* II.19: "sesame-, pyramid- and round-cakes, many-knobbed *popana*, lumps of salt and a snake . . . " [σησαμαῖ ταῦτα καὶ πυραμίδες καὶ τολύπαι, καὶ πόπανα πολυόμφαλα χόνδροι τε ἁλῶν καὶ δράκων]), are in the Demeter Sanctuary at Corinth, where several variants of the model *liknon* filled with cakes and fruit have been found: R. S. Stroud, "The Sanctuary of Demeter and Kore on Acrocorinth Preliminary Report I: 1961–1962," *Hesperia* 34, 1965 (pp. 1–24), pp. 23–24 and pl. 11:d, e, g.

[18] For these rivals of the ribbed cake for the title of *omphalota popana*, the concentric circle or target cakes, see V. G. Callipolitis, ««Τράπεζαι προσφορῶν» τοῦ Μουσείου Μυτιλήνης», Λεσβιακά 3, 1959, pp. 41–54, where he discusses offering stands on which were carved different foods, including cakes—on one example three target cakes—and gathers examples of other model cakes, and *idem*, "Naïscos de Némésis, trouvé en Macédoine," *Marsyas, Studies in the History of Art*, Supplement I, *Essays in Memory of Karl Lehmann*, Locust Valley, New York 1964, pp. 59–62, three target cakes in the field beside a relief of Nemesis. The way in which the "three cakes" of Attic inscriptions or other bloodless offerings would be placed on an offering

curious evolution takes place in Samos, the home, with Athens, of the best plakountas. In 2nd-century B.C. Samian banquet reliefs, we do not see the ribbed and knobbed mallow-pod shape of the central cake, which is here larger than ever, but rather a low, thick, circular crust above which rises a smooth swelling, very much the result obtained when following Cato's 2nd-century recipe.[19] It seems clear that the cake in 2nd-century Samos is a Samian plakounta, on the way to losing its crust as it has in modern times.

But most other depictions of cakes in art are too vague for positive identification. Some of the vagueness may have been intentional, since we know that a great variety of cakes of different shapes and names were offered to different divinities at different festivals;[20] the craftman may have sometimes wanted prudently to convey the mere idea of pastry.

Survivals of the plakounta beyond classical antiquity separate into three branches. In the first, cake and name survive together, as in the Rumanian *platchynta*. In the second, sheets or cake survive under another name: modern Greek *phyllo* or German *strudel* for the sheets, Turkish *börek*, modern Greek *galaktoboureko*, American *Napoleon* or French *mille-feuilles* for the cake. In the third, the name survives for a related dessert, often layered and sometimes with a cheese-and-honey filling: Hungarian *palacsinta*, Czech *palaczinki*, Austrian *palatschinken torte*.

The identification of Antiphanes' ten thousand veils with phyllo or strudel thus not only restores the ancient and honorable ancestry of the most characteristic dessert of Greece, the Balkans, and the Near East but happily trails after it the identification of related things, words, and processes in both Greece and Rome.

But if *plakounta* and *placenta* only meant, throughout classical antiquity, first the cake of the ten thousand veils and then just cake, "placenta" means for us, as the *Oxford English Dictionary* puts it:

> The spongy vascular organ, of flattened circular form, to which the foetus is attached by the umbilical cord, and by means of which it is nourished in the womb, in all higher mammals, and which is expelled in parturition; the afterbirth.

---

table is well illustrated on a krater from Spina, Alfieri and Arias (footnote 12, pp. 62–63 above), pl. 66. E. Paul (*Antike Welt in Ton: Griechische und römische Terrakotten des Archäologischen Institutes in Leipzig*, Leipzig, n.d. but latest bibliographical reference 1959) illustrates in no. 269 (p. 93 and pl. 75) a Hellenistic terracotta tray with fruit and three target cakes, no provenience. B. M. Kingsley (*The Terracottas of the Tarentine Greeks, an Introduction to the Collection in the J. Paul Getty Museum*, n.p. 1976) shows in no. 12 (cover) a goddess, probably Demeter or Persephone, carrying fruit and target cakes; it may be the same cakes that are glimpsed in the *liknon* painted on two walls of the House of the Vettii in Pompeii: K. Schefold, *Vergessenes Pompeji*, Bern/Munich 1962, figs. 92:2 and 93. Some *monomphala* may also be among the cakes in the model *likna* of the Demeter Sanctuary in Corinth: see footnote 17, p. 64 above.

[19] For reliefs in Samos, see R. Horn, *Samos*, XII, *Hellenistische Bildwerke aus Samos*, Bonn 1972, pls. 68, 69, 71, 84–93.

[20] For lists of such cakes see C. A. Lobeck, *Aglaophamus*, Königsberg 1829, II, pp. 1060–1085 and E. Orth, "Kuchen," *RE* XI, ii, 1922 (cols. 2088–2099), col. 2088. For a discussion of cakes see L. Deubner, *Attische Feste*, Berlin 1932, pp. 154–155 and H. Payne, *Perachora* I, Oxford 1940, pp. 67–69.

The organ is further described in R. W. Johnstone and R. J. Kellar's *Textbook of Midwifery*, 20th ed., London 1965, p. 71:

> The placenta at term is a roundish, flat organ about nine inches in diameter and three quarters of an inch in thickness at the centre.[21]

How this organ came to be called "placenta" is curious because of its very lack of direct connection with classical antiquity.

In ancient Greece the placenta was called χόριον. It included all the embryonic membranes (not only the one modern anatomy calls "chorion") and their thickened, blood-exchanging attachment to the uterus now called "placenta". The treatise *On the Nature of the Child*, part of the Hippocratic Corpus, describes the development of embryonic membranes in section XVI:

> When flesh has formed, then since the contents of the womb have increased, the membranes increase as well, especially those outside, and pouch ["vascularize"]. And the blood which comes down from the mother, attracted by the flesh's aspiration, and adds to the flesh's growth, whatever of this blood is not used up is distributed among the pouches. And when these membranes pouch and receive blood, that is called *chorion*.[22]

Compare R. D. Frandson, *Anatomy and Physiology of Farm Animals*, Philadelphia 1965, p. 350:

> The extra-embryonic membranes or *placenta* develop as a means of meeting the increasing need for more nutrition . . .

and on p. 351:

> In the hemochorial placenta . . . not only the fetal vessels but also the chorion of the fetal placenta are invaginated into pools of the maternal blood.

Galenos of Pergamon (Galen), physician to Marcus Aurelius, continued to write in Greek, the language of medicine.[23] In his careful *On the Anatomy of the Uterus*, X, he gives a fine description of embryonic membranes and placenta, which he continues to call *chorion*; his description of placental villi is as good as most modern illustrations. Galen does use the word *plakounta*, but nutritionally, not anatomically, in his treatise *On the Effects of Foods* (i.3.2), in a subsection on pastry.

---

[21] For the appearance of the placenta, see R. Warwick, P. Williams, *et al.*, *Gray's Anatomy*, 35th ed., Edinburgh/Norwich 1973, p. 105, fig. 2:46 and p. 613, fig. 6:36.

[22] *Hippocrate*, XI, *De la génération, De la nature de l'enfant, Des maladies* IV, *Du foetus de huit mois*, R. Joly, ed. and tr., Paris 1970, pp. 53–83, for the treatise περὶ φύσιος παιδίου.

[23] One of the few physicians to write in Latin was Celsus in the 1st century after Christ; he calls the afterbirth *secundae* (*de medicina* v.25.13 and vii.29.9).

Plakounta and *placenta* largely disappear from Byzantine Greek and Mediaeval Latin.[24] We only occasionally find a provincial use of *placentula*, a bun, or of *plakountarios*, *placentarius*, a cakemaker with a second meaning of jester (sayer of pleasant, in the sense of funny, sayings). As for Mediaeval anatomy, it follows Galen, for good or ill.

It is not until the 16th century that a group of young experimenters in North Italian universities, to which they came from all over Europe, dared to rebel against Galen (who had been a considerable rebel in his time). Their leader was the great Andreas Vesalius, a fifth-generation Flemish physician who obtained the chair of anatomy in the most celebrated medical school of the time, Padua, at the age of 22, after a brilliant public dissection. He was 27 when he published his revolutionary *de humanis corporis fabrica (On the Structure of the Human Body)*. Among Vesalius' students was Gabriele Fallopio, who in turn had as disciples two other great anatomists, Fabrizio d'Acquapendente and William Harvey. It was Gabriele Fallopio (who had himself become a professor in Padua) in his *Observationes anatomicae*, published—in Latin of course—in 1561, who first used the term *placenta* anatomically,[25] as *placenta uterina*, womb-cake, which it is still called in German: *Mutterkuchen, Fruchtkuchen.*

How did Gabriele Fallopio coin the word? And did he mean it to express plakounta, or just cake? Although the organ's alternation of membranes and spongy tissues, and even its appearance with one rough and one smooth side, would fit plakounta, it is difficult to ascertain which pastries were common in 16th-century Padua and whether *placenta* was still a cake-name there, despite the absence of the word from official and literary language. If not, since *placenta* had dropped out of Mediaeval Latin, how did Fallopio arrive at the word? We remember here that Andreas Vesalius, Fallopio's teacher, was renowned for his erudition and his deliberate use of classical Latin.[26] It may be that the student put into his own text some dissection-room nickname originally bestowed by the learned Vesalius.

At any rate, the *Oxford English Dictionary* assures us that it was not until 1677 that the word made its first appearance in English, in botany, and that it was as late as 1691 before it was first used in anatomy.

[24] Mediaeval Latin: J. F. Niermayer, *Mediae latinitatis lexicon minus: a Mediaeval Latin-French/English Dictionary*, Leiden 1976; R. E. Latham, *Revised Mediaeval Word-List from British and Irish Sources*, London 1965; C. de F. Du Cange *et al.*, *Glossarium mediae et infimae latinitatis*, 2nd ed., Paris 1937–1938. Byzantine Greek: E. A. Sophocles, *Greek Lexicon of the Roman and Byzantine Periods*, New York 1887.

[25] M. Wegscheider, "Geschichte der Geburtshilfe," in M. Neuburger and J. Pagel, *Handbuch der Geschichte der Medizin*, Jena 1905.

[26] For Vesalius' learning in ancient literature, see L. Edelstein, "Andreas Vesalius the Humanist," *Bulletin of the History of Medicine* 14, 1943, pp. 547–561; for Vesalius' circle, *André Vésale, renovateur de l'anatomie humaine*, Brussels 1957 (an exhibition catalogue with wide-ranging introductory essays). Sources used for the history of Greek medicine in this study include Joly (footnote 22, p. 66 above); F. J. Herrgott, tr., *Soranus d'Éphèse, Traité des Maladies des Femmes, et Moschion, son abbréviateur et traducteur*, Nancy 1895; W. G. Spencer, tr. *Celsus De Medicina*, London/Cambridge, Mass. 1935–1938; C. M. Goss, "Galen of Pergamon: On the Anatomy of the Uterus," *Anatomical Record* 144.2, October 1962; and "Galeni de alimentorum facultatibus," *Corpus medicorum graecorum*, G. Helmreich, ed., IV, ii, Leipzig/Berlin 1923. For a general overview of Greek medicine see E. D. Philips, *Greek Medicine*, London/Southampton 1973.

APPENDIX 2: AGORA DATED DEPOSITS

Deposit	Cat. No.	Inv. No.	Subject	Date
A 16:3 Well	**7** **17**	T 3476 a–c, e T 3476 d	Dancing Maenad Kalathiskos Dancer?	Last quarter 4th century?
A 19:5 Pit	**60**	T 3494	Two lions and horse	5th and last quarter 4th century?
C 20:2 Fill with figurines	**10** **89** **109** **110**	T 2830 T 2829 A 1204 T 2765	Dancing Maenad? Gorgoneion Gorgoneion, positive Gorgoneion, positive	Mixed 4th century to second quarter 2nd century or even later
D 17:4 Cistern	**85**	T 2925 a and b	Gorgoneion	Mixed to first quarter 1st century
E 14:1 Cistern	**41** **42**	T 883 a and c T 883 b	Banquet Banquet	Mixed to fourth quarter 3rd century
F 19:1 Well	**57**	T 2070	Griffin	5th century after Christ
G 5:2 Cistern	**102**	T 1595	Uncertain	3rd and 4th centuries after Christ
G 13:4 Well (Group A)	**43**	T 653 a and b	Banquet	Third quarter 4th through first quarter 3rd century? [and down to *ca.* 265 (S. I. R.)]
G 14:2 Well	**88**	T 2177	Gorgoneion	Mixed early 4th to first quarter 1st century [to 2nd century (S. I. R.)]
H–K 12–14 Middle Stoa Building Fill (MSBF)	**2** **11** **13** **24** **26** **32** **37** **45** **53** **62** **84**	T 388 T 3361 T 389 T 3187 T 377 T 3360 MC 14 T 421 T 376 + T 3362 T 3237 T 405 + T 429	Dancing Maenad Dancing Maenad? Dancing Maenad? Ship with Triton or Ketos Nike driving Chariot Chariot Group Chariot Group? Assembly of Gods? Griffins and Deer Lion or Griffin attacks Gorgoneion	Second half 4th century to mid-2nd century [to first quarter of 2nd century (S. I. R.)]

I 16:1 Well	**48**	T 337	Person and object	Mixed 5th and 4th centuries dumped on use fill of Roman period
J 11:1 Dumped fill	**5** **9** **20** **22** **92**	T 3119 T 3120 T 3118 T 3121 T 3109	Dancing Maenad Dancing Maenad? Nereid? Ship Gorgoneion?	To last quarter 4th century
J 12:2 Well	**36**	T 453	Chariot Group?	To early 3rd century after Christ
J 12:3	**58**	T 508	Griffin	To mid-3rd century
M–N 15:1 South Stoa II Building Fill (SSIIBF)	**51** **70**	T 3233 T 3287	Person, fallen? Predator	To early third quarter 2nd century [S. I. R.]
N 16:2 Fill	**91**	T 3324	Gorgoneion?	Third quarter 4th century?
N 20:3 Well	**104**	T 3050	Mold or positive	To 1st century after Christ
N 20:6 Cistern	**4**	T 1612	Dancing Maenad	3rd into early 2nd century
N 20:7 Cistern	**30**	T 1621	Chariot Group	To first quarter 2nd century [and early second quarter (S. I. R.)]
O 16:4 Fill	**39**	T 3416	Chariot Group?	To last quarter 4th century? [late 4th or early 3rd century (S. I. R.)]
O 20:3 Well	**72**	T 1842	Predator	3rd century
P–R 6–12 Stoa of Attalos Building Fill (SABF)	**19** **50** **64** **75**	T 2986 T 2985 T 2989 T 3043	Amazon Person and pattern Lion or Griffin and Prey Lion	Second half of 4th to mid-2nd century
R 13:11 Well	**15**	T 4164	Nike?	Third quarter 4th century?

S 21:1 Well	**105**	T 1963	Mold or positive	To 1st century after Christ
U 26:1 Fill	**69**	T 1975	Predator and prey	3rd [and early 2nd century (S. I. R.)]

CONCORDANCE

AGORA INVENTORY NUMBERS AND CATALOGUE NUMBERS

Inv. no.	Cat. no.	Inv. no.	Cat. no.	Inv. no.	Cat. no.
A 99	**21**	T 1965	**61**	T 3121	**22**
A 1204	**109**	T 1975	**69**	T 3151	**52**
MC 13	**71**	T 2024	**81**	T 3155	**29**
MC 14	**37**	T 2047	**61**	T 3156	**55**
T 136	**83**	T 2070	**57**	T 3187	**24**
T 139	**82**	T 2142	**54**	T 3198	**25**
T 266	**101**	T 2177	**88**	T 3228	**14**
T 330	**103**	T 2197 a, b	**79**	T 3233	**51**
T 337	**48**	T 2349	**44**	T 3236	**66**
T 376	**53**	T 2353	**100**	T 3237	**62**
T 377	**26**	T 2380	**78**	T 3256	**93**
T 388	**2**	T 2595	**28**	T 3287	**70**
T 389	**13**	T 2596	**38**	T 3313	**97**
T 405	**84**	T 2765	**110**	T 3324	**91**
T 421	**45**	T 2829	**89**	T 3340	**86**
T 429	**84**	T 2830	**10**	T 3360	**32**
T 453	**36**	T 2918	**85**	T 3361	**11**
T 508	**58**	T 2920	**85**	T 3362	**53**
T 574	**107**	T 2925 a, b	**85**	T 3373	**40**
T 617	**34**	T 2948	**35**	T 3386	**1**
T 628 a, b	**56**	T 2965	**94**	T 3389	**12**
T 653 a, b	**43**	T 2981	**90**	T 3415	**65**
T 769	**67**	T 2985	**50**	T 3416	**39**
T 883 a, c	**41**	T 2986	**19**	T 3417	**80**
T 883 b	**42**	T 2989	**64**	T 3418	**96**
T 981	**33**	T 3003	**63**	T 3443	**8**
T 1059	**108**	T 3008	**31**	T 3476 a, b, c, e	**7**
T 1287	**16**	T 3023	**3**	T 3476 d	**17**
T 1392 a, b	**49**	T 3033	**45**	T 3494	**60**
T 1553	**68**	T 3043	**75**	T 3564	**59**
T 1595	**102**	T 3045	**6**	T 3657	**99**
T 1612	**4**	T 3048	**47**	T 3660	**23**
T 1621	**30**	T 3050	**104**	T 3774	**46**
T 1654	**74**	T 3061	**95**	T 3786	**87**
T 1842	**72**	T 3083	**106**	T 3787	**98**
T 1860	**76**	T 3109	**92**	T 3788	**18**
T 1862	**77**	T 3118	**20**	T 3984	**82**
T 1925	**27**	T 3119	**5**	T 4164	**15**
T 1963	**105**	T 3120	**9**	T 4167	**73**

PLATES

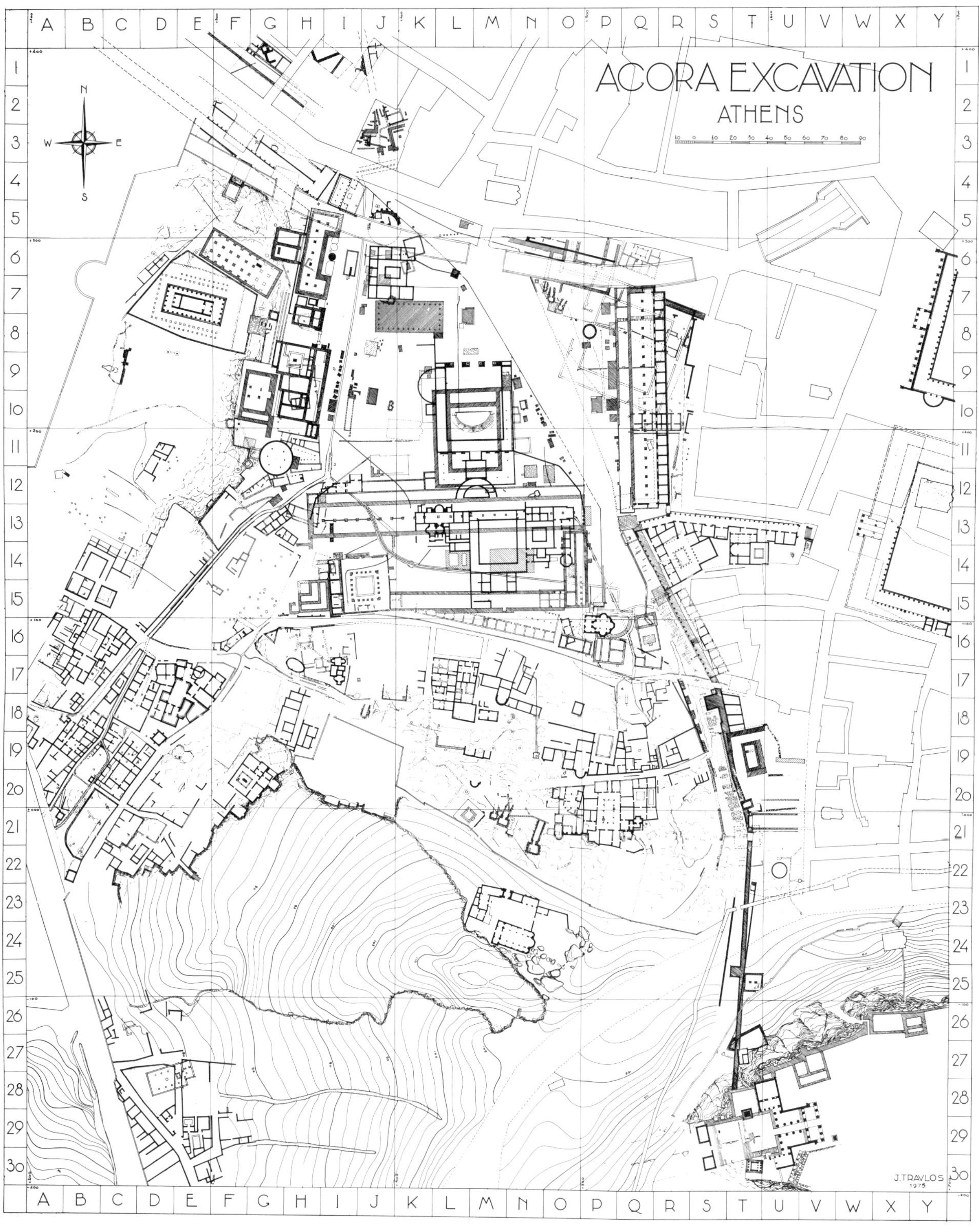

AGORA EXCAVATION
ATHENS
N
W E
S
J.TRAVLOS
1975

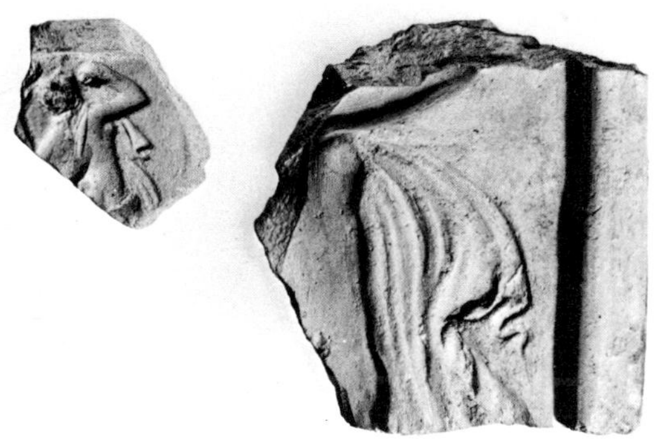

1, **7** (molds)   1:4

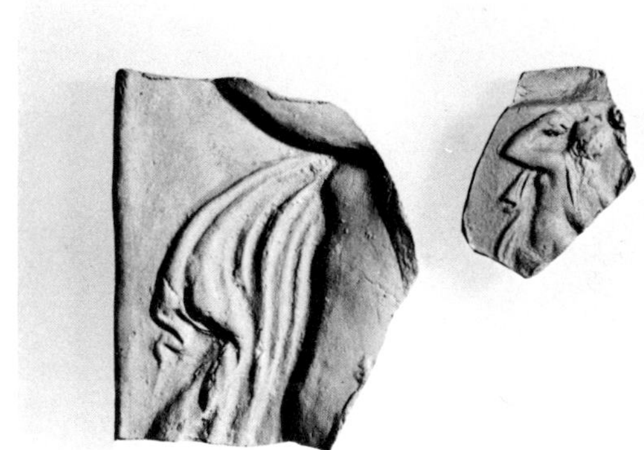

7, **1** (casts)   *ca.* 1:4

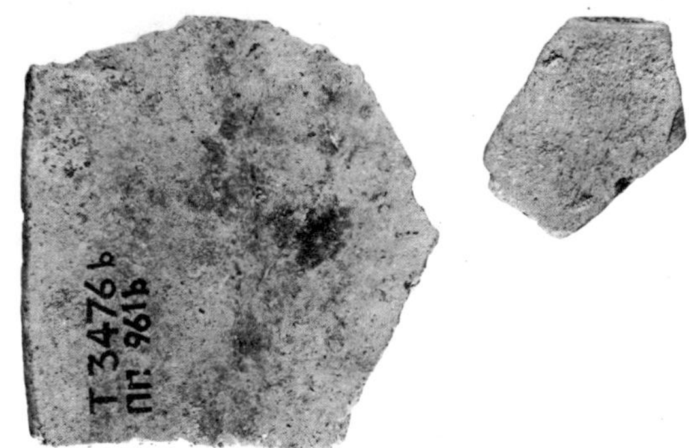

7, **1** (backs)   *ca.* 1:4

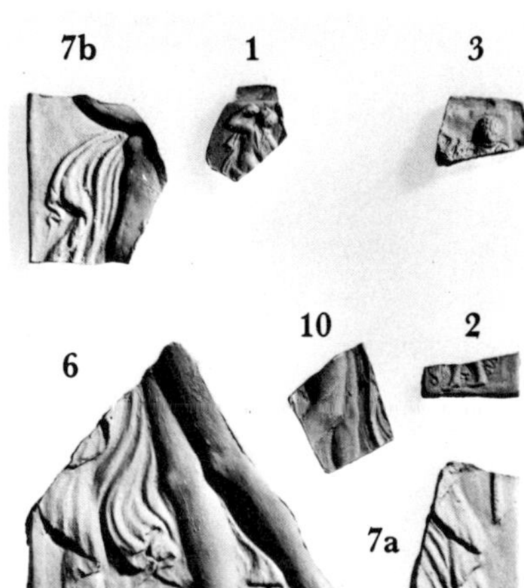

1–3, **6**, **7**, **10** (casts)   1:8

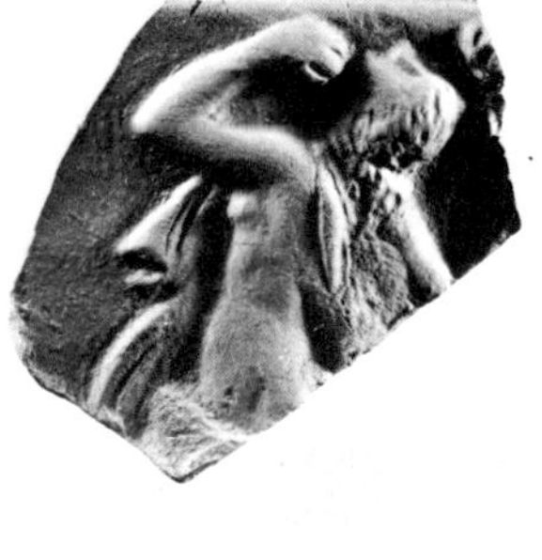

1 (cast)   1:2

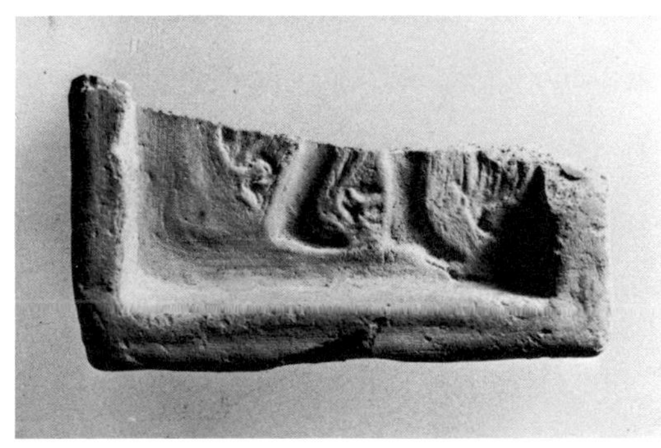

2 (mold)   1:2

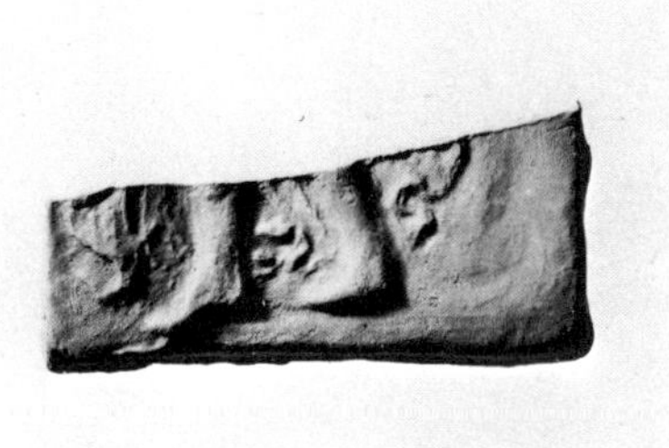

2 (cast)   1:2

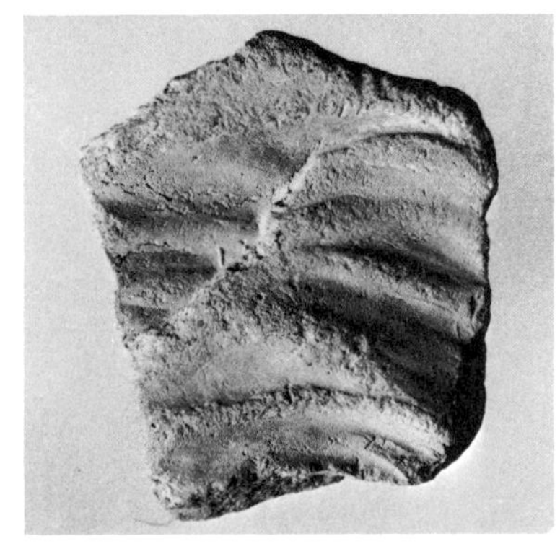

5 (mold)   1:2

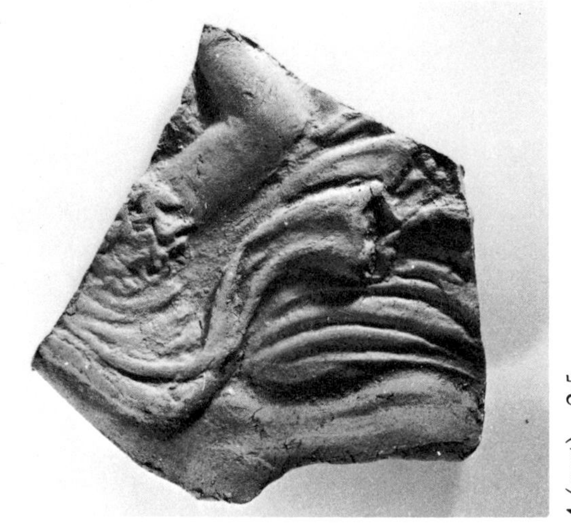

4 (cast)   2:5

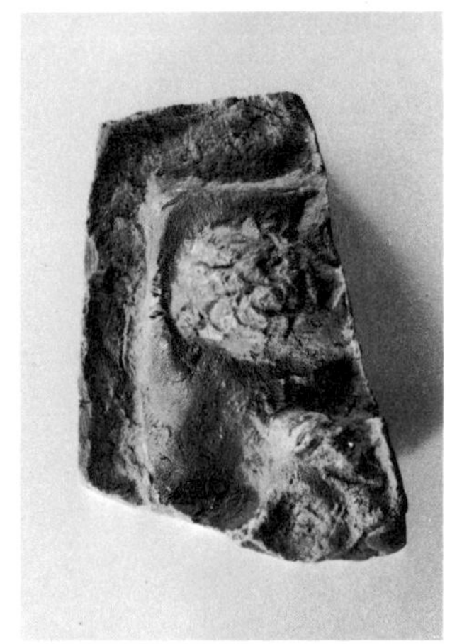

3 (cast)   1:2

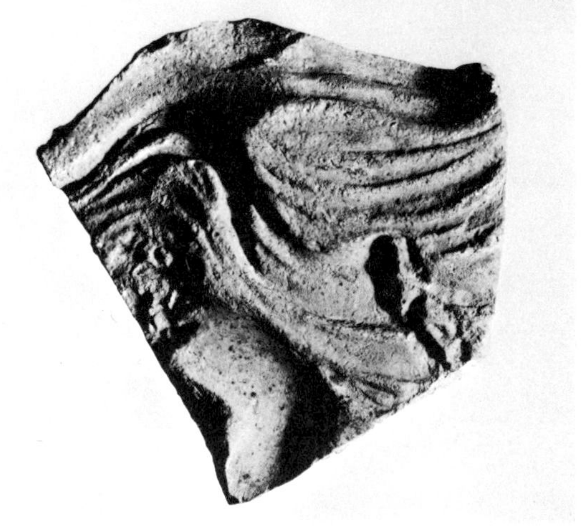

4 (mold)   2:5

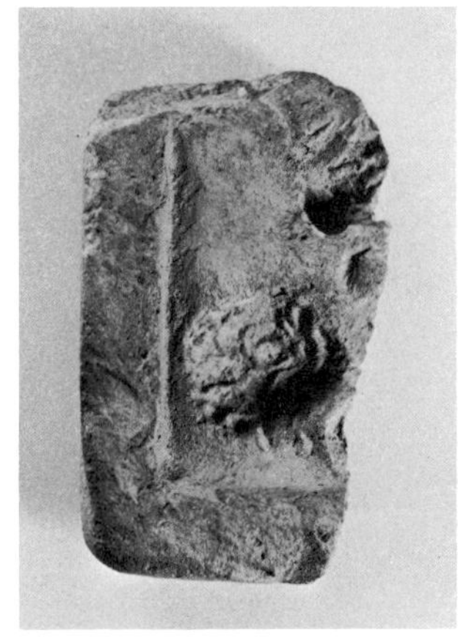

3 (mold)   1:2

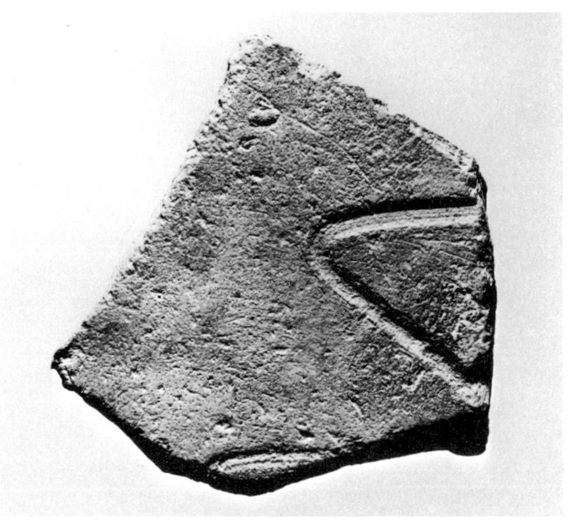

4 (back)   2:5

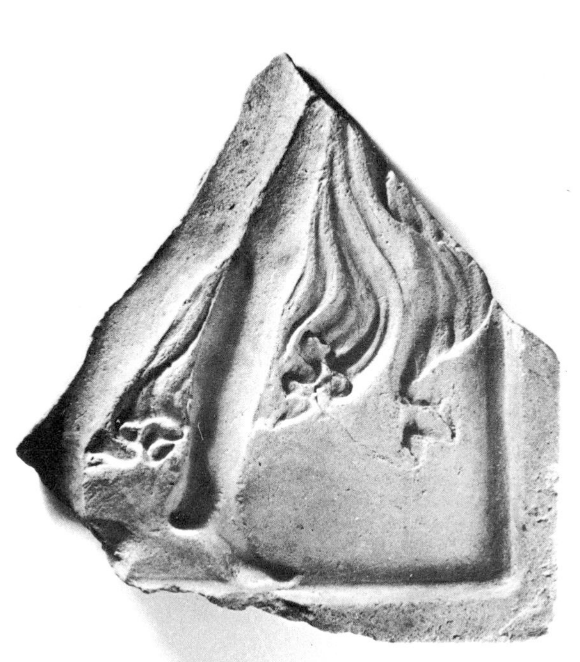

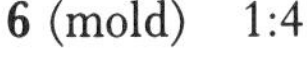

6 (mold)   1:4

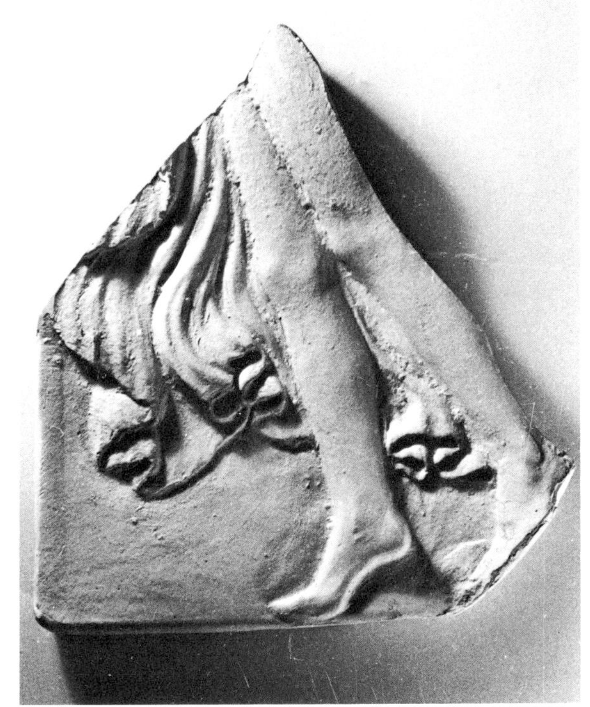

6 (cast)

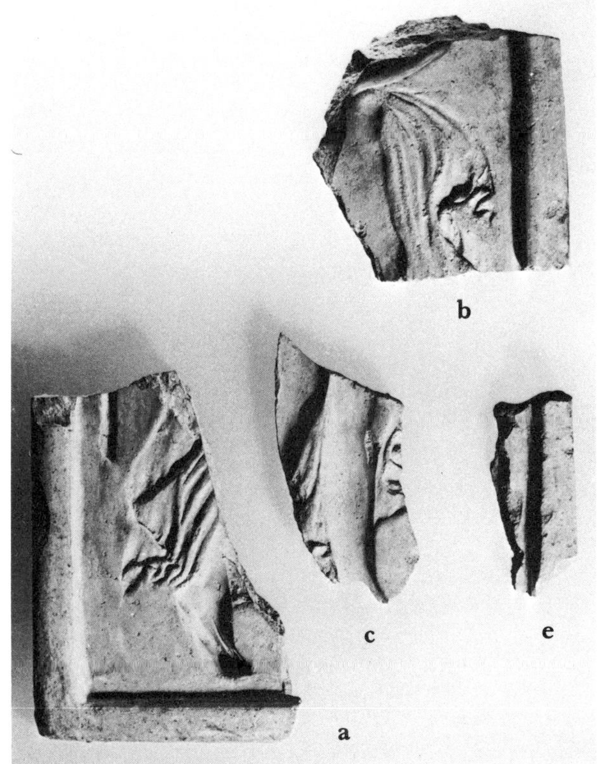

7 (mold)

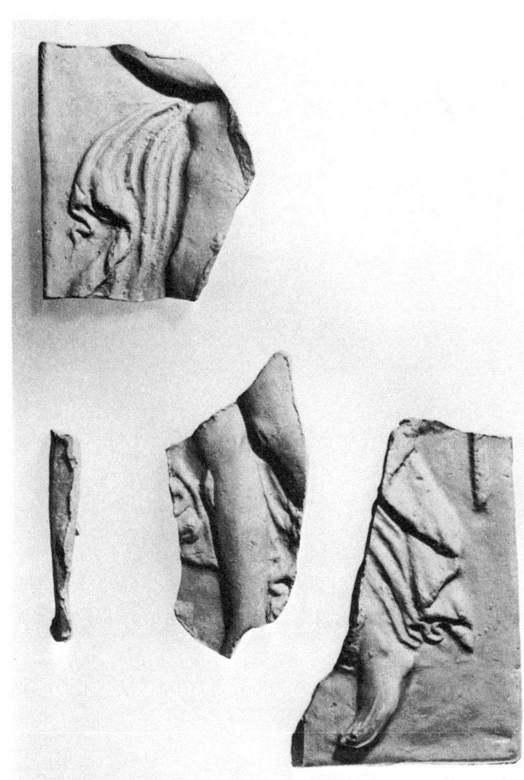

7 (cast)

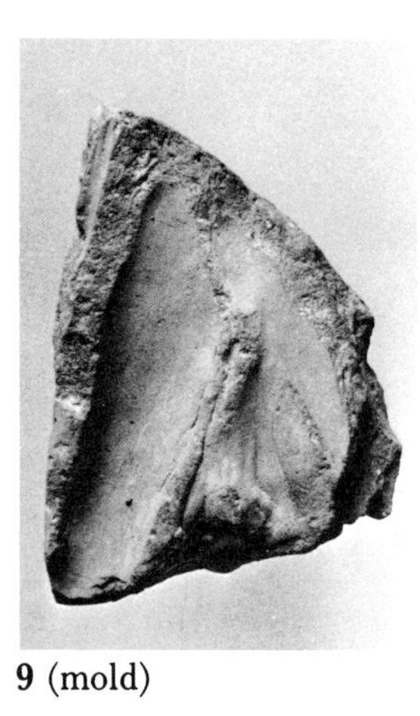

9 (mold)

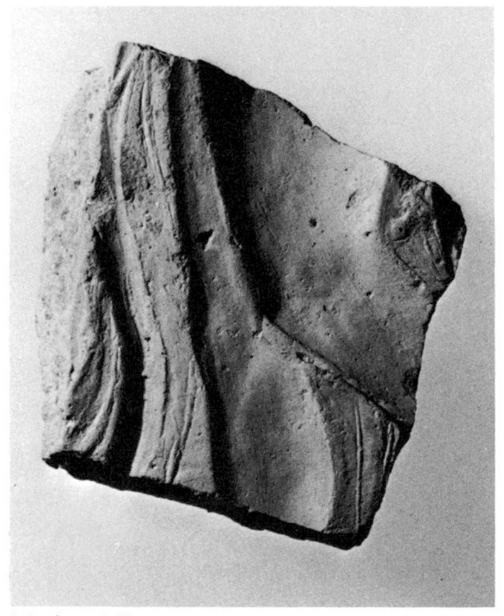

10 (mold)

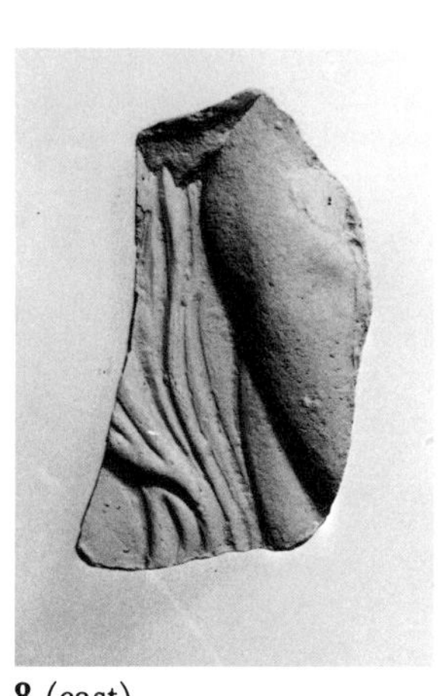

8 (cast)

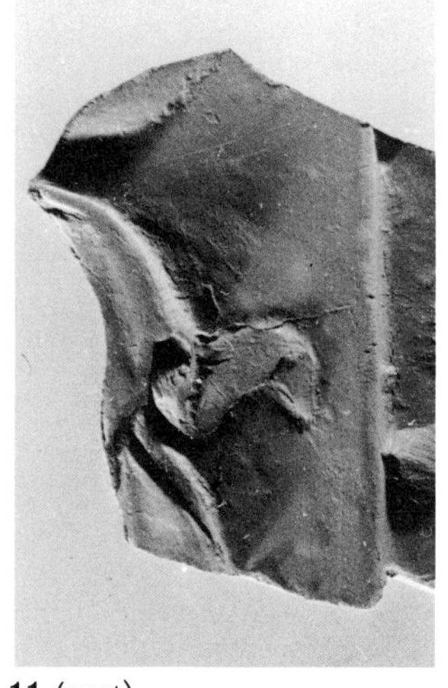

11 (cast)

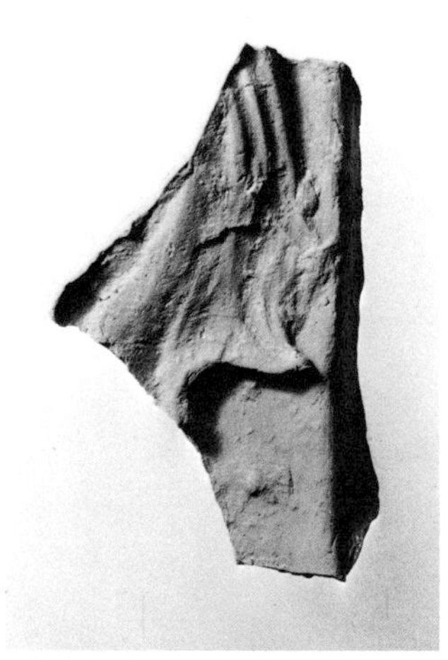

12 (cast)

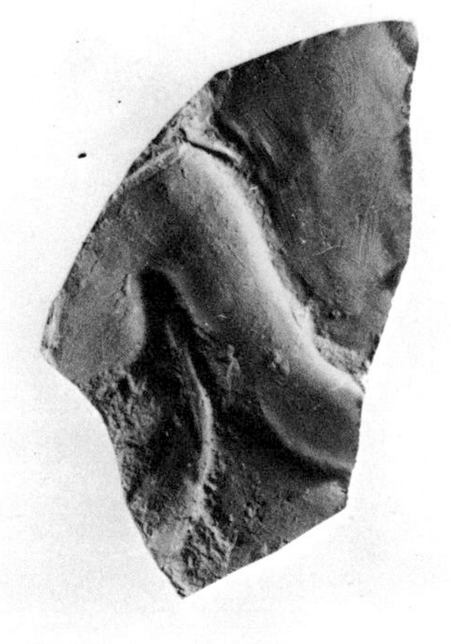

13 (mold)

14 (cast)

Scale 1:2

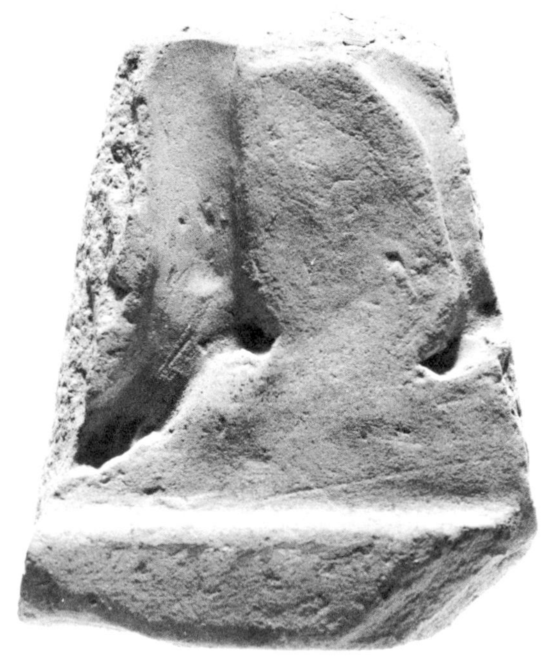

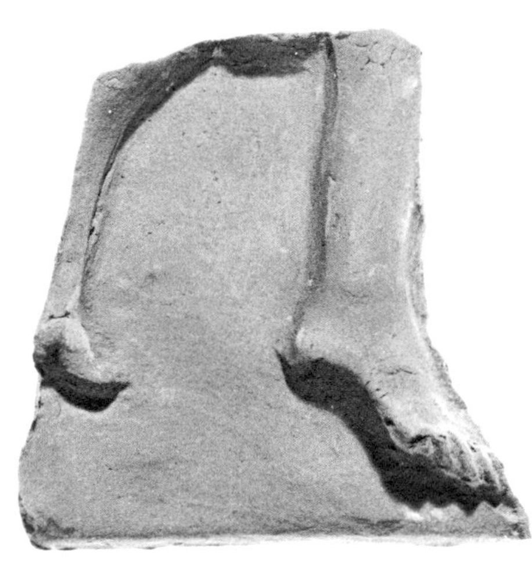

15 (cast)   1:1

15 (mold)   1:1

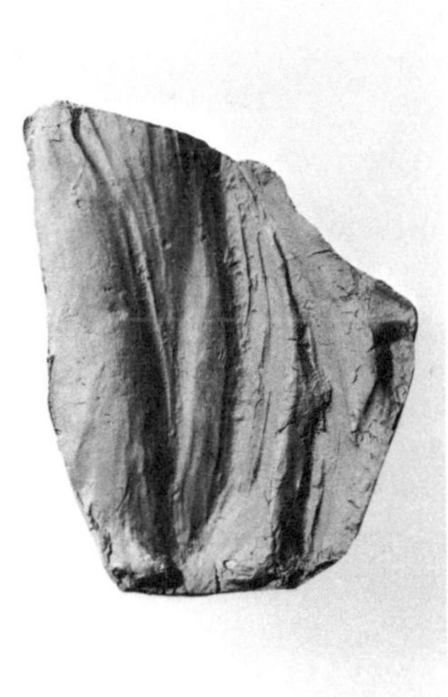

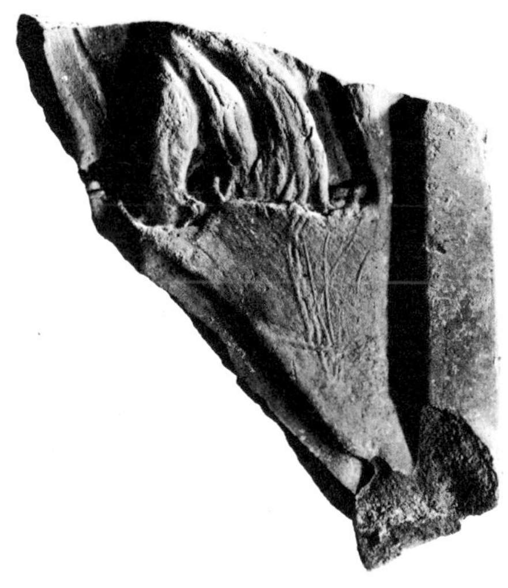

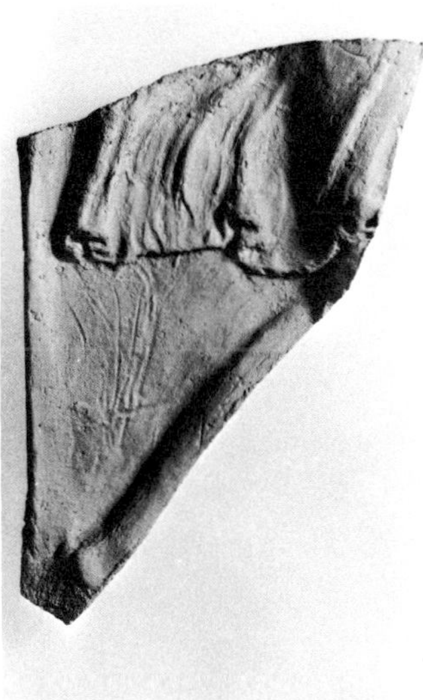

16 (cast)   1:2   **17** (mold)   2:5   **17** (cast)   2:5

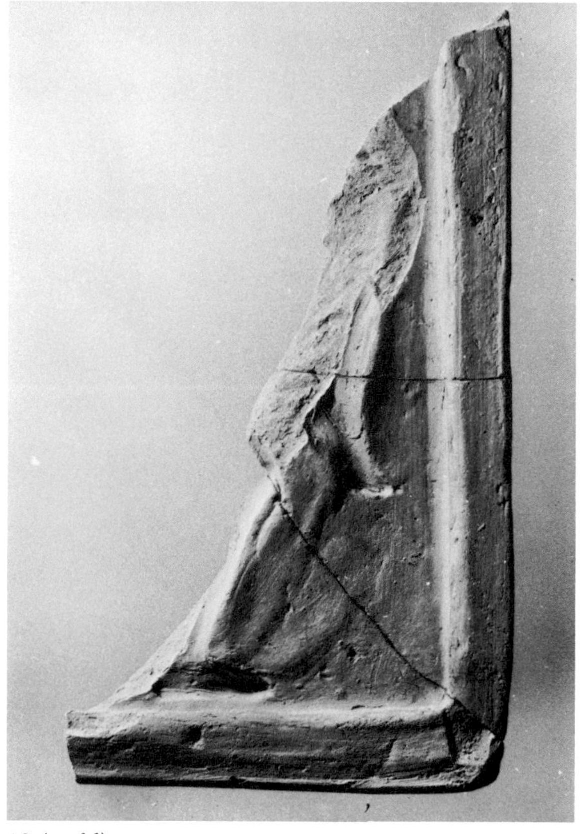
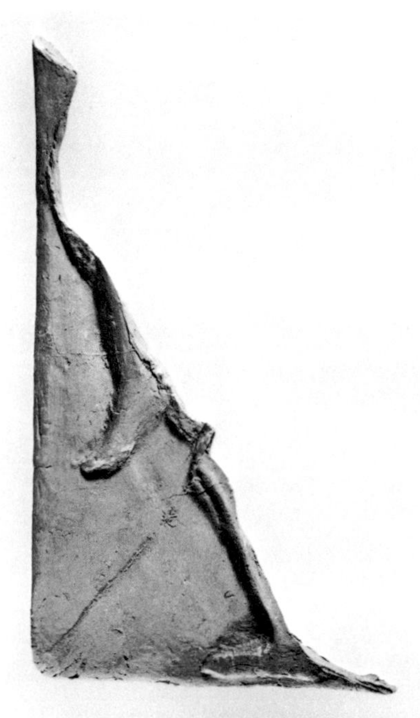

18 (mold)

18 (cast)

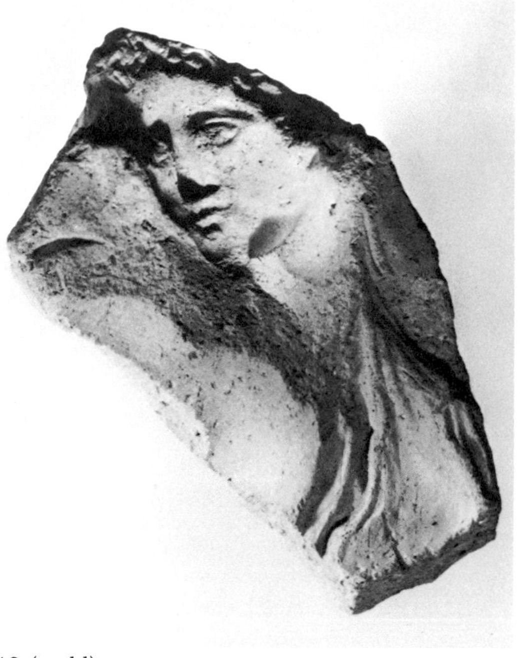
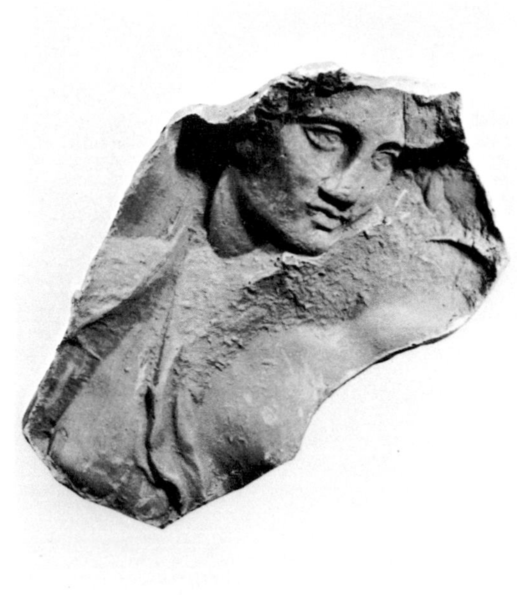

19 (mold)

19 (cast)

Scale 2:5

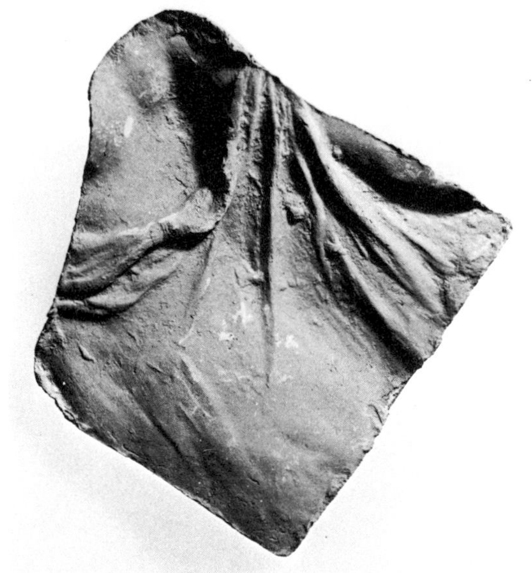

20 (cast)　2:5

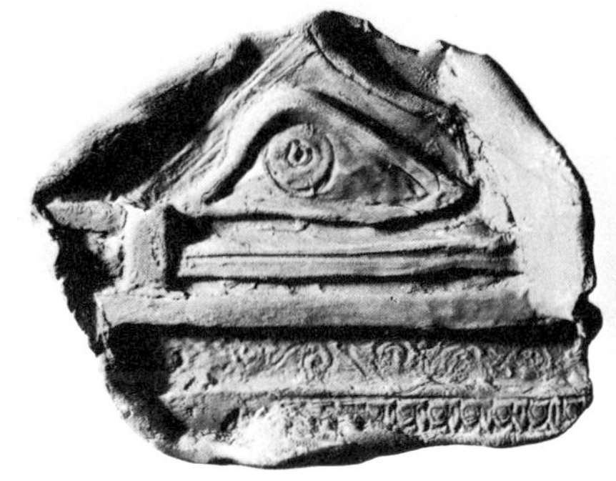

21 (cast)　1:2

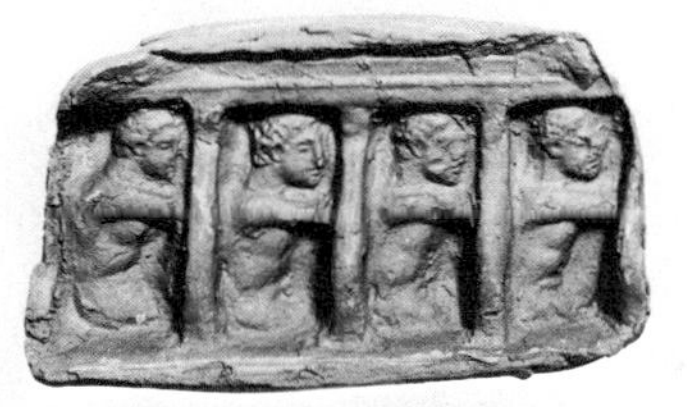

23 (cast)　1:2

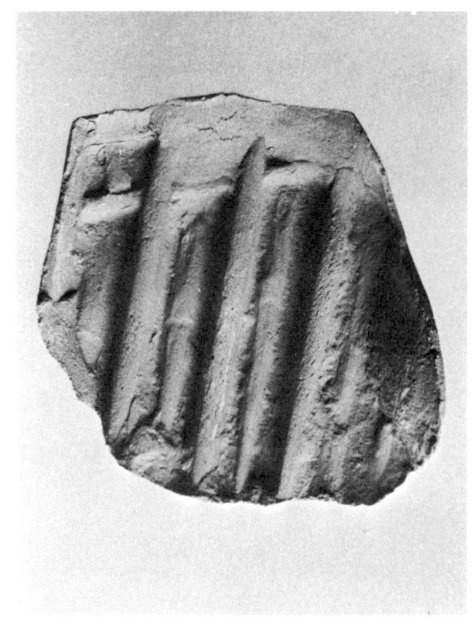

22 (cast)　1:2

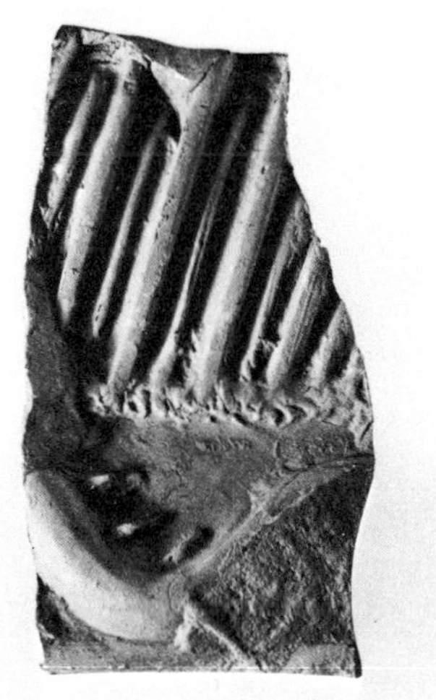

24 (cast)　2:5

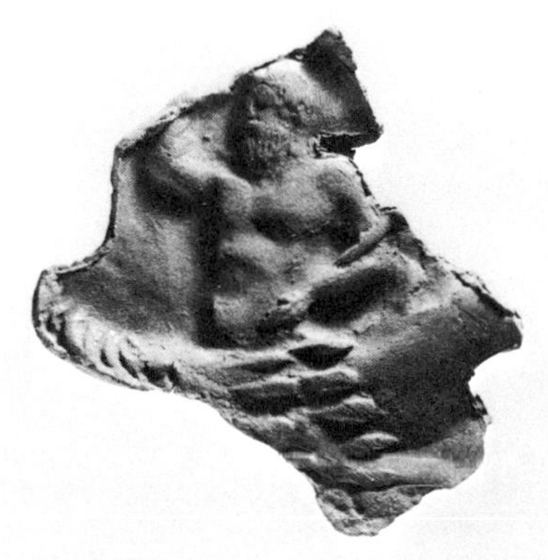

25 (cast)　2:5

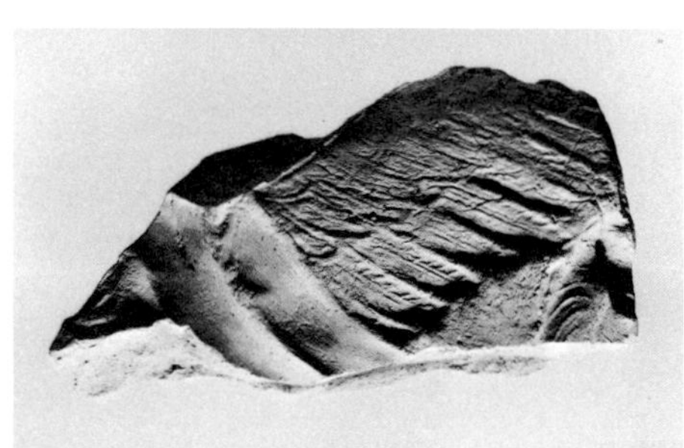

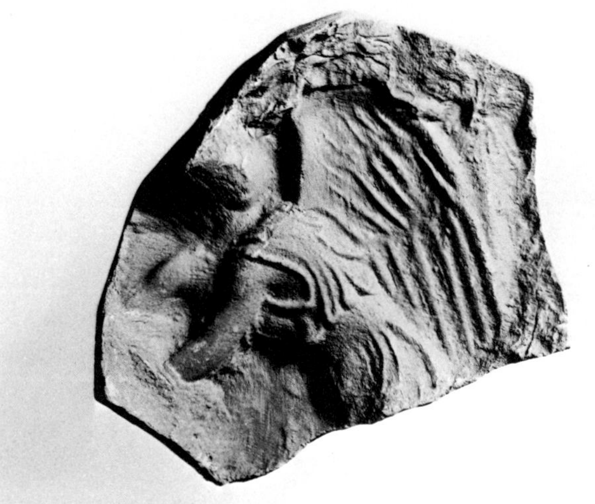

26 (mold)   2:5

27 (cast)   1:2

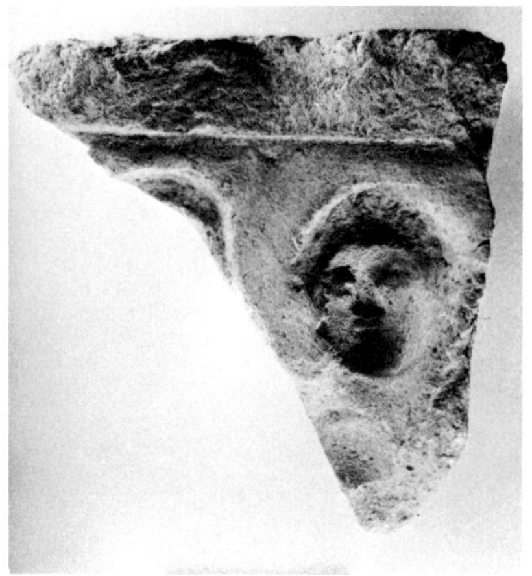

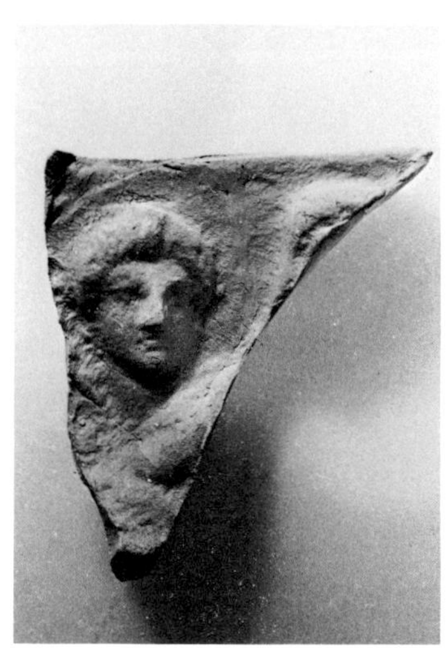

28 (mold)   2:5

28 (cast)   2:5

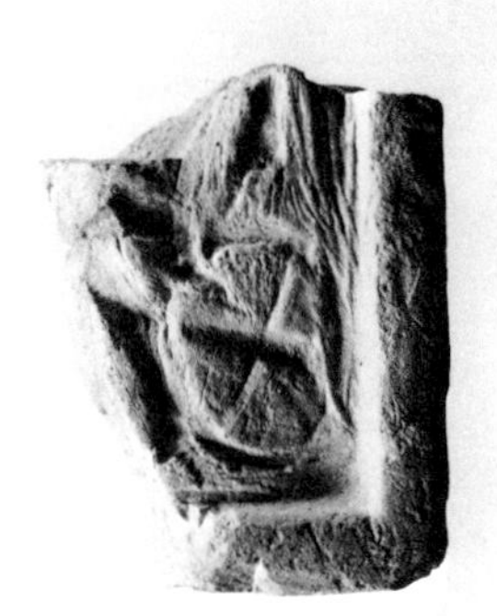

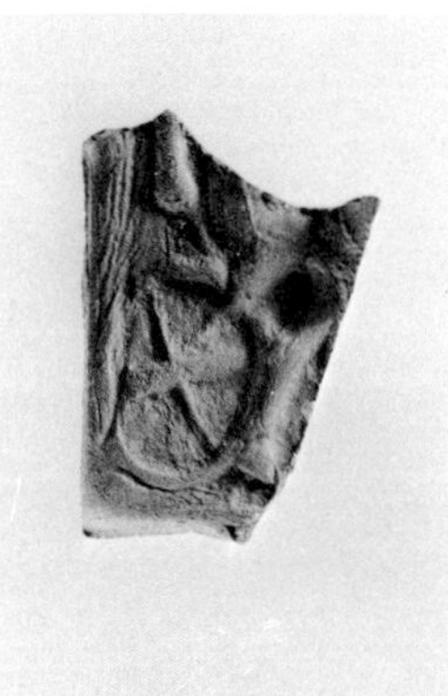

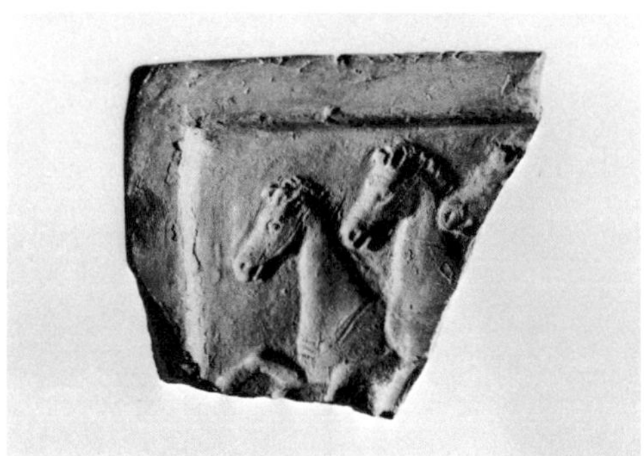

29 (mold)   1:2

29 (cast)   1:2

30 (mold)   1:2

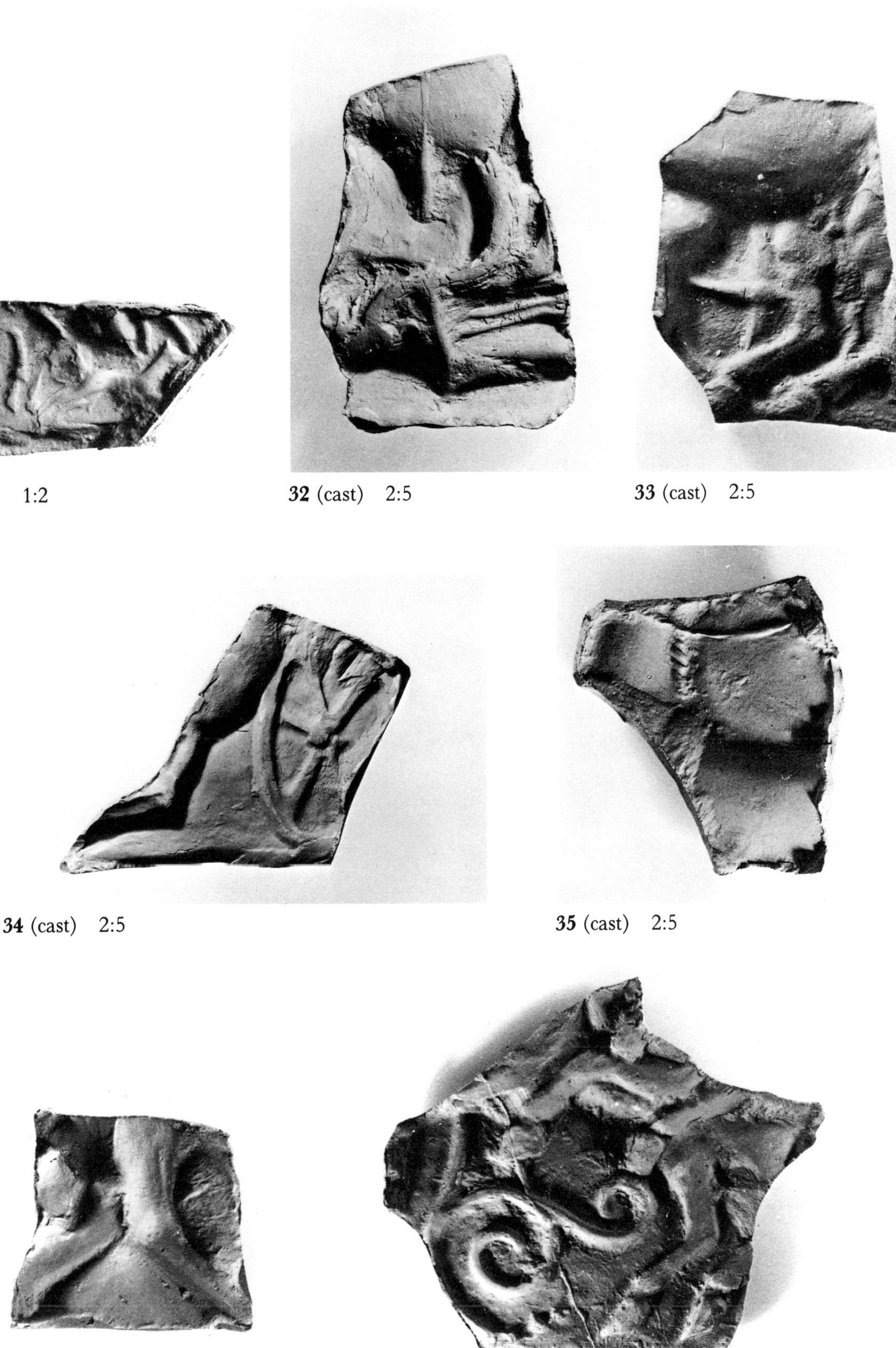

31 (cast)   1:2

32 (cast)   2:5

33 (cast)   2:5

34 (cast)   2:5

35 (cast)   2:5

36 (cast)   1:2

37 (cast)   2:5

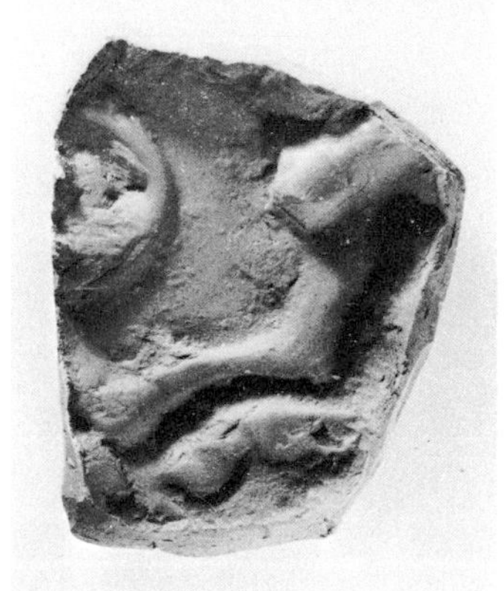

38 (cast) 2:5

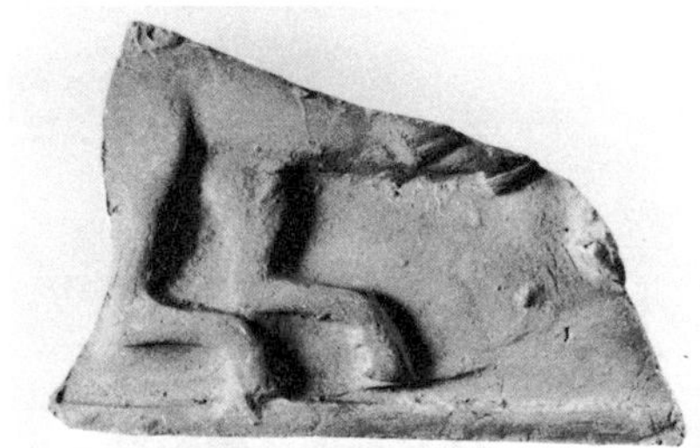

39 (cast) 1:2

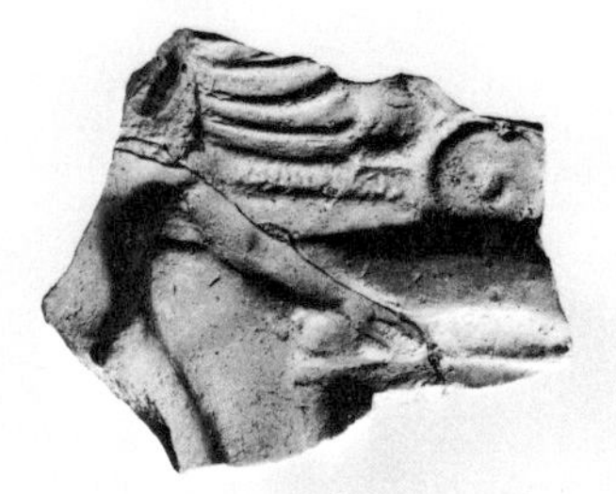

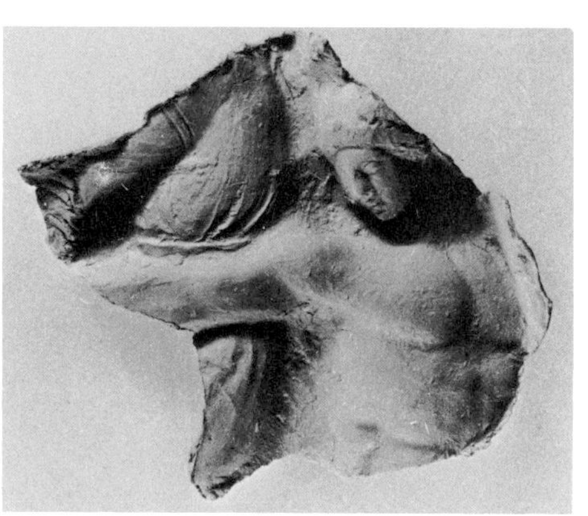

40 (cast) 2:5

41 (T 883 c, mold) 2:5

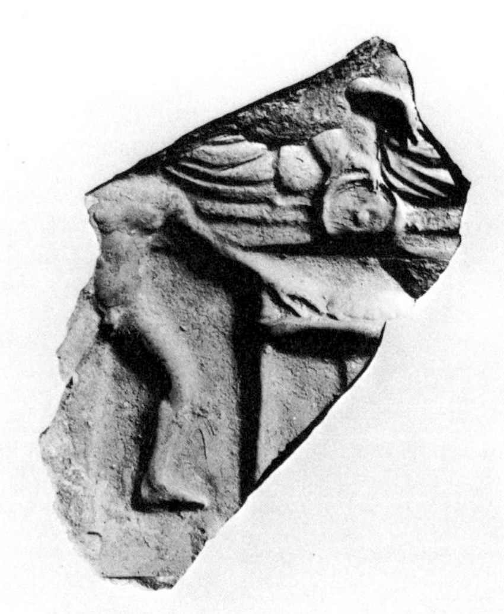

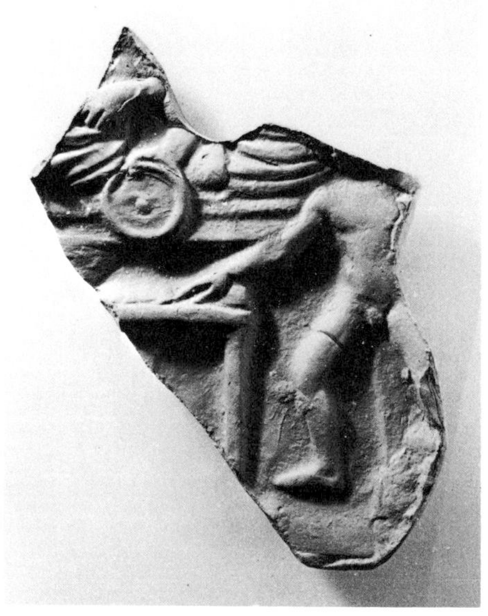

41 (T 883 a, mold) 2:5   **41** (T 883 a, cast) 2:5

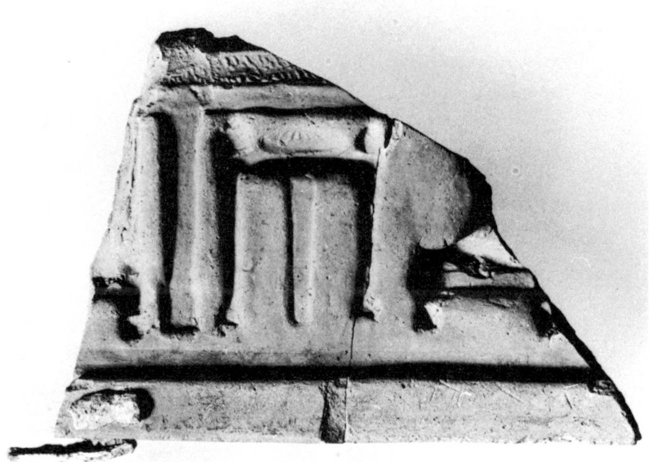

42 (mold)   2:5

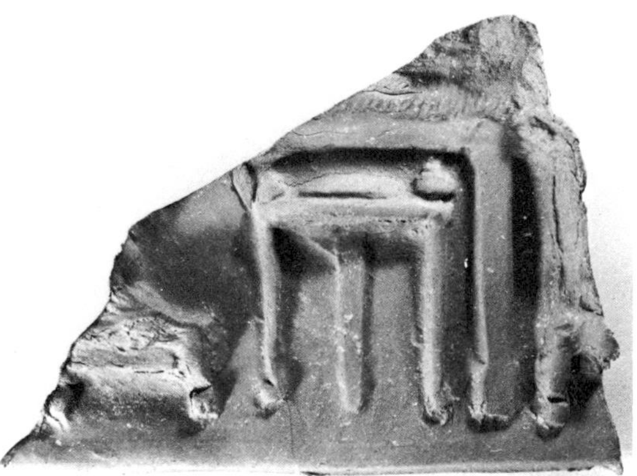

42 (cast)   2:5

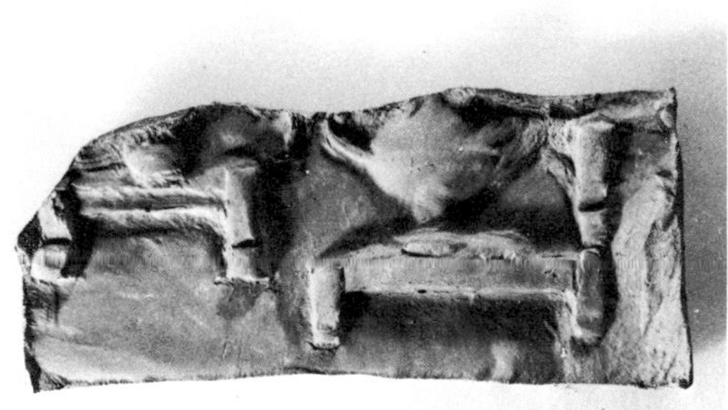

43 (a, cast)   2:5

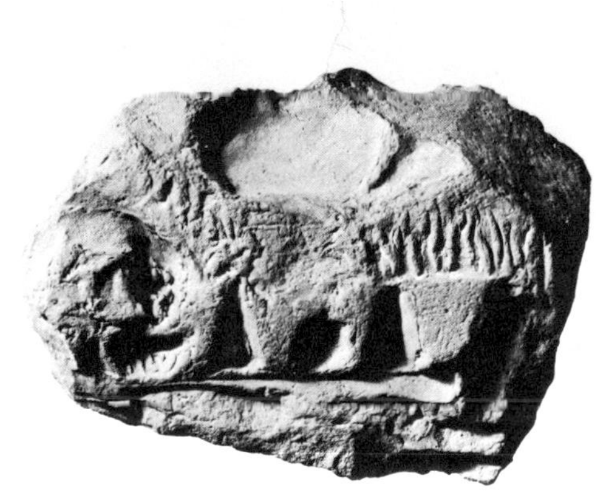
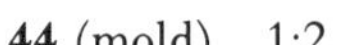

44 (mold)   1:2

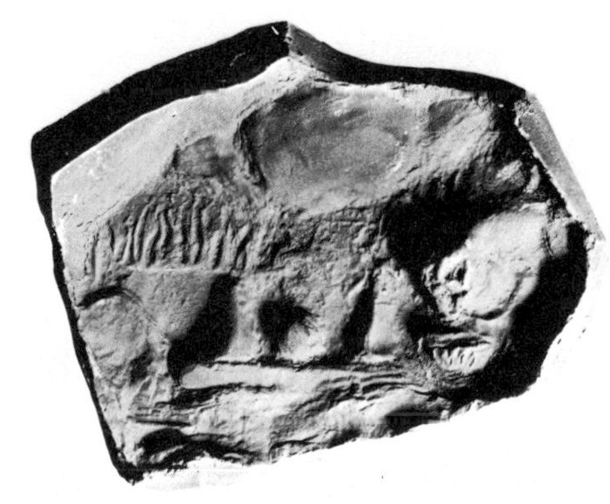

44 (cast)   1:2

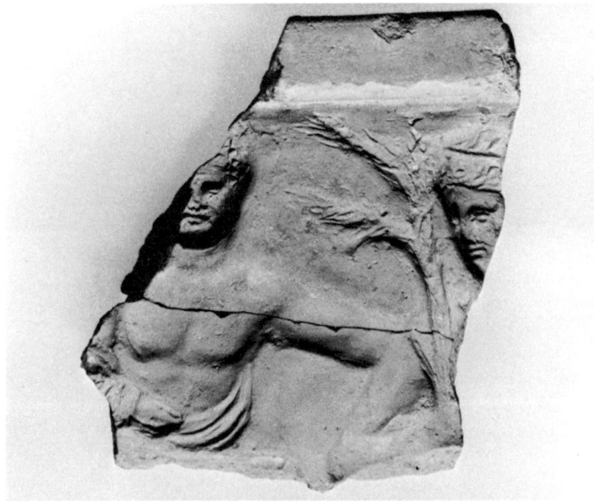

45 (mold)   2:5

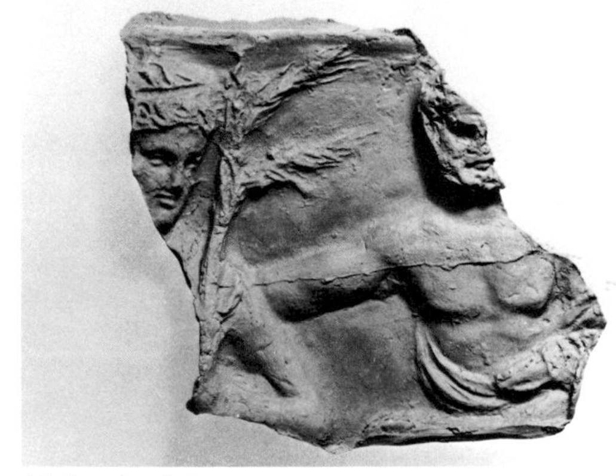

45 (cast)   2:5

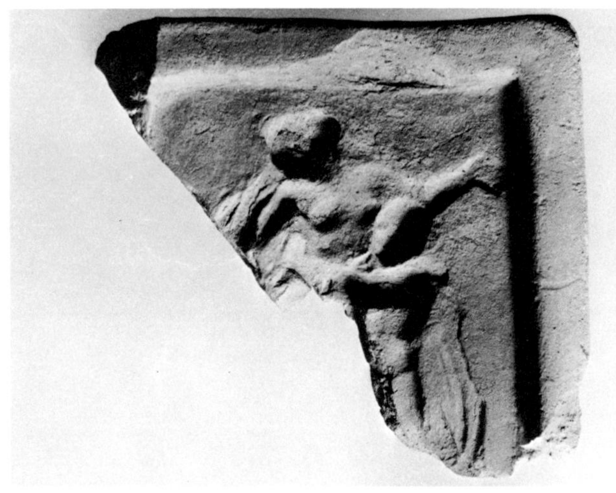

46 (mold)   1:2

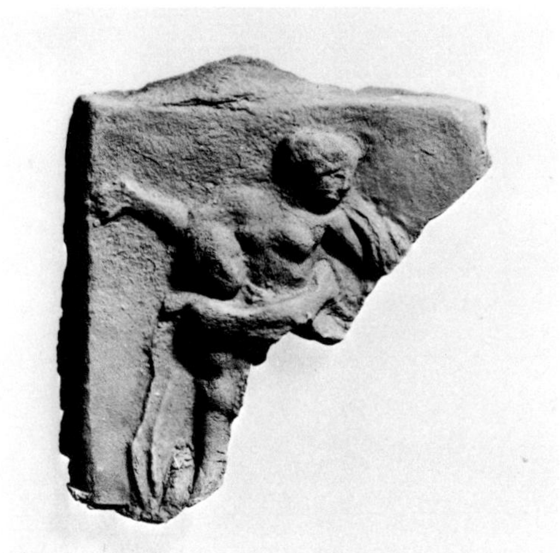

46 (cast)   1:2

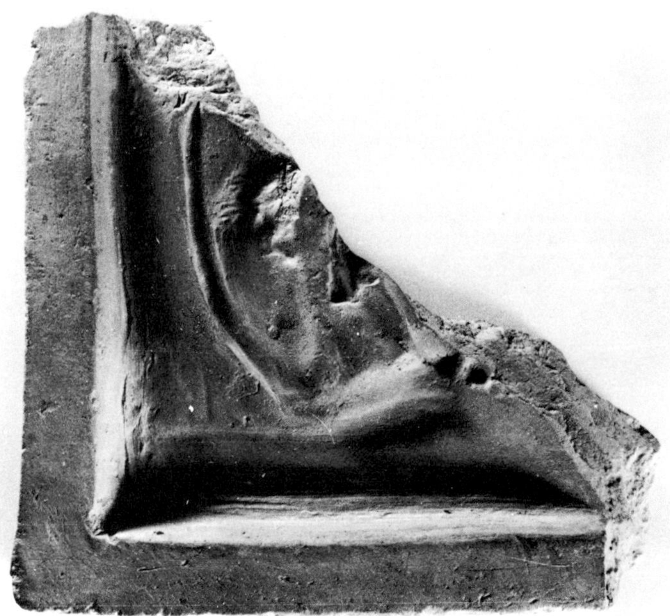

47 (mold)   2:5

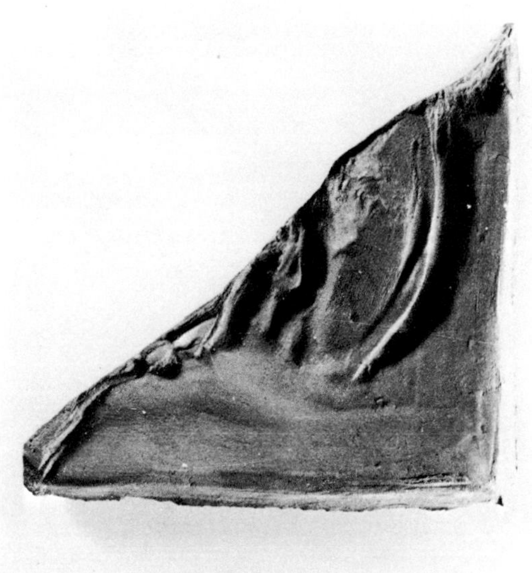

47 (cast)   2:5

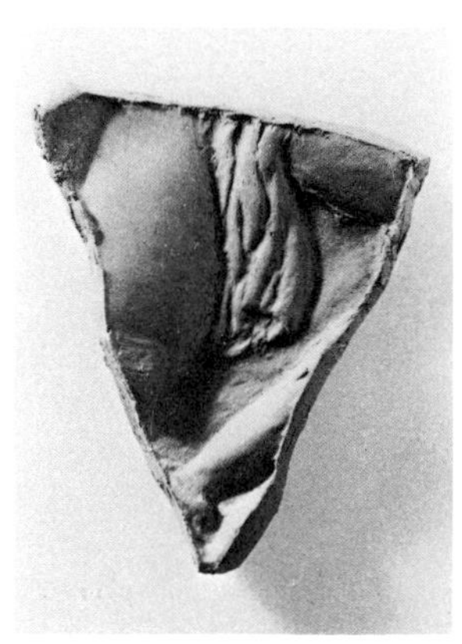

48 (cast)   2:5

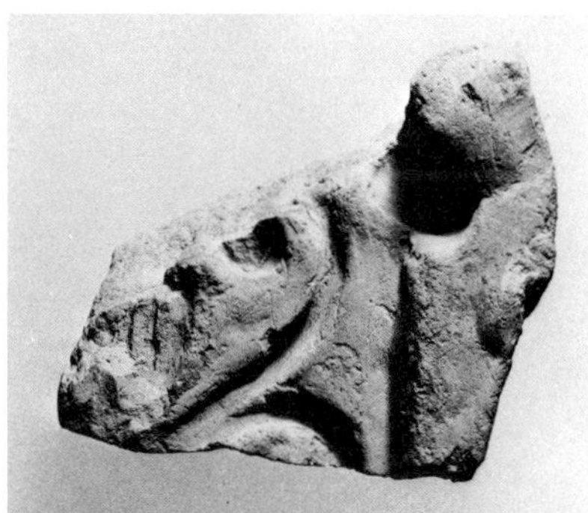

49 (b, mold)   2:5

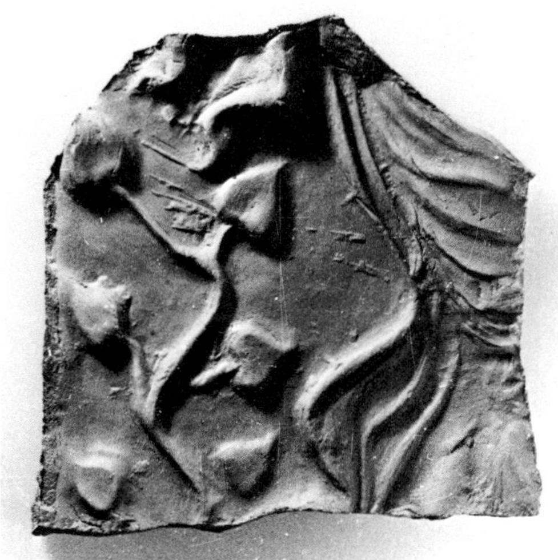

49 (a, cast)   2:5

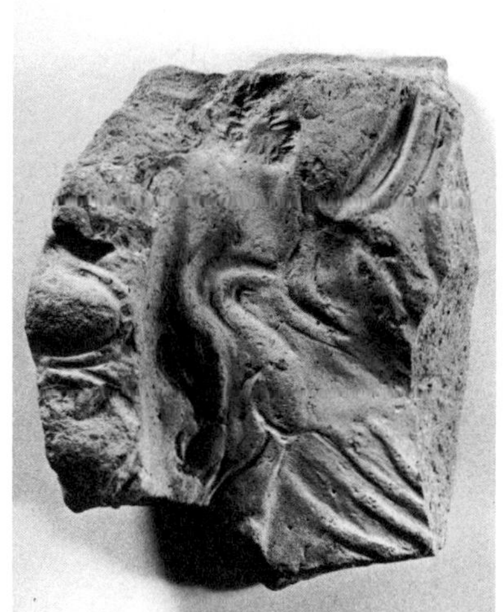

50 (mold)   2:5

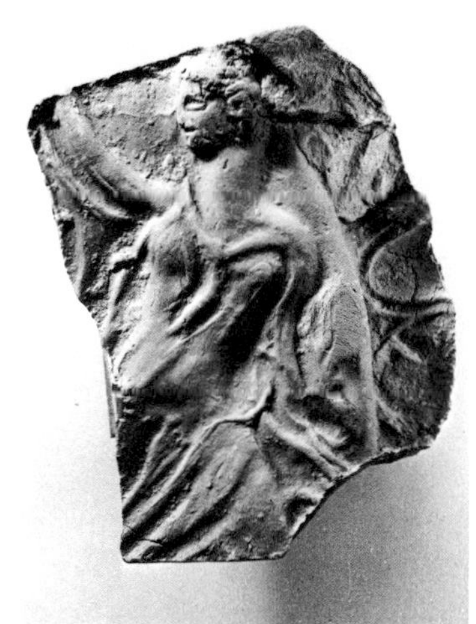

50 (cast)   2:5

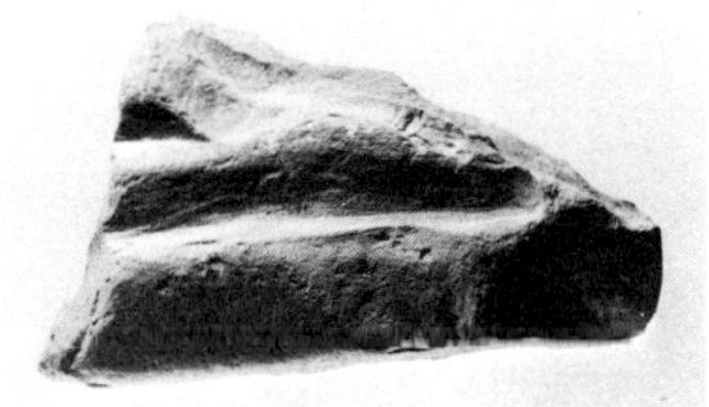

51 (mold)   1:2

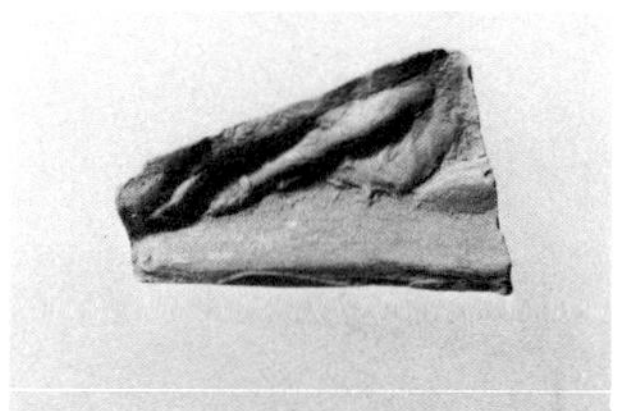

51 (cast)   1:2

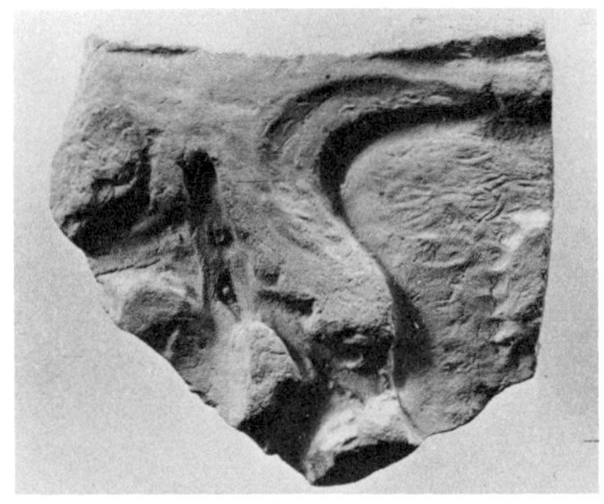

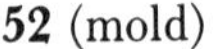

52 (mold)

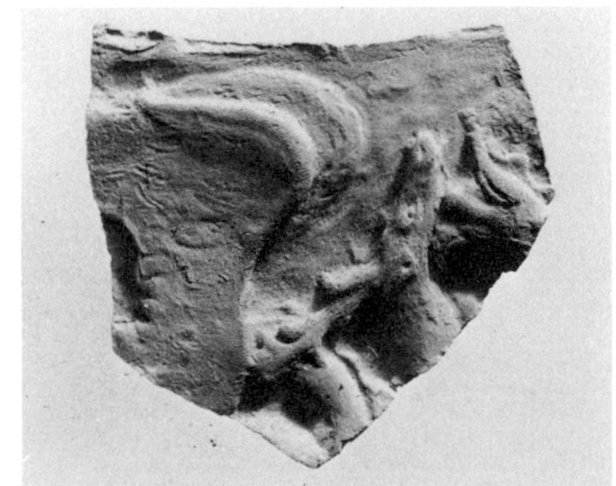

52 (cast)

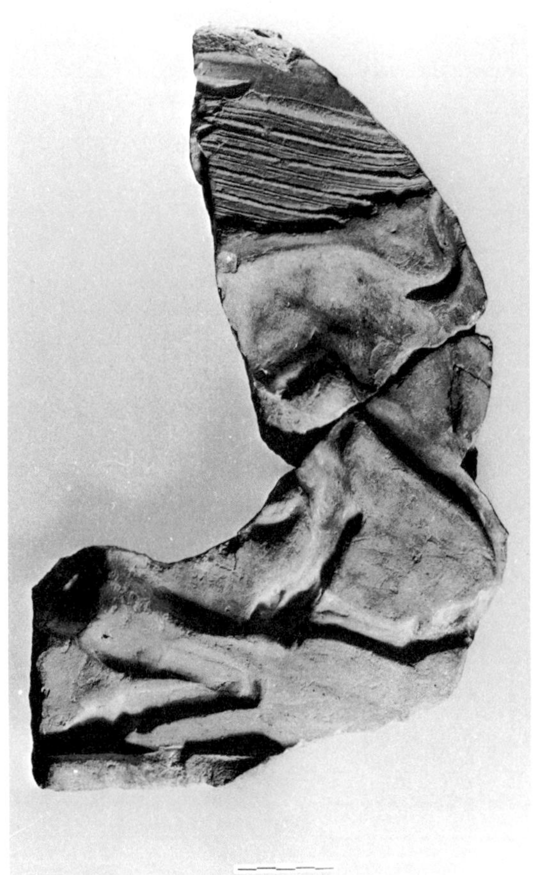

53 (mold)

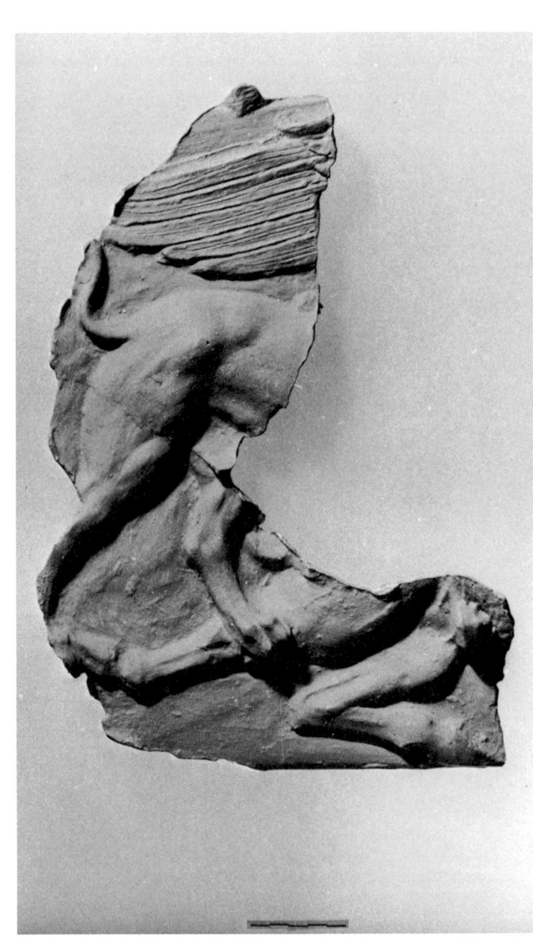

53 (cast)

Scale   1:2

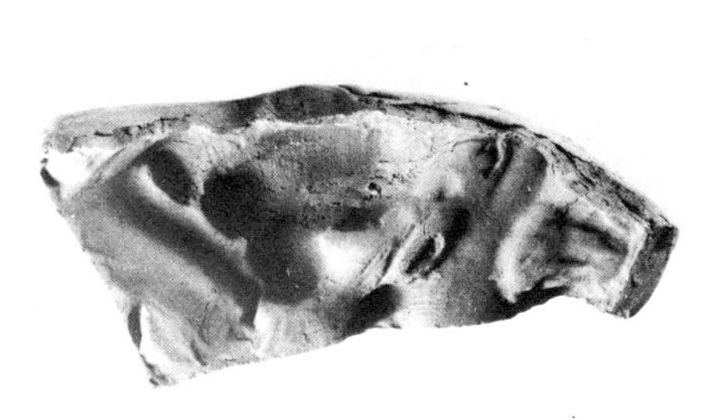

54 (cast)   2:5

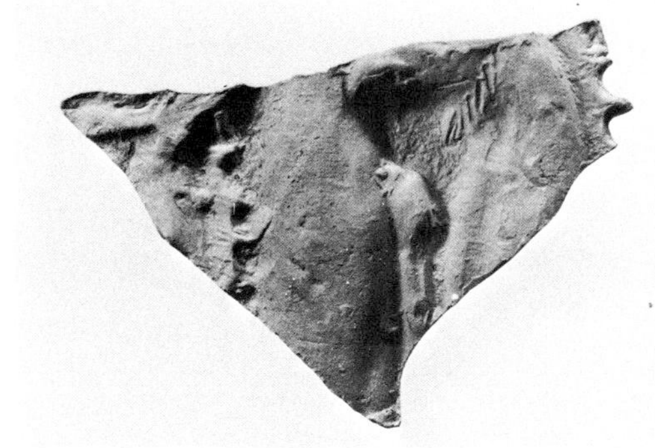

55 (cast)   2:5

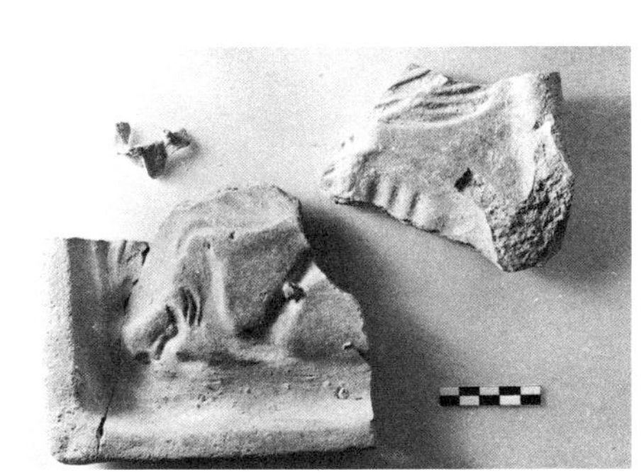

56 (mold)   1:5

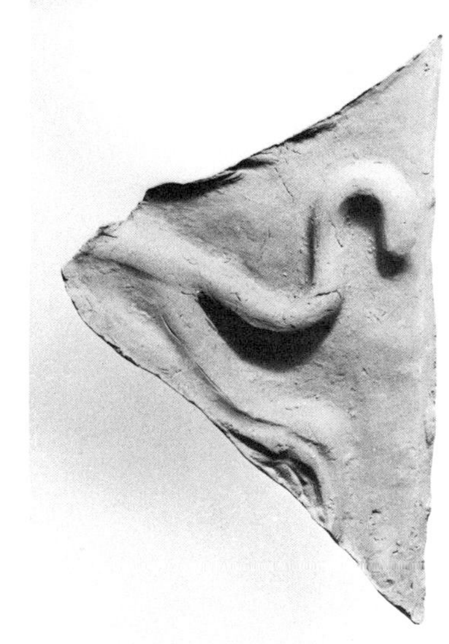

57 (cast)   2:5

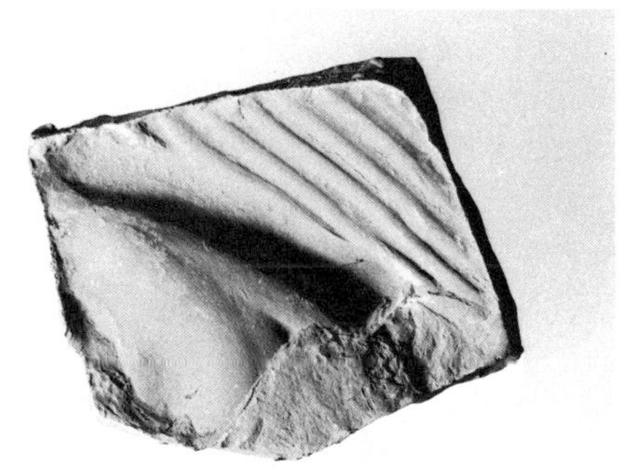

58 (cast)   2:5

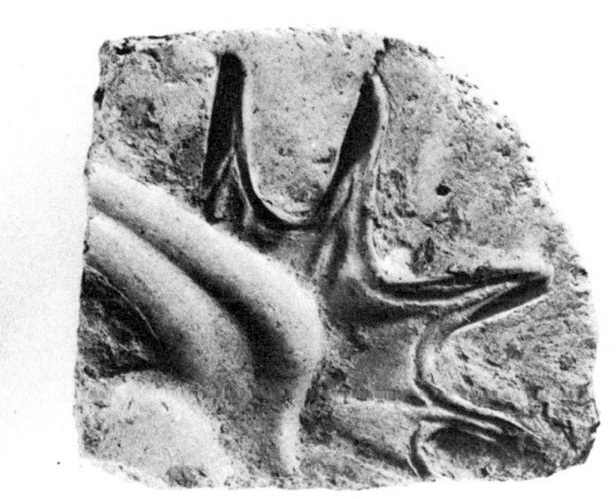

59 (mold)   1:2

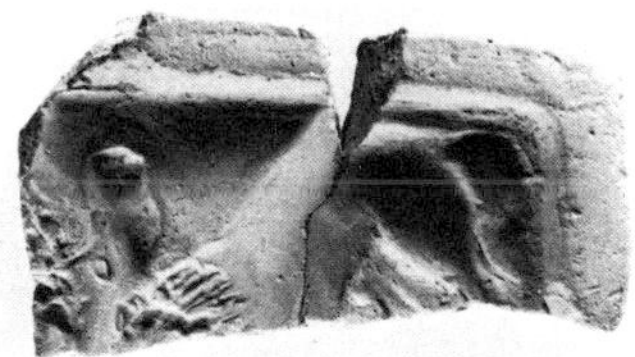

60 (mold)   2:5

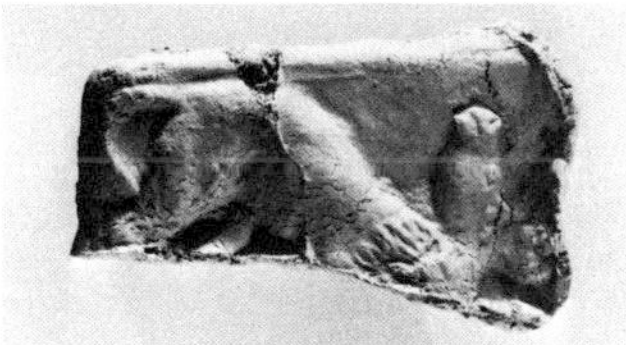

60 (cast)   2:5

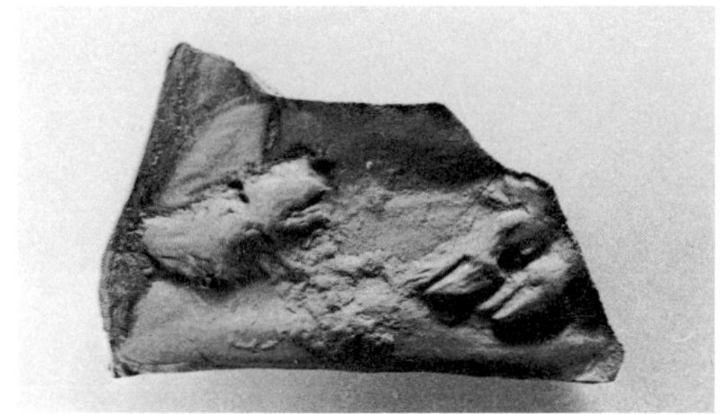

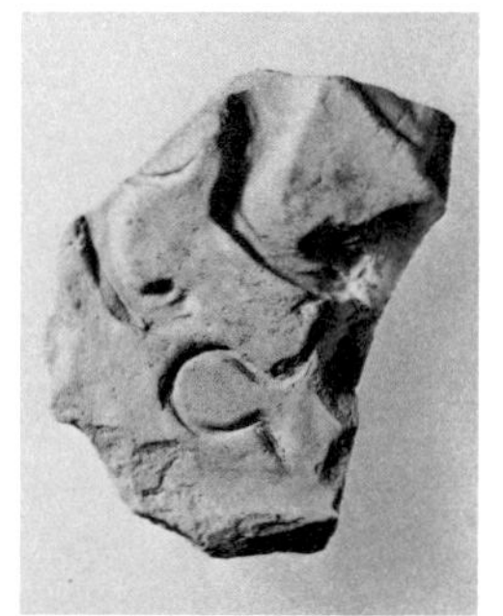

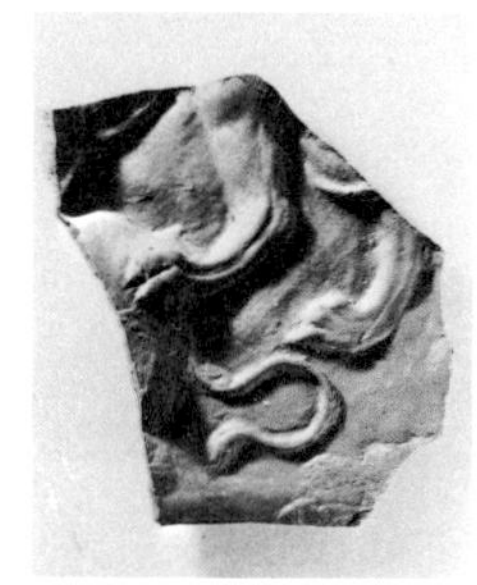

61 (T 2047, cast)   2:5

61 (T 1965, mold and cast)   1:5

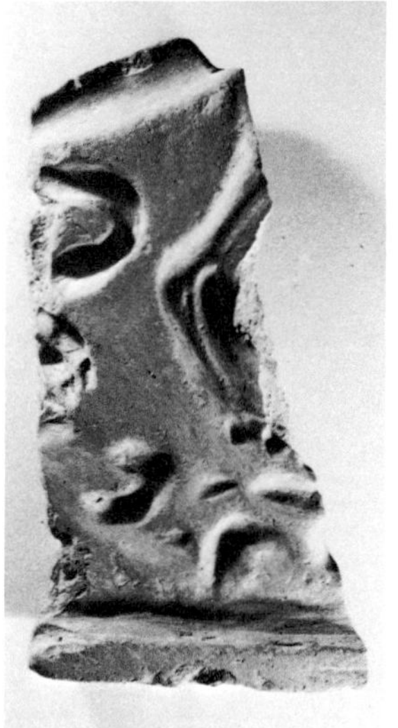

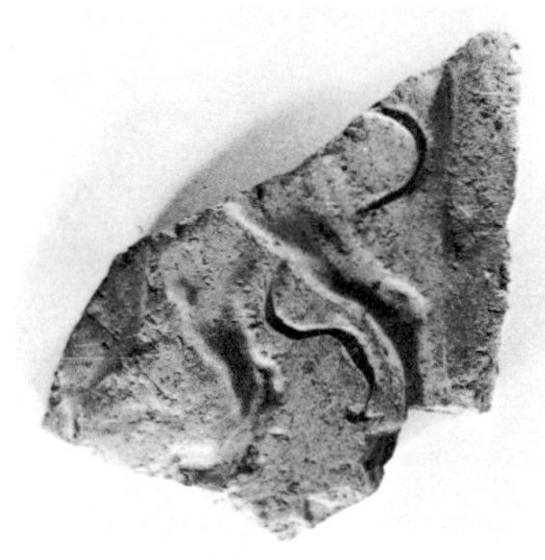

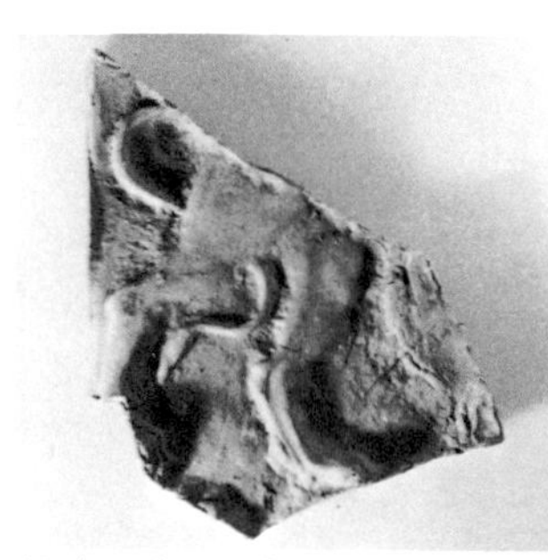

63 (mold)   1:5

63 (cast)   1:5

62 (mold)   1:5

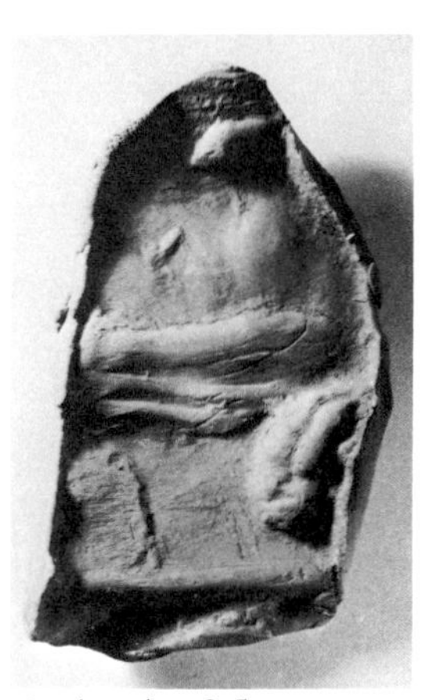

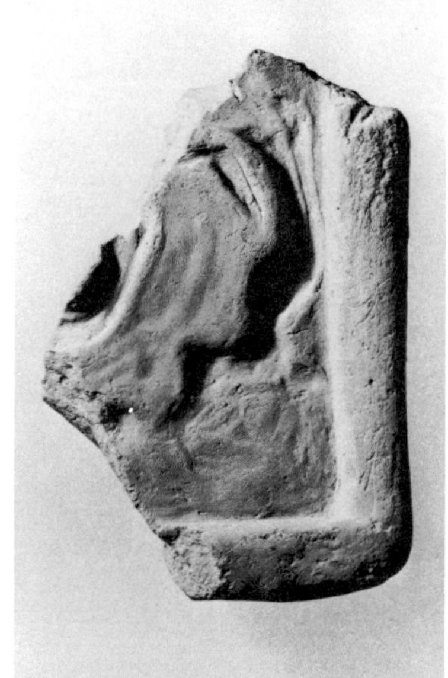

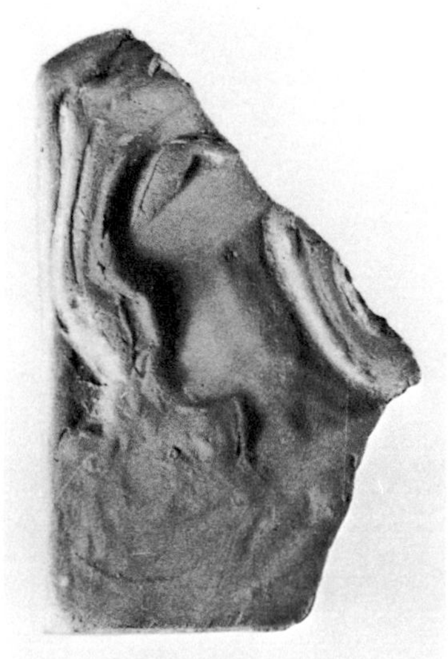

64 (cast)   2:5

65 (mold)   2:5

65 (cast)   1:2

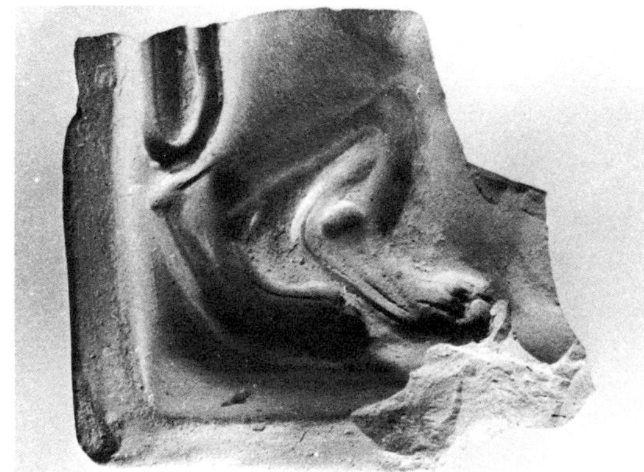

66 (mold)   2:5

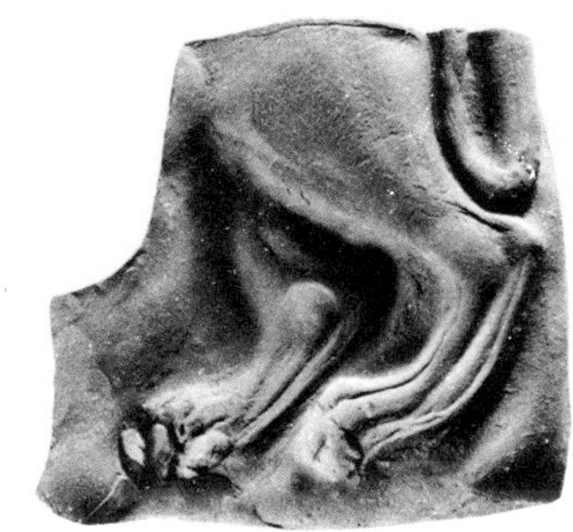

66 (cast)

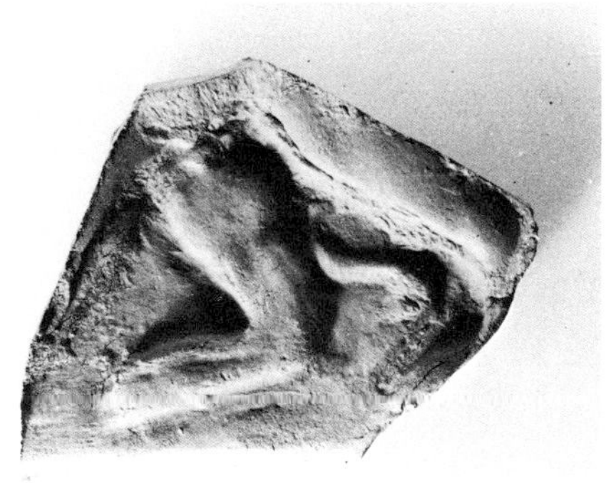

67 (cast)   1:2

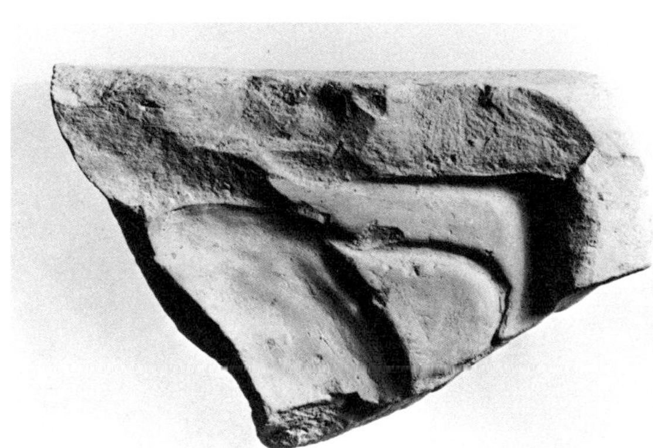

68 (mold)   1:2

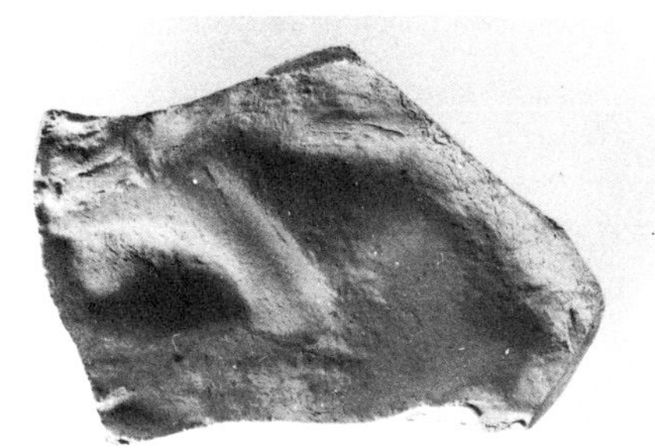

69 (cast)   1:2

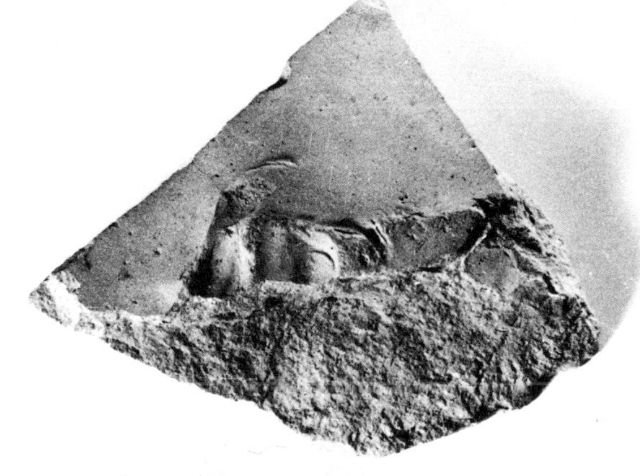

70 (mold)   2:5

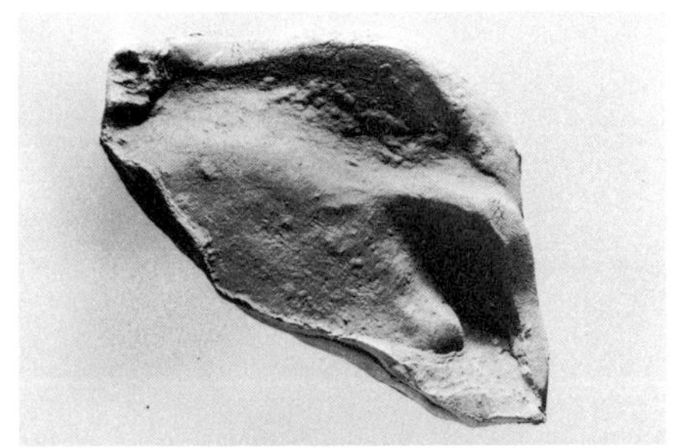
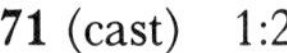

71 (cast)   1:2

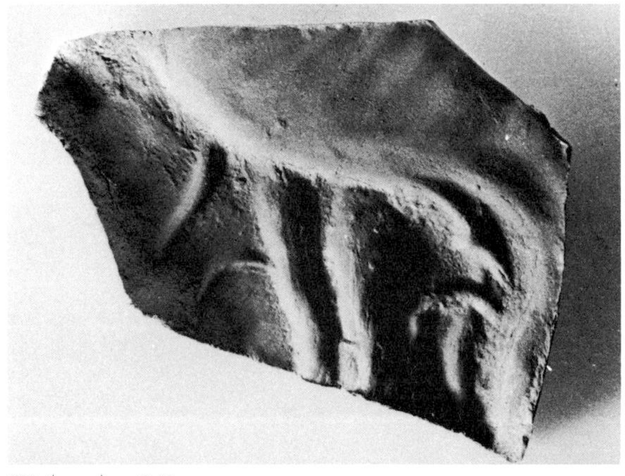

72 (cast)   2:5

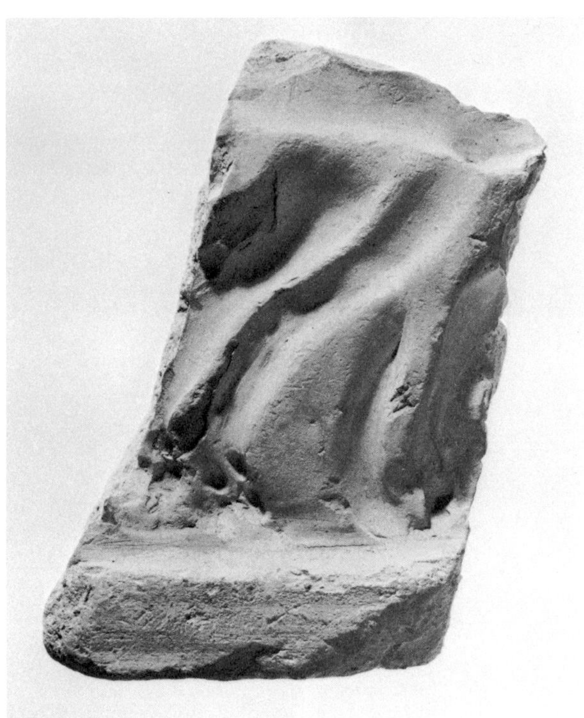

73 (mold)   3:5

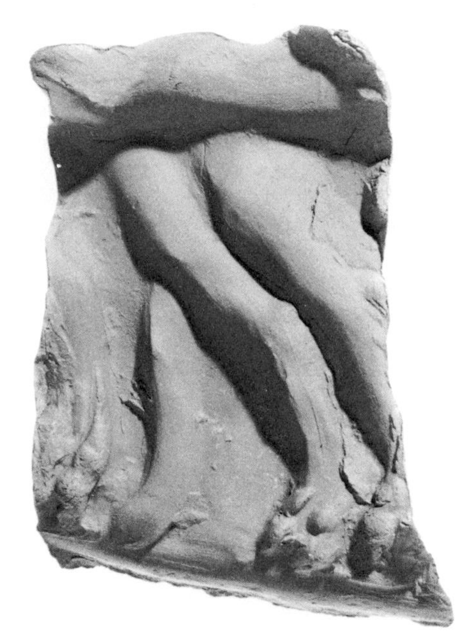

73 (cast)   3:5

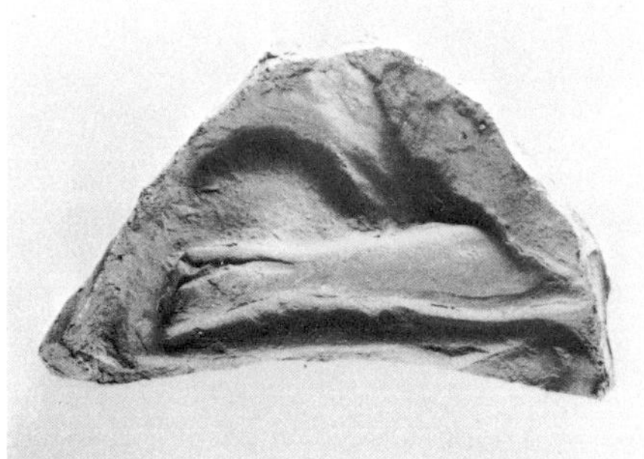

74 (cast)   4:5

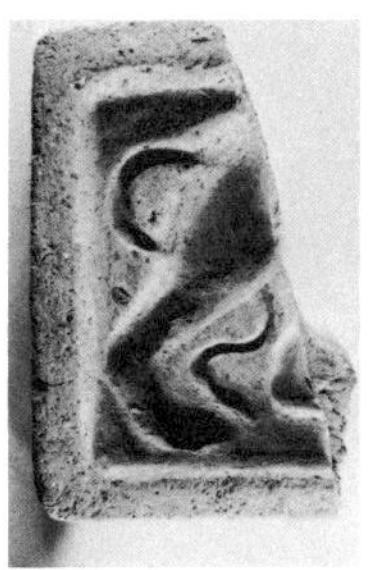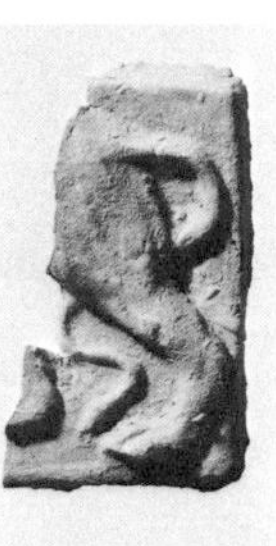

75 (mold and cast)   1:5

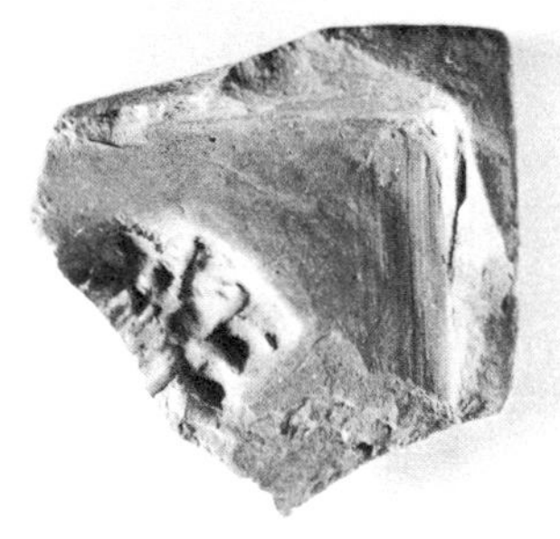

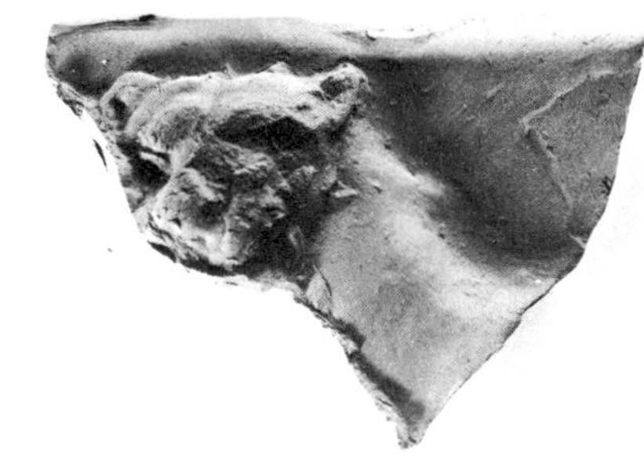

76 (mold)   1:2   **77** (cast)   2:5

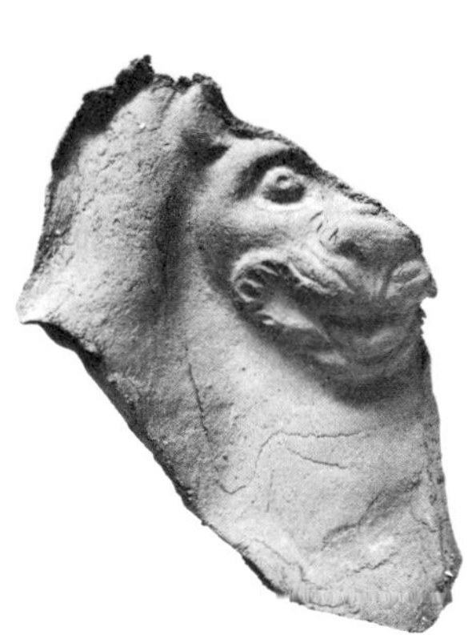

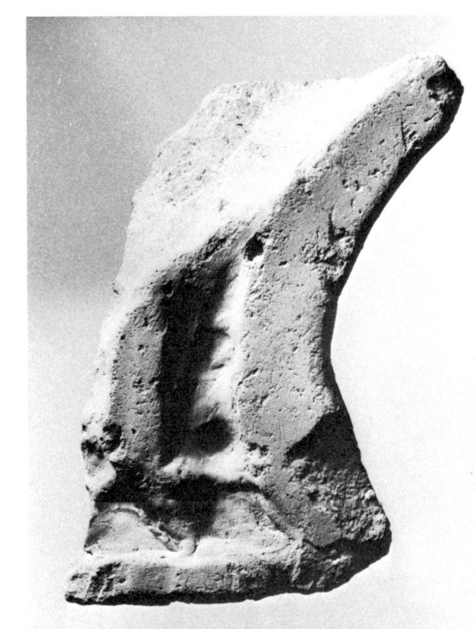

78 (cast)   1:2

80 (mold)   2:5

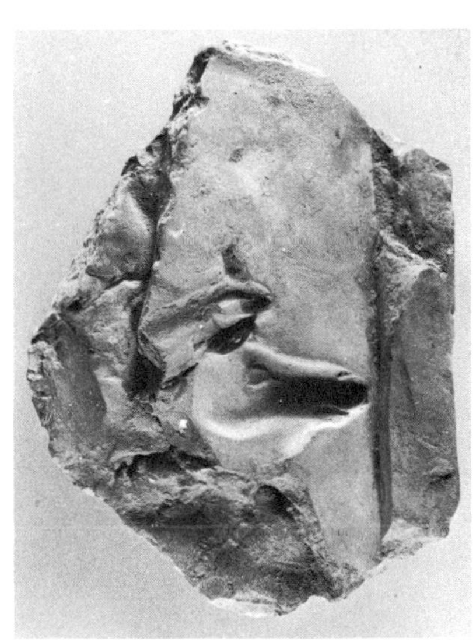

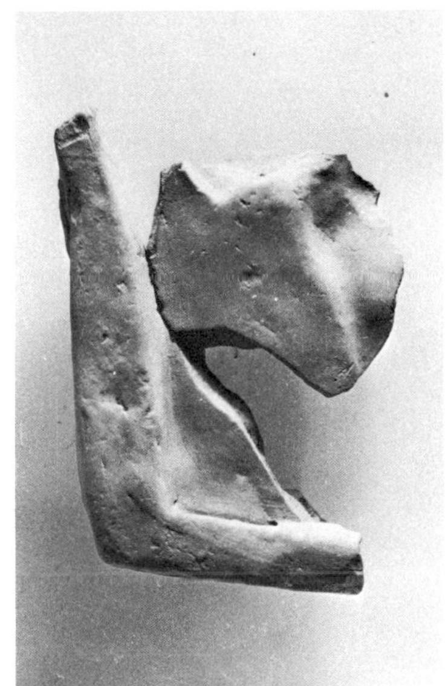

79 (a, mold)   2:5   **79** (b, mold)   2:5

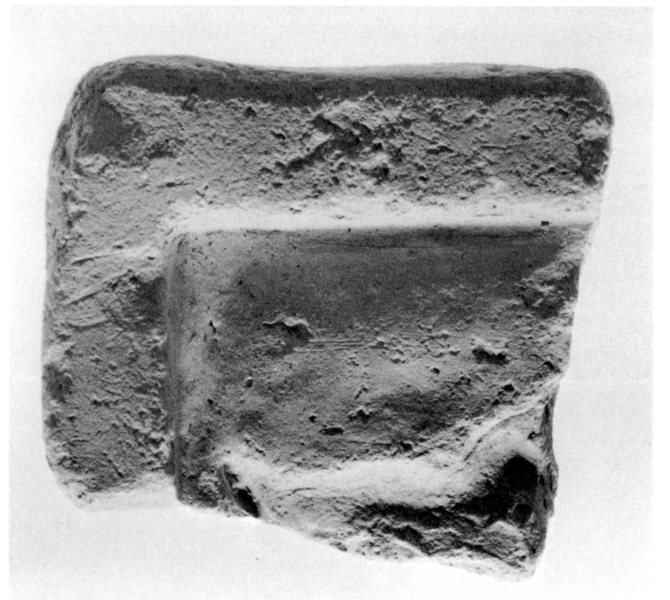

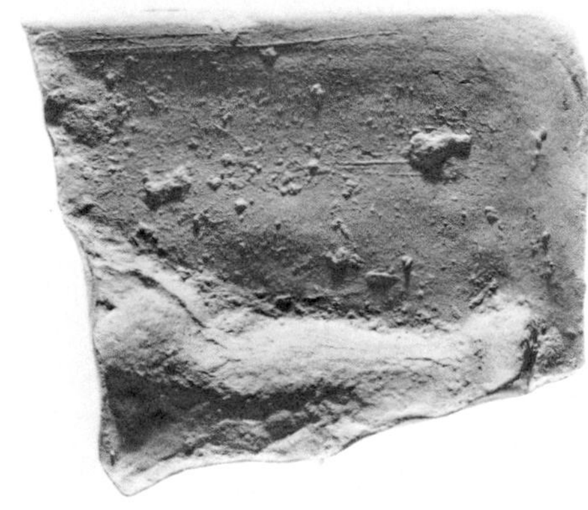

82 (mold)   7:10

82 (cast)   7:10

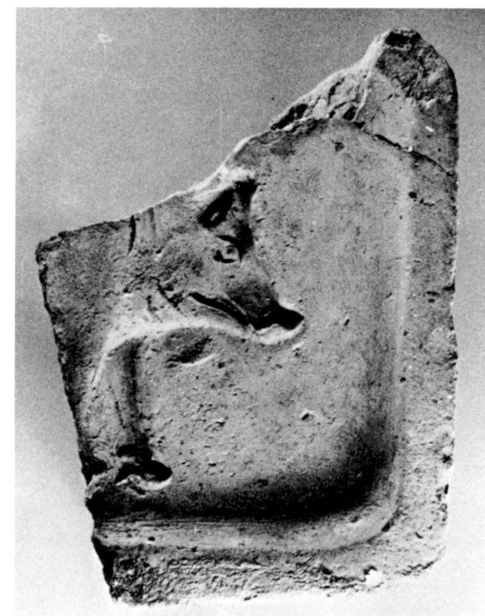

81 (mold)   2:5

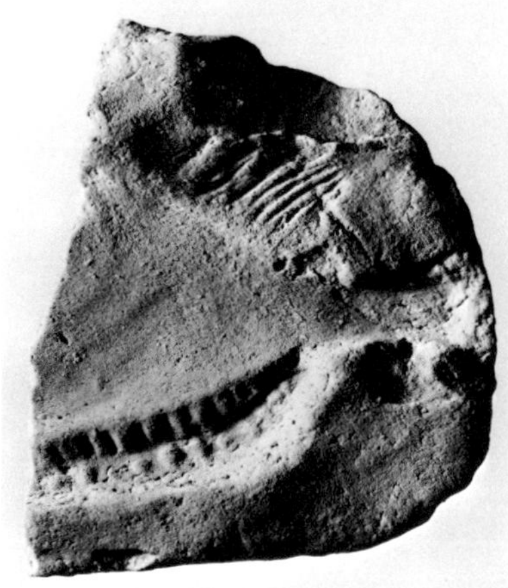

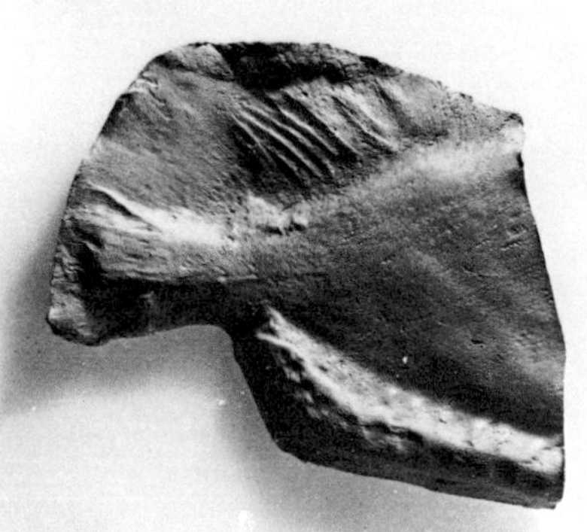

83 (mold)   2:5

83 (cast)   2:5

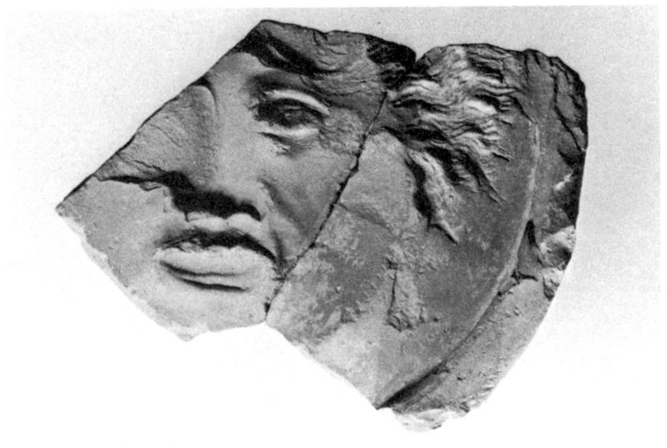

84 (mold)   2:5

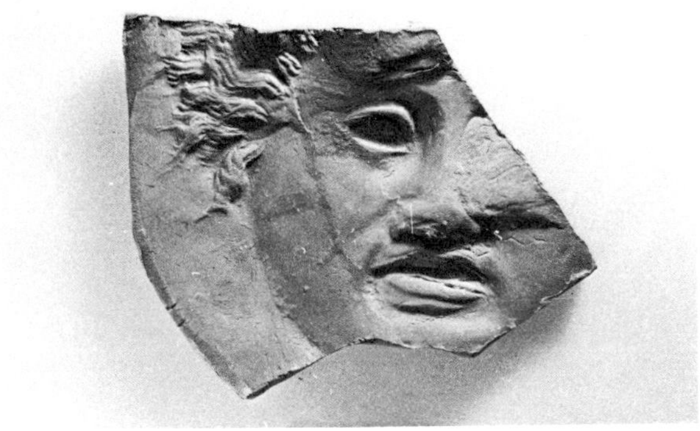

84 (cast)   2:5

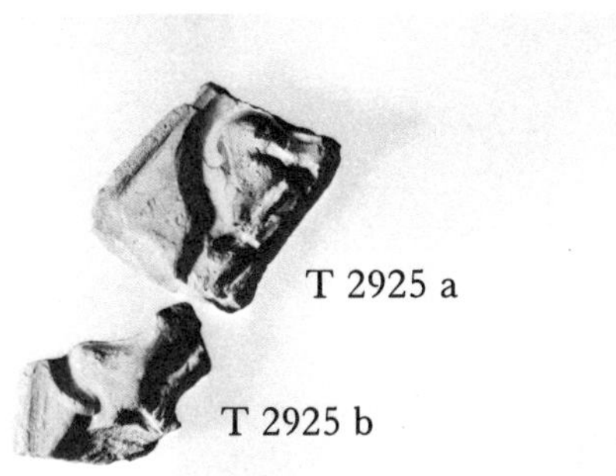

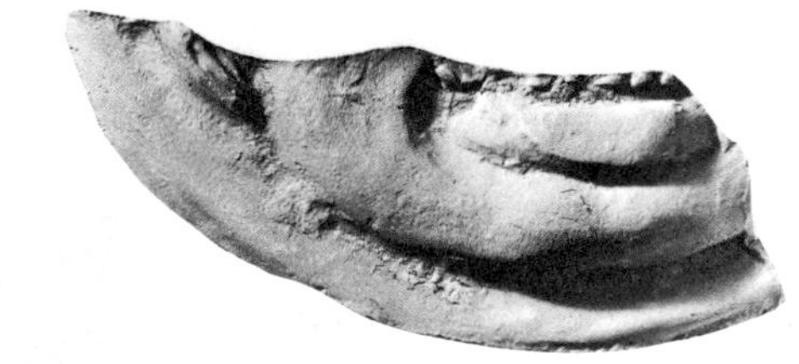

86 (cast)   2:5

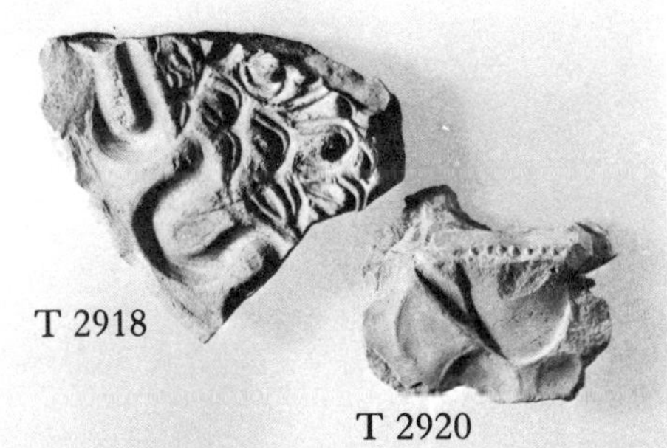

85 (mold)   1:5

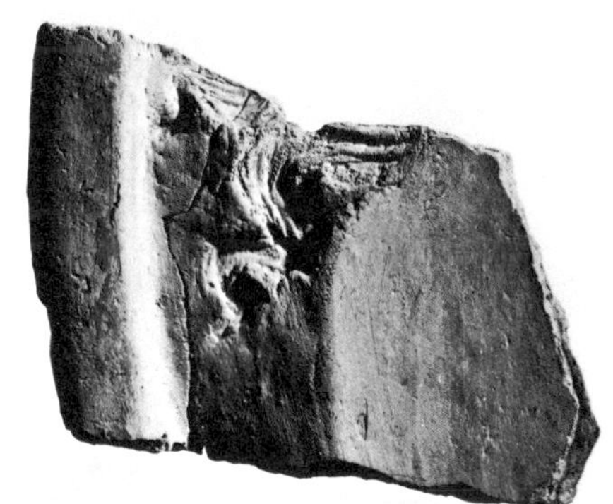

87 (mold)   2:5

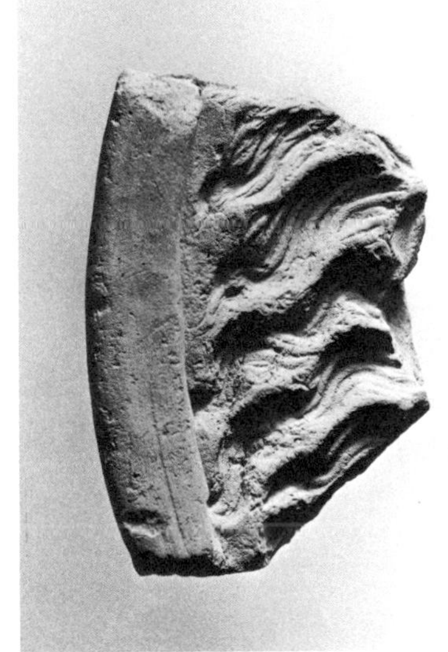

88 (mold)   1:2

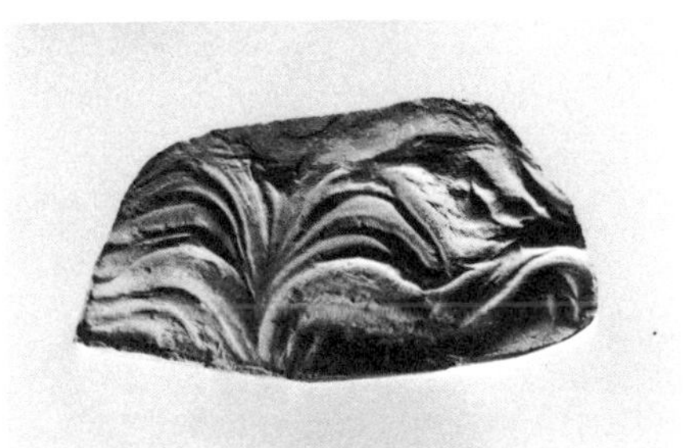

89 (cast)   2:5

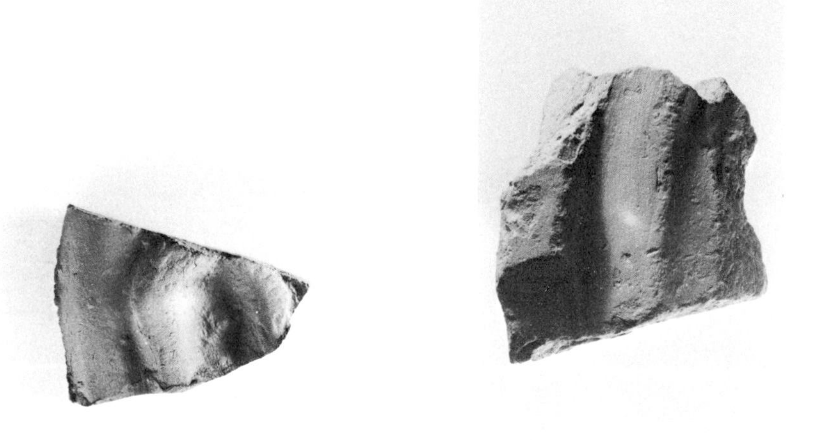

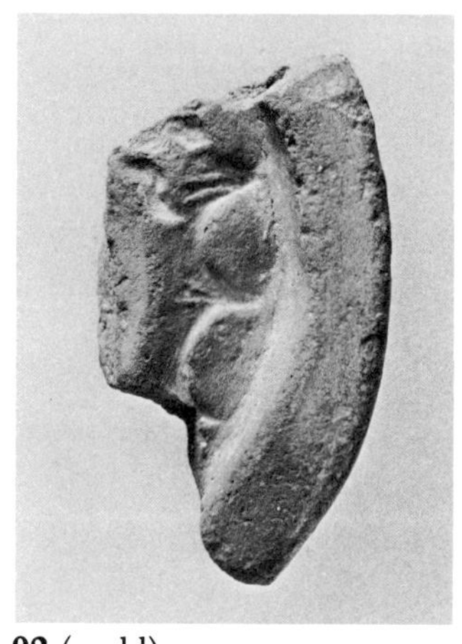

90 (cast)   **91** (mold)   **92** (mold)

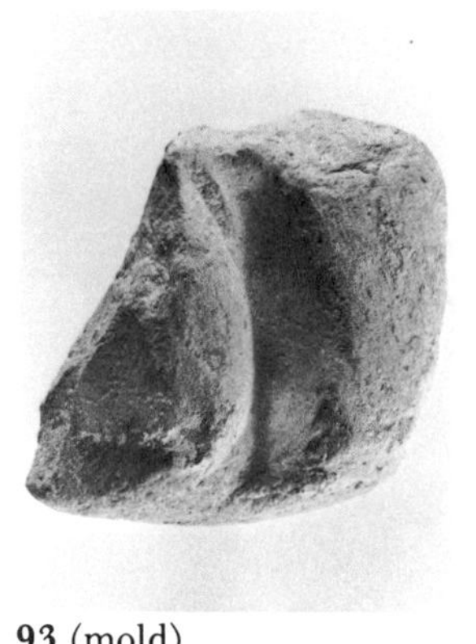

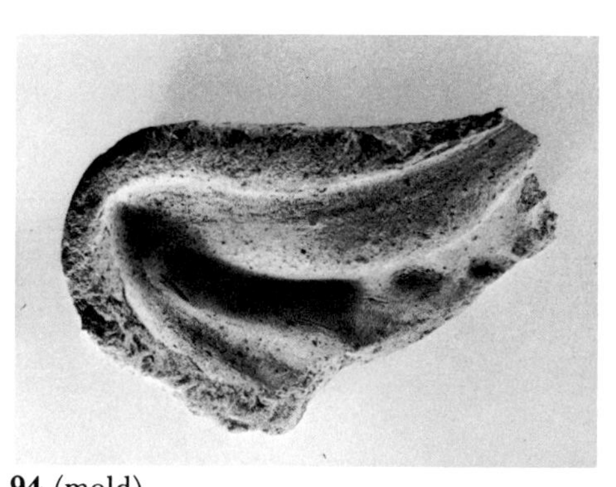

93 (mold)   **94** (mold)

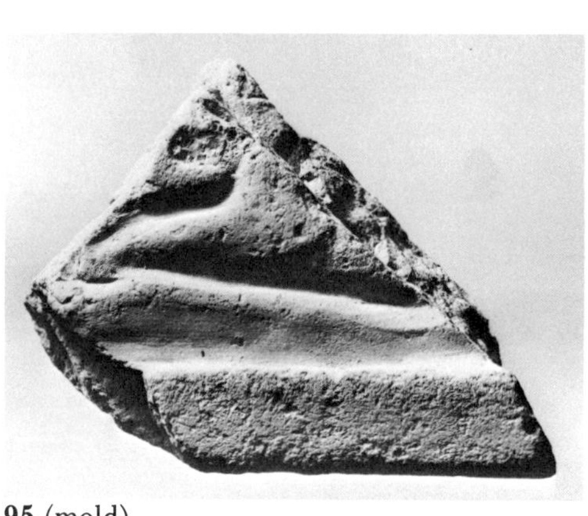

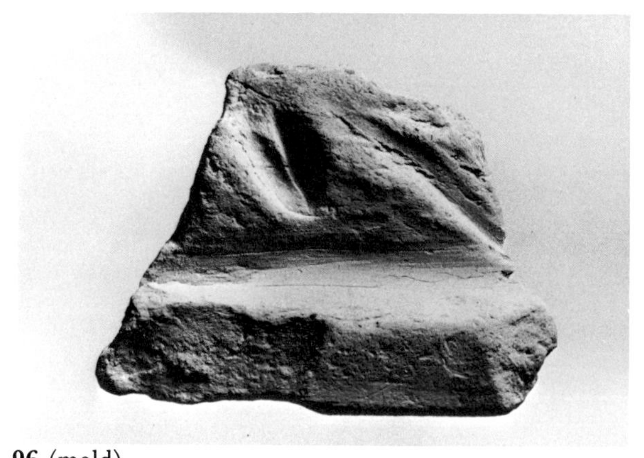

95 (mold)   **96** (mold)

Scale 1:2

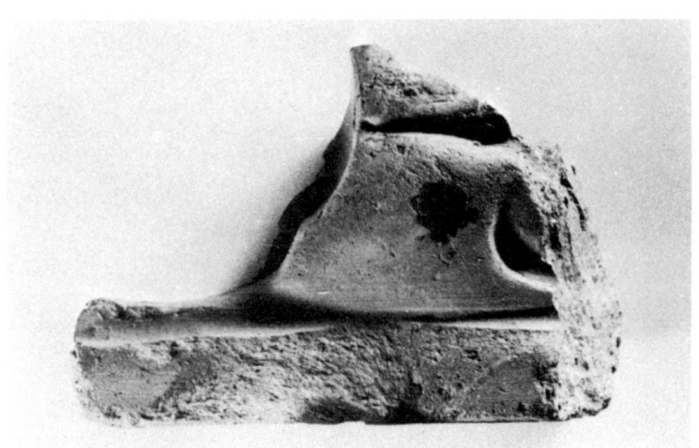

97 (mold)   1:2

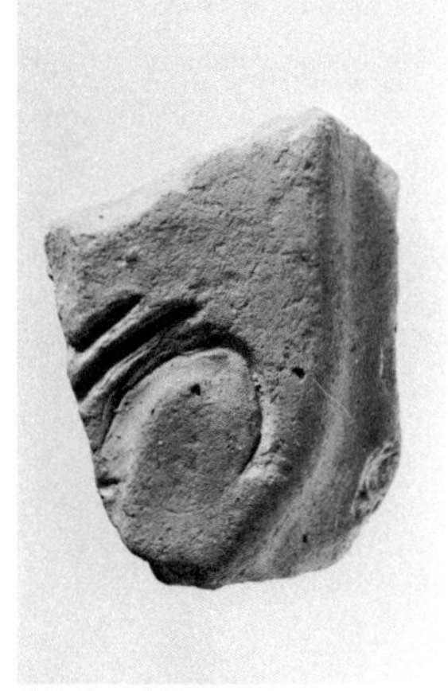

98 (mold)   1:2

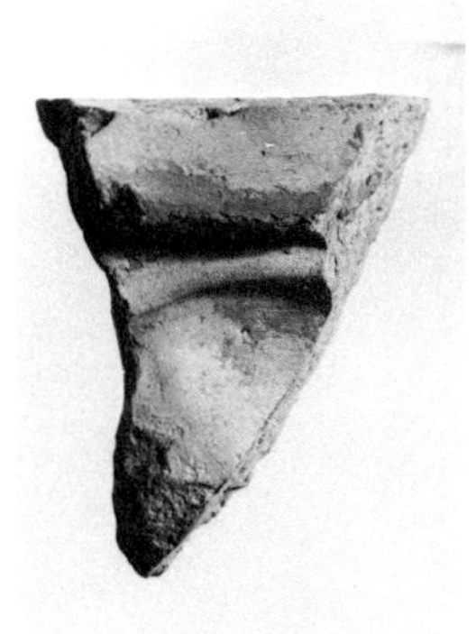

99 (mold)   2:5

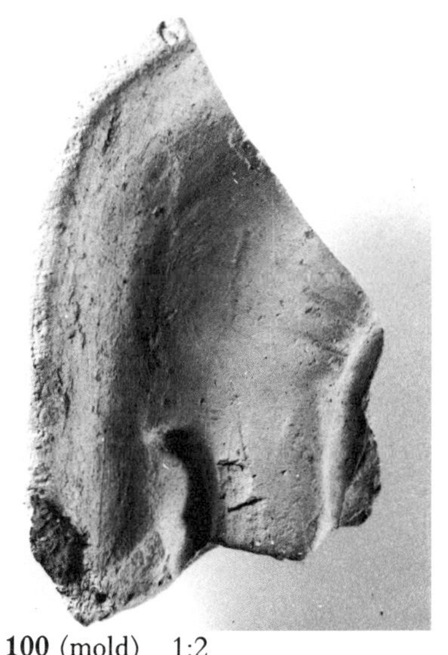

100 (mold)   1:2

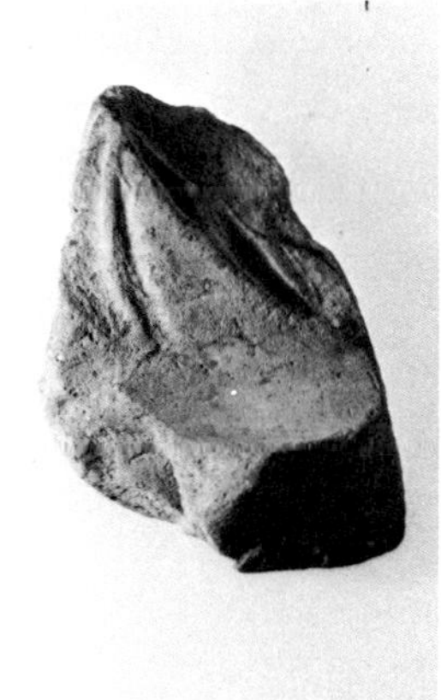

101 (mold)   1:2

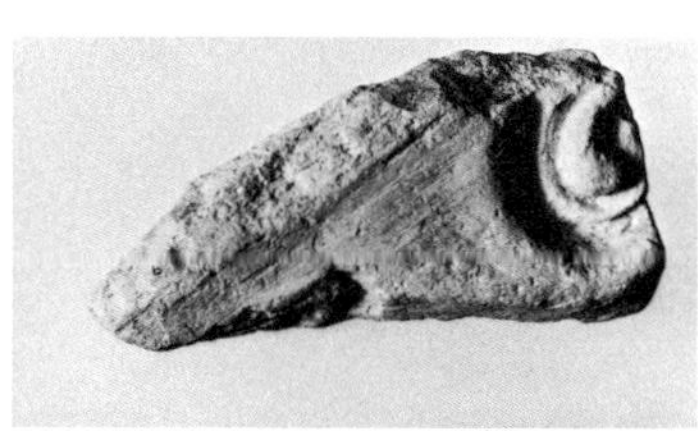

102 (mold)   1:2

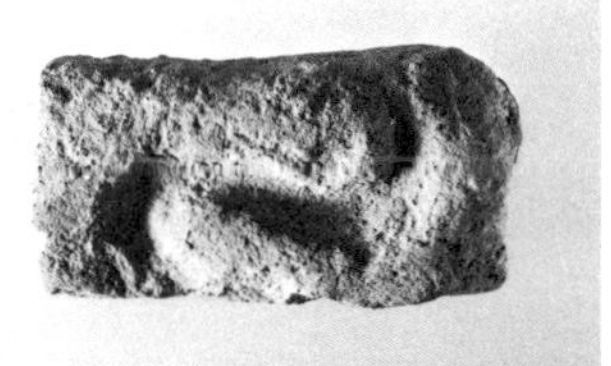
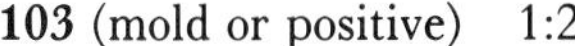

103 (mold or positive)   1:2

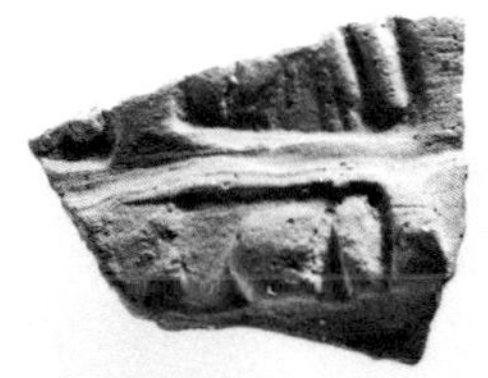

104 (mold or positive)   1:2

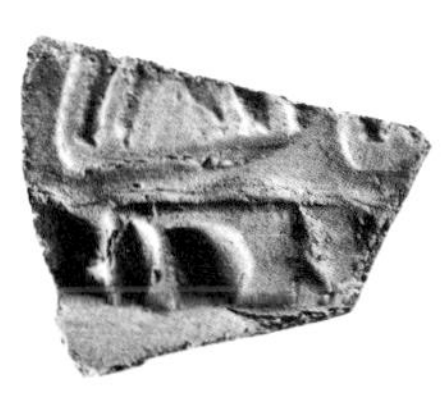

104 (cast)   1:2

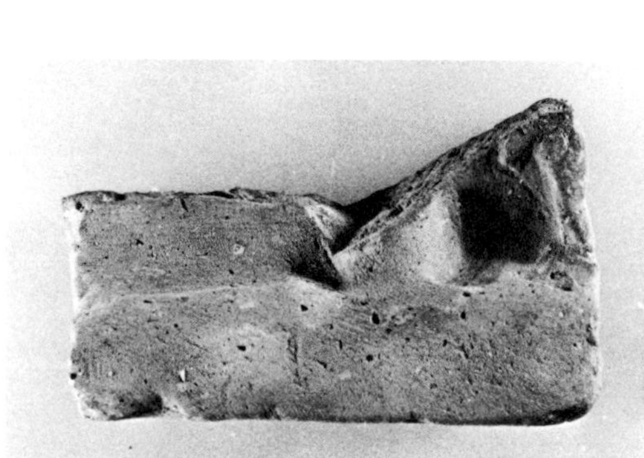

105 (mold or positive)   1:2

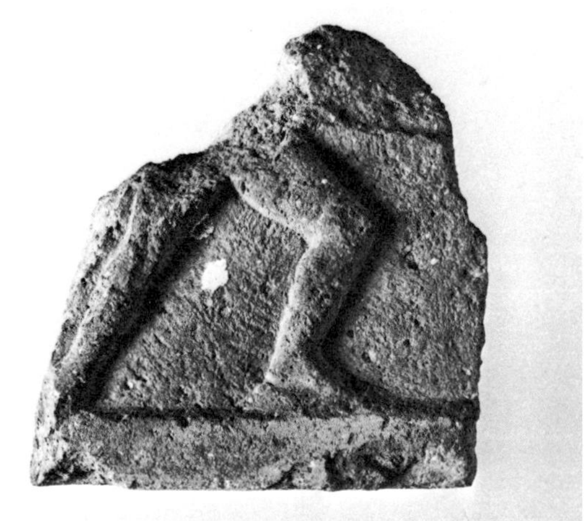

106 (positive)   2:5

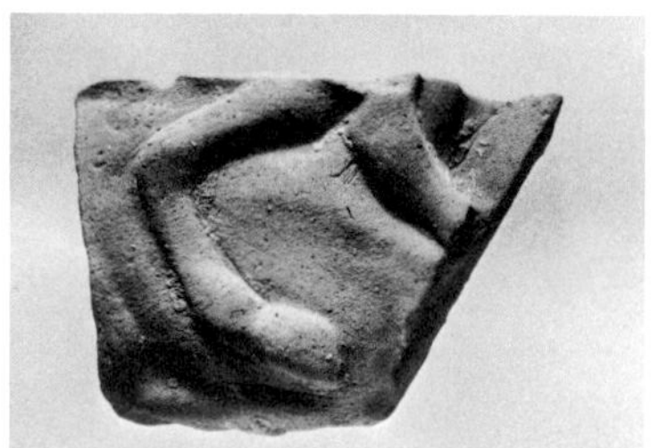

107 (positive)   1:2

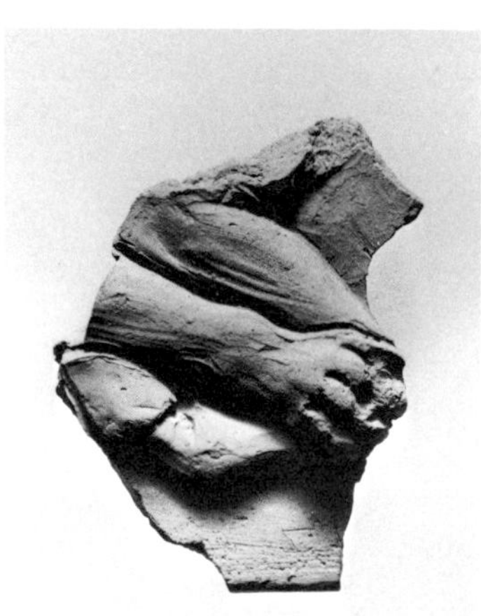

108 (positive)   1:2

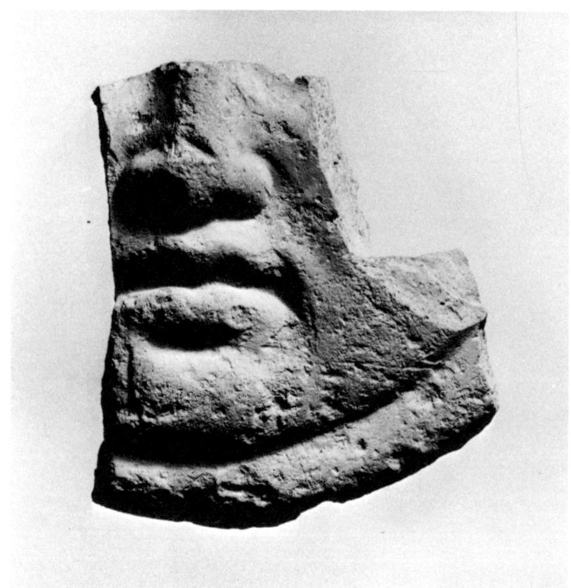

109 (positive)   2:5

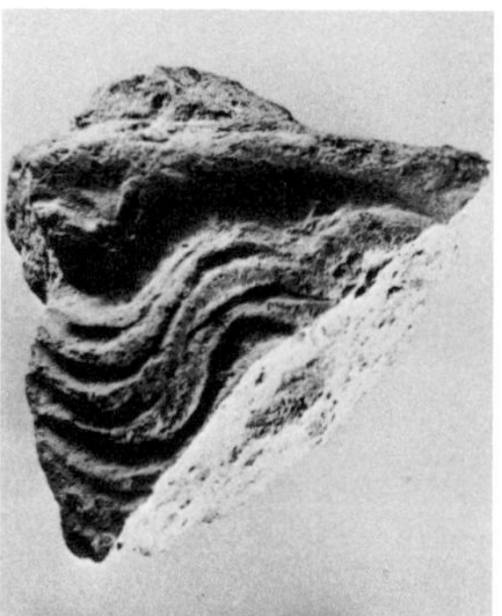

110 (positive)   1:2

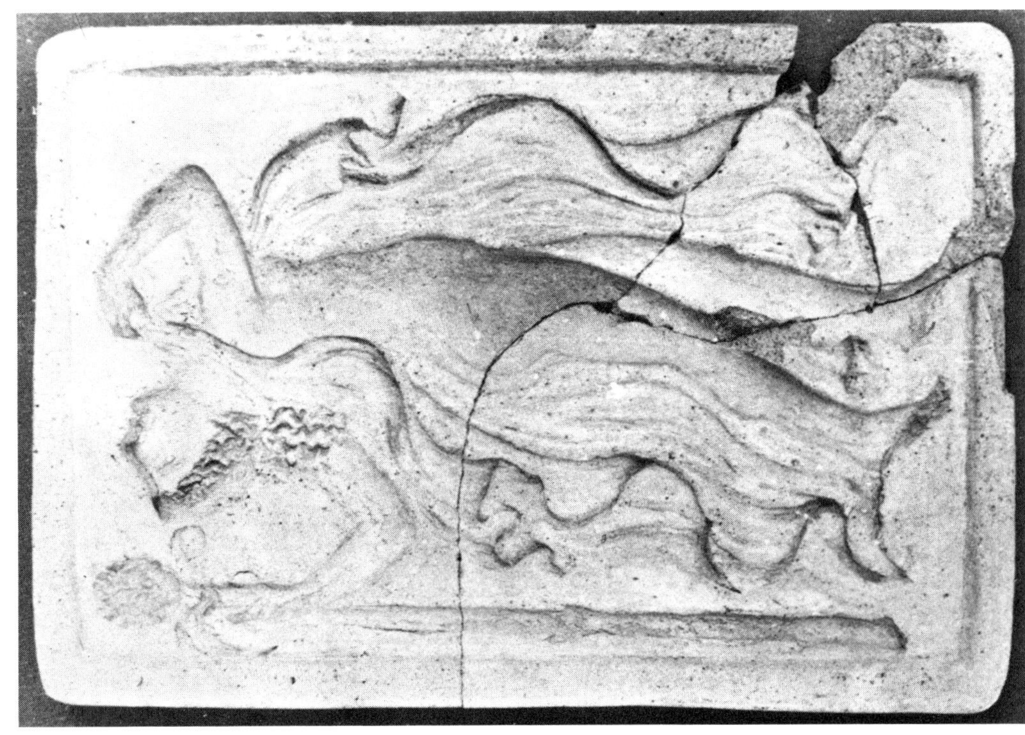

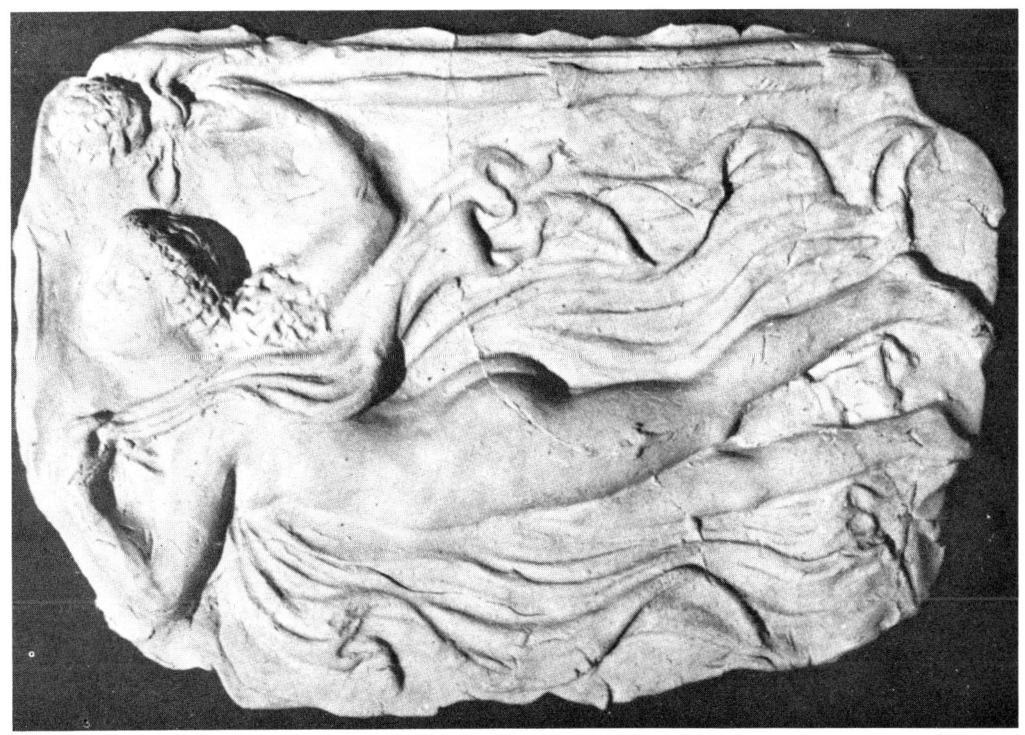

Cast and mold (Dancing Maenad) from Chalkis (Ἀρχ Ἐφ 1980, pl. 54)

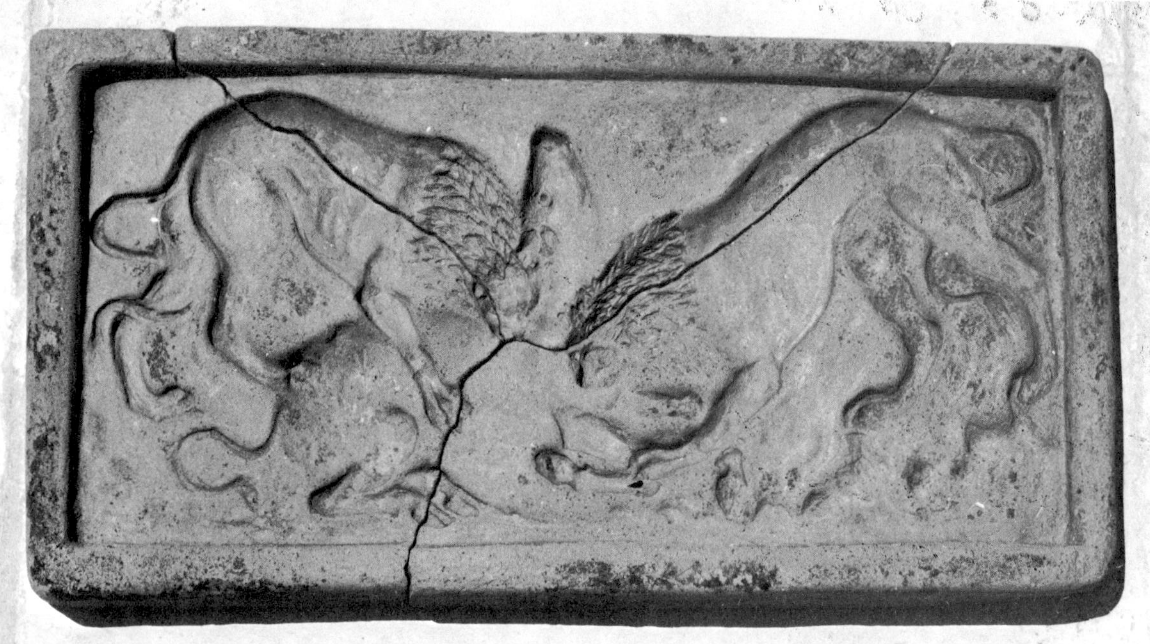

a. Mold (Lions Attacking a Cow) from Agrileza,
   Laurion (*Archaeological Reports 1984–85*,
   p. 119, fig. 29)

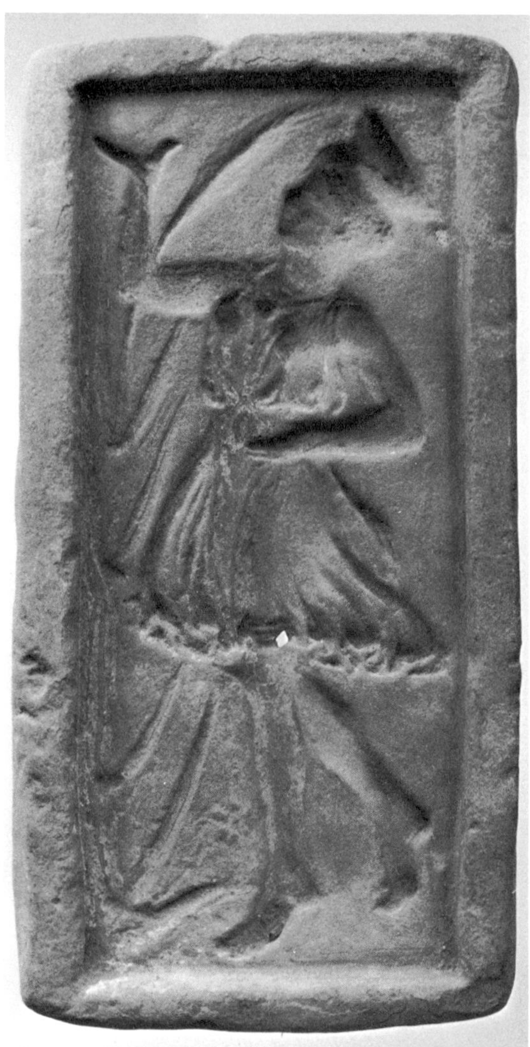

b. Mold (Kalathiskos Dancer) from Eretria
   (Δελτ 20, 1965, Β΄ [1967], pl. 335)

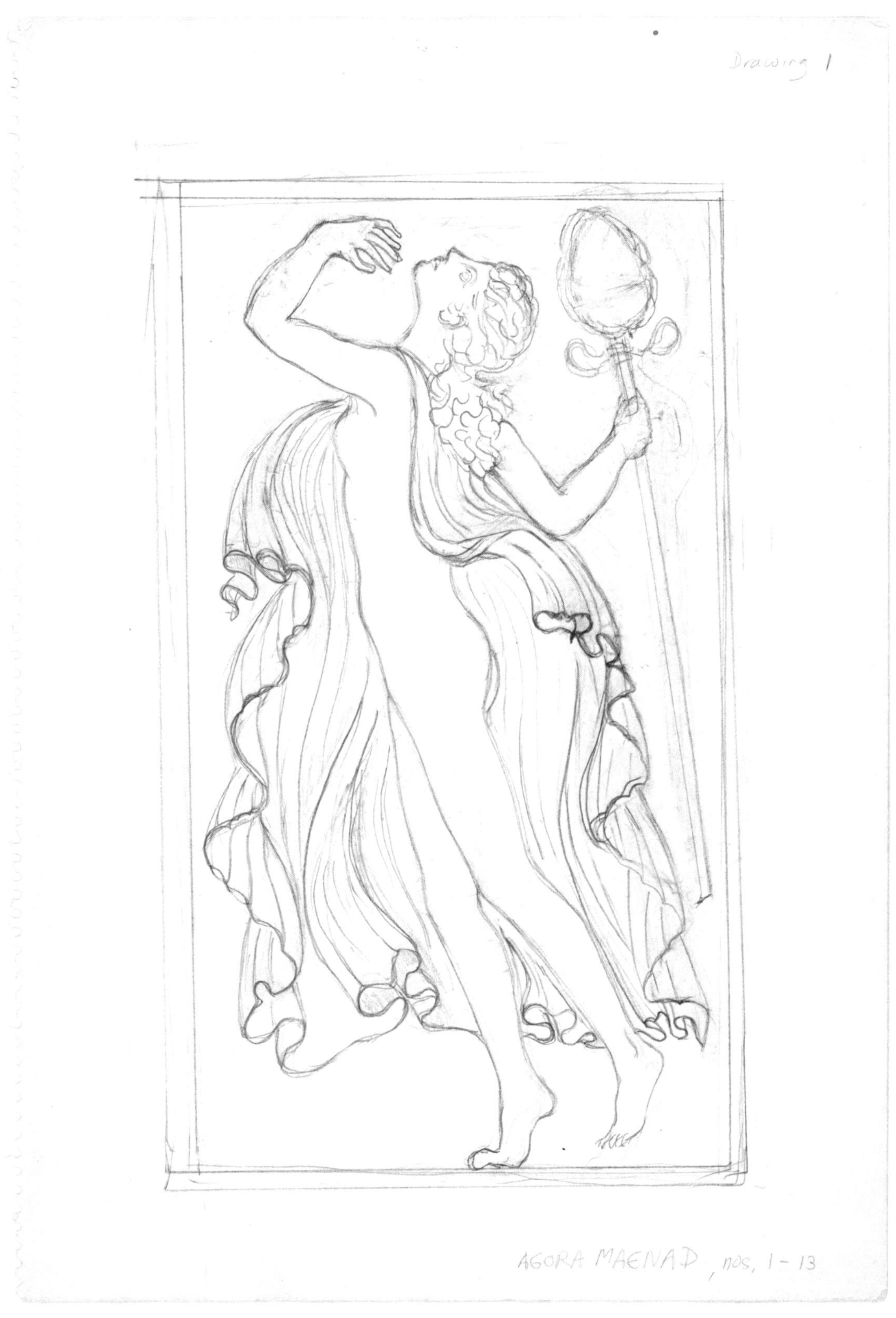

Drawing No. 1: Dancing Maenad (**1–13**)

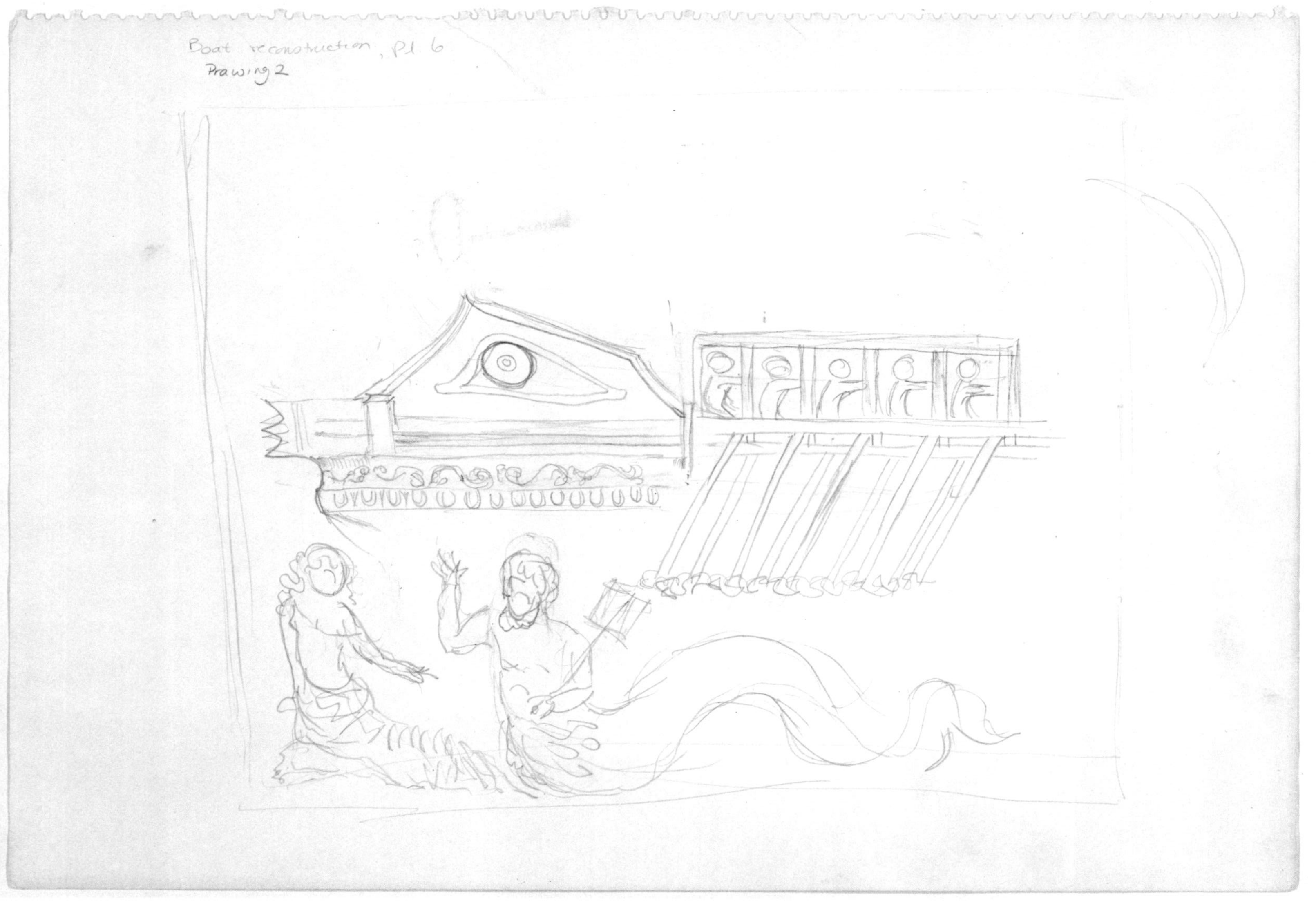

Drawing No. 2: Ship (21–24)

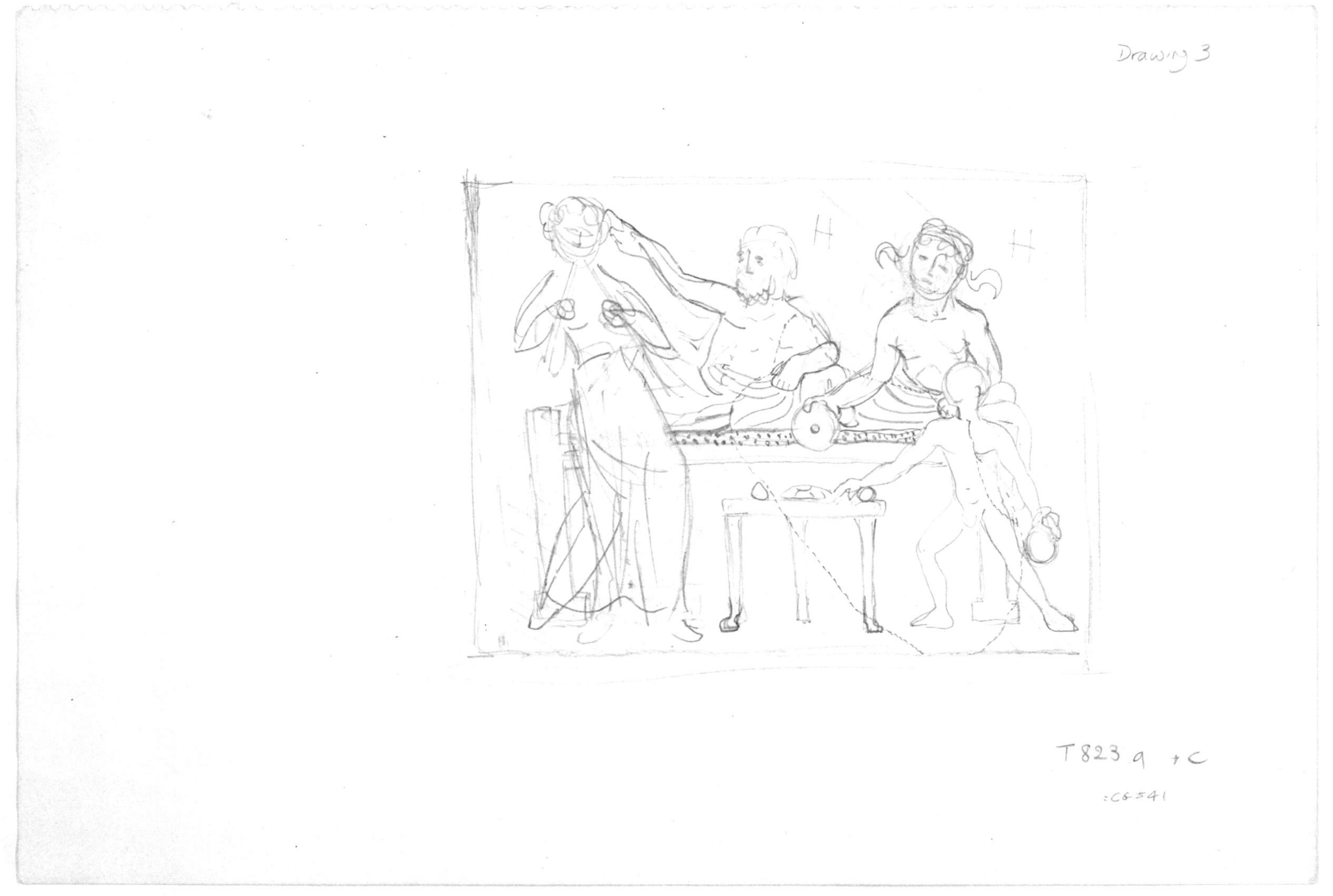

Drawing No. 3: Banquet (**41**)

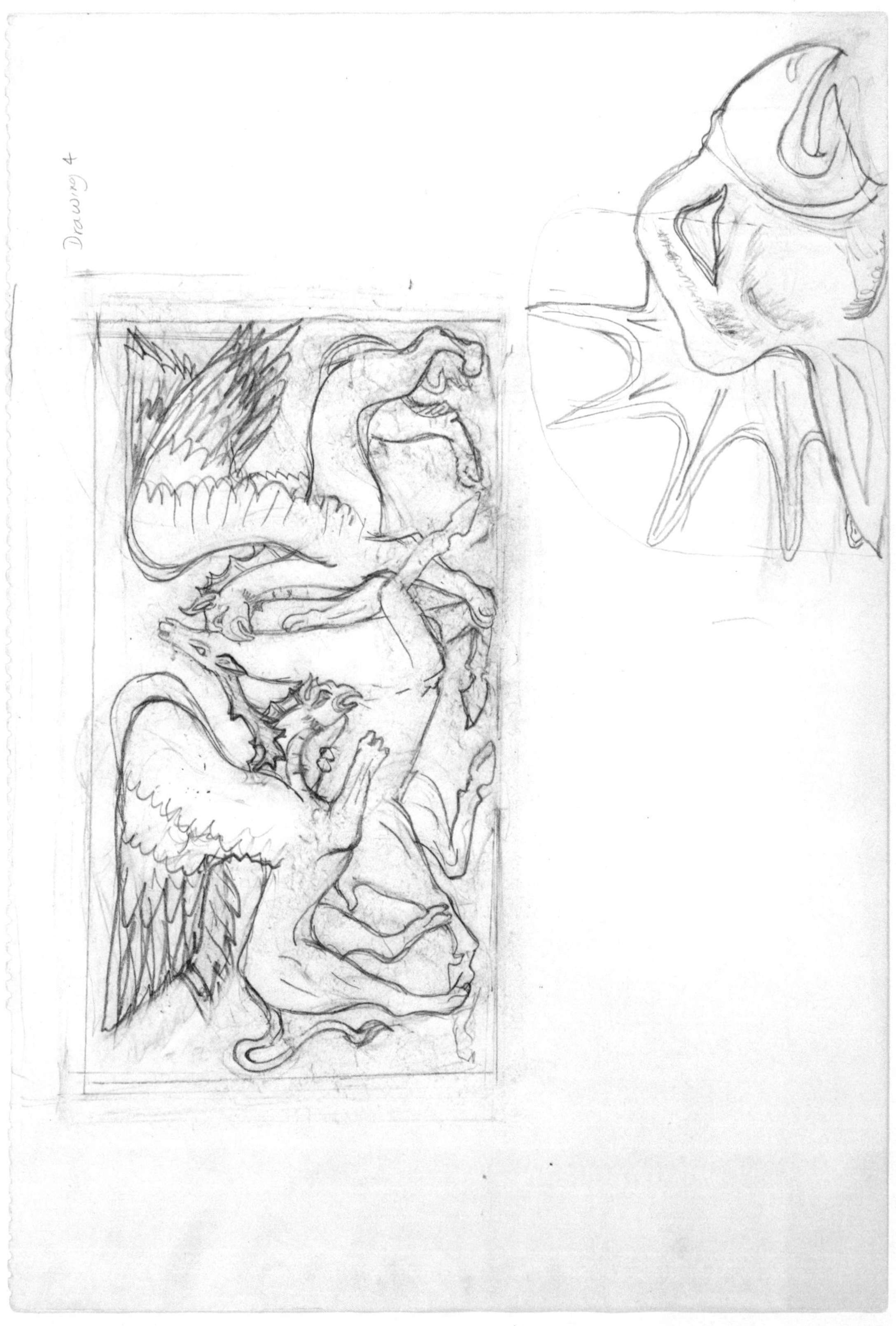

Drawing No. 4: Griffins Attacking a Deer (**52–56, 59**)

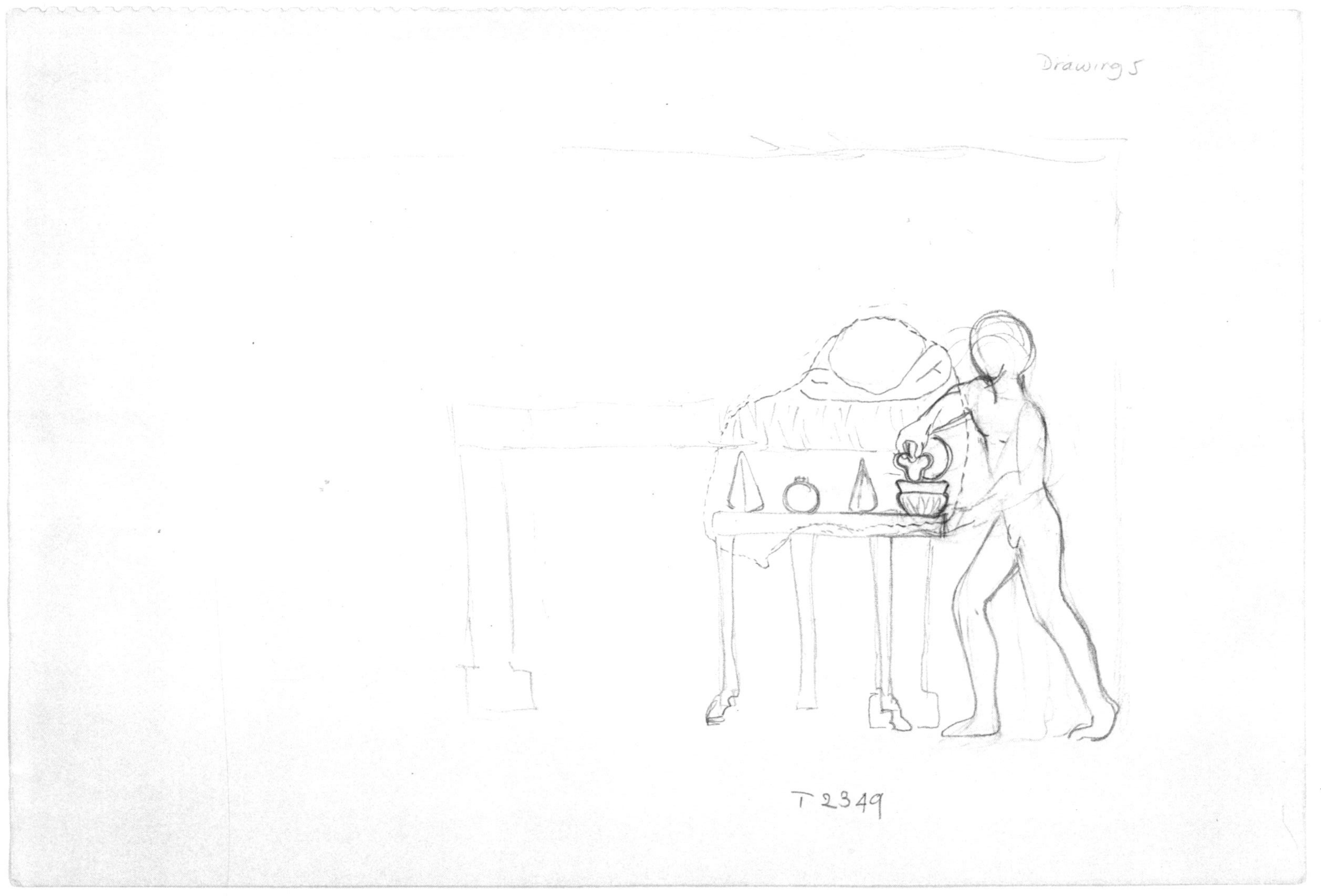

Drawing No. 5 Banquet (**44**)

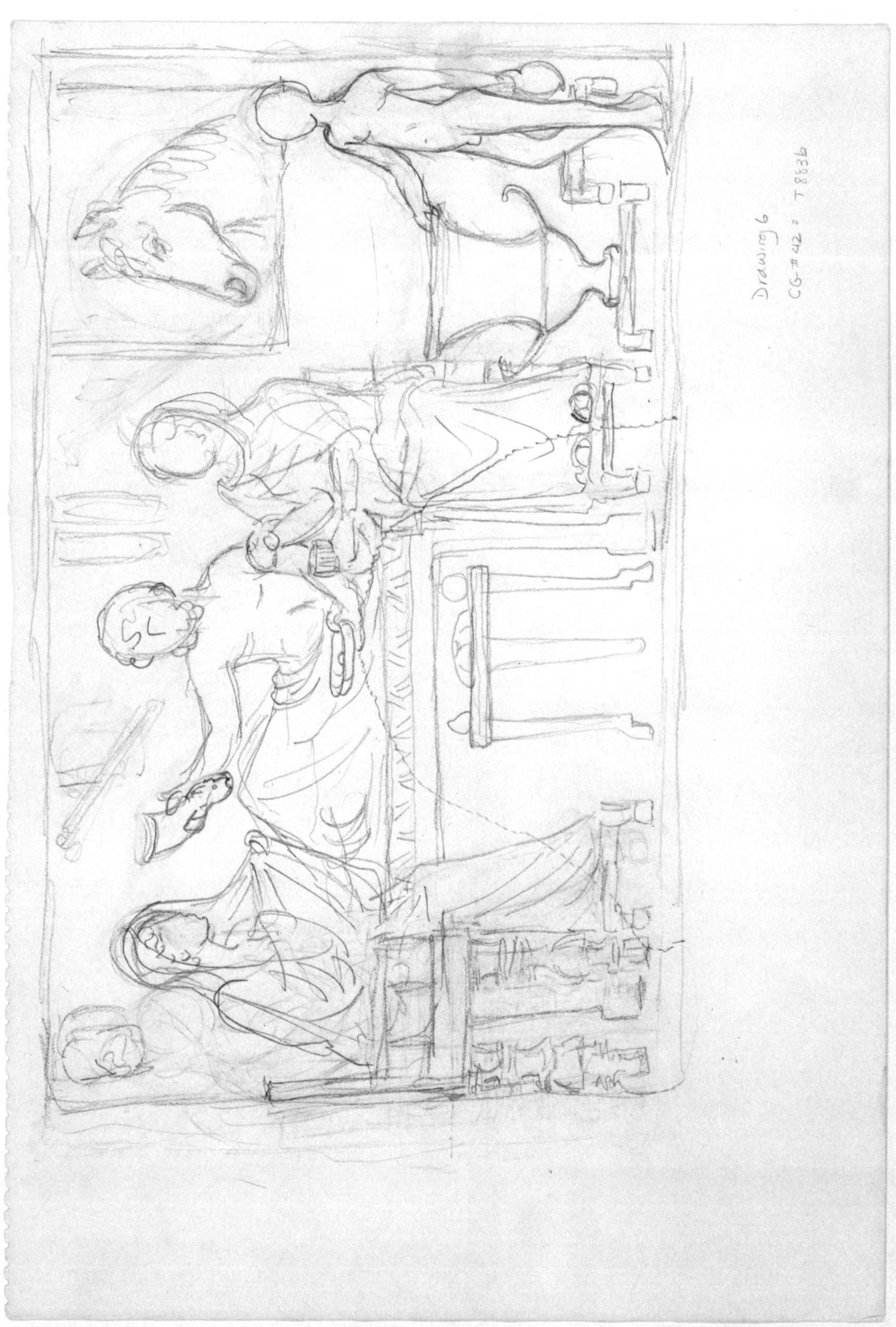

Drawing No. 6: Banquet (**42, 43**)

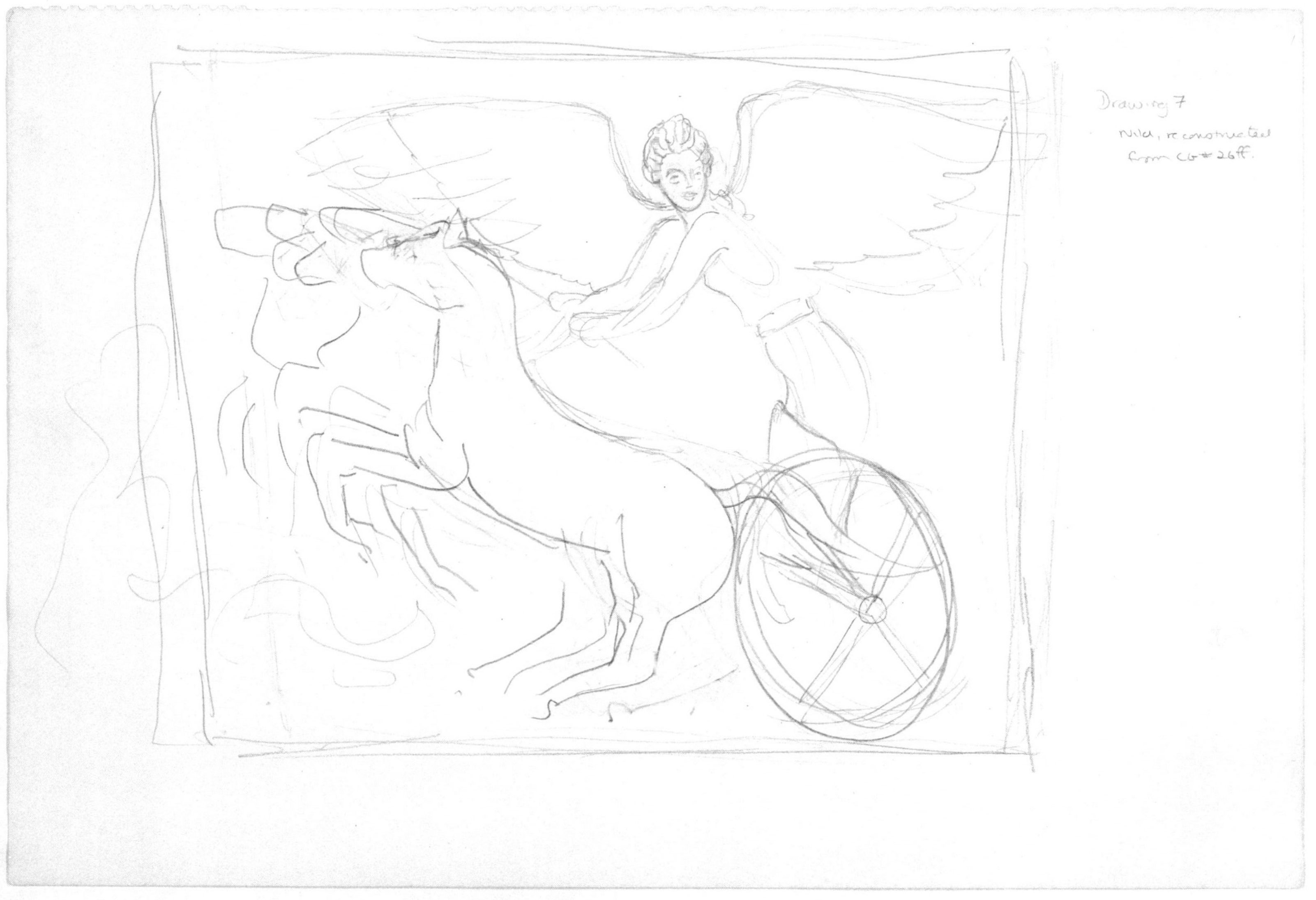

Drawing No. 7: Nike and Chariot (**26–39**)

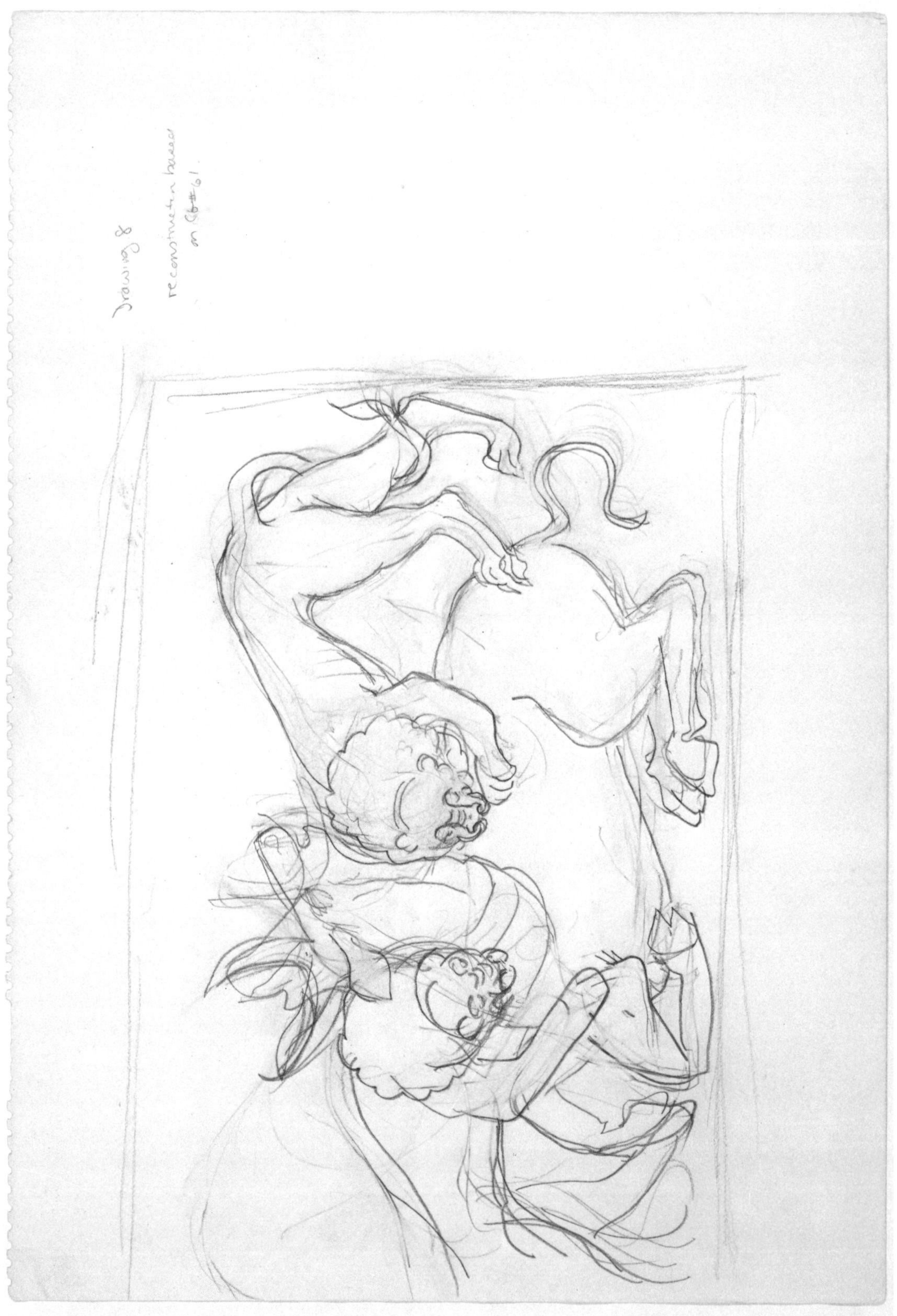

Drawing No. 8: Lions Attacking a Bull (61)